Radhakrishnan

Radhakrishnan

His Life
and
Ideas

K. SATCHIDANANDA MURTY

and

ASHOK VOHRA

State University of New York Press

Published by
State University of New York Press, Albany

©1990 State University of New York

For information, address State University of New York Press,
State University Plaza, Albany, N.Y., 12246

Library of Congress Cataloging-in-Publication Data

Murty, K. Satchidananda.
    Radhakrishnan: his life and ideas / K. Satchidananda and Ashok
Vohra.
        p.   cm.
    Includes bibliographical references.
    ISBN 0-7914-0343-2.—ISBN 0-7914-0344-0 (pbk.)
    1. Radhakrishnan, S. (Sarvepalli), 1888-1975.   2. Presidents—
India—Biography.   3. Philosophers—India—Biography.   I. Vohra,
Ashok, 1949-   .   II. Title.
DS481.R2M87   1990
954.04'092—dc20
    [B]   89-39718
                                                                  CIP

10 9 8 7 6 5 4 3 2 1

Contents

Preface

The ancient Greeks expected a biography to be encomiastic. Aristoxenus of Tarantum (b. 370 B.C.) was the first who gave a new shape, outside and beyond encomia, to biography. In Indian culture, apart from the legendary lives of great religious personalities like the Buddha, Mahāvīra, Nāgārjuna and Śaṅkara, what may be called biographies are very few. One may consider Bāṇa's life of King Harsha and Bilhana's life of Vikramāṅkadeva to be biographies, but these are laudatory through and through.

In 1928 in his *Aspects of Modern Biography*, André Maurois outlined what ought to be the characteristics of a true biography: (1) it should expose the whole story, letting the chips fall where they may, (2) it should not classify people into rigid psychological types, as every person is complex, (3) however great the subject of a biography may be, as he cannot but be human, he is bound to have his doubts, failings, motives, and wretched secrets, even though he may be as "normal" as most of us are.

If a biography is to be, as Edmund Gosse said, "the faithful portrait of a soul in its adventures through life,"* it would be almost impossible to write one of some people. The subject of this biography is of that sort. On the other hand, it may be said of a philosopher or a scientist that "the essential in the being" of such a man lies "in *what* and *how* he thinks, not in what he does or suffers." This is what Albert Einstein said about himself. Radhakrishnan, for inscrutable reasons, said very little about himself. Perhaps following Einstein's example, he declared that for understanding and evaluating what he wrote, it is not necessary to know about his life history. A biography of his, unless it is by a member of his family, would not be able to give many details of his life not already known publicly. It is, of course, possible to discover through inference possible motives of actions, compare behavior and achievement with professed ideals, and thereby evaluate the character of any person. Such an attempt, to some extent, has been made in this work. Joseph Epstein has pointed out that "human character" is the great subject of all biography.

Encyclopaedia Britannica, 11th ed.

In April 1981 the Publications Division, Ministry of Information and Broadcasting, India, requested K. Satchidananda Murty to write a biography of Radhakrishnan for publication in their *Builders of Modern India* series. He agreed, and by the end of April 1982 he had not only read all that was available in print about Radhakrishnan's life, but also managed to collect details about it from those who worked or studied with the latter, as well as those who personally knew him in Madras, Waltair, Mysore, Calcutta, Banaras, Oxford and New Delhi. But for a complex of reasons he could not begin writing the biography then, and later opted out from that commitment.

When the Government of India declared September 5, 1988 to September 5, 1989 as Radhakrishnan's Birth Centenary Year, Murty's interest in this matter was rekindled. But because of his many commitments, he requested Ashok Vohra to collaborate with him. He asked him to produce a first draft on the basis of the material accumulated by him and gather more from recent publications. Vohra complied, and his draft of the first sixteen chapters, later revised by Murty, along with the latter's draft of the last chapter were then discussed by both, jointly edited and finalized. Thus both are *equally* responsible for the contents of this book.

While heading Andhra University from 1931 to 1936, Radhakrishnan also taught in its philosophy department. In the early 1940s while Professor P.T. Raju, one of the most eminent students of Radhakrishnan was teaching in the department, Murty had studied in it. From 1949 Murty served on its faculty for thirty-five years. But it was only after Radhakrishnan had become vice-president that Murty was introduced to him by Dr. S. Gopal, who was also once a faculty member of Andhra University. During Radhakrishnan's fifteen year stay in New Delhi, Murty had the privilege of meeting him a number of times, and received kindness and encouragement from him.

Biographers may have idolatry admiration or just goodwill for their subjects. In this case the authors confess that they are critical admirers of Radhakrishnan's intellectual and practical achievements. While they believe he was a great man, they think that he was as human as anyone else.

March 21, 1989

Acknowledgments

The authors are grateful to the following persons who have kindly provided them with information about Radhakrishnan in their correspondence or conversations with K. Satchidananda Murty mostly in 1981:

A.J. Alston (London)
T. Bullaiah (Rajahmundry)
Nikhil Chakravorty (New Delhi)
Professor Debiprasad Chattopadhyaya (Calcutta)
Ms. Winifred H. Dawes (Bristol)
Professor S. Gopal (Madras)
The Late K.D.D. Henderson (Salisbury)
Dr. Vernon Katz (London)
Ms. Vina Majumdar (New Delhi)
Mrs. Lakshmi N. Menon (Trivandrum)
Professor Hiren Mukherjee (Calcutta)
A. Radhakrishna Murti (Vijayawada)
The Late Professor T.R.V. Murti (Varanasi)
Professor D. Narasimhaiah (Mysore)
Dr. Ch. G.S.S. Srinivasa Rao (Madras)
The Late Professor K.B. Ramakrishna Rao (Mysore)
T. Ramalingeswara Rao (Madras)
Dr. B. Gopal Reddy (Nellore)
S. Satyanarain (Kakinada)

The authors are indebted to (1) the authorities of Andhra University for making available in 1981-1982 to Murty the minutes of the meetings of various university bodies during Radhakrishnan's vice-chancellorship, (2) the late Shri Bangorey for giving to Murty copies of C.R. Reddy-Radhakrishnan correspondence deposited with Andhra University, (3) the authorities of Nehru Memorial Museum and Library, New Delhi, for making available photocopies of Radhakrishnan's papers, and (4) the chairman and member-secretary of the Indian Council of Philosophical Research for the council's financial assistance to Ashok Vohra towards typing expenses.

On Professor Murty's request, in the early eighties Dr. O. Deenammal (Department of Philosophy, Andhra University) analyzed the material relating to Radhakrishnan's vice-chancellorship of Andhra University and prepared notes on it, while Dr. M.V. Krishnayya (Department of Philosophy, Andhra University) gathered information about Radhakrishnan's diplomatic and political life from some books, periodicals and newspapers. Mrs. Asha Vohra was helpful to Vohra in finalizing the draft of chapters one to sixteen and in checking the typescript. The authors are much obliged to all these individuals for their cooperation. On Murty's request, Shri H.Y. Sharada Prasad, Secretary, Indira Gandhi Memorial Trust, New Delhi, kindly read chapters twelve to fifteen. The authors are grateful to him.

Our thanks also to the authors, editors and contributors of the publications cited in our references, on which our work depended. Except the authors, no person or institution mentioned here is responsible for the views or facts contained in this book.

We are grateful to SUNY Press, especially to Mr. William Eastman, for the keen interest shown by them in the publication of the book.

I.

Early Life

Close to the border between the States of Andhra Pradesh and Tamilnadu, located in the latter, not far from the very famous pilgrim center of Tirupati in the former, and fifty miles northwest of one of the four metropolitan cities of India, Madras, is a small town called Tiruttani. Until the linguistic states of Andhra Pradesh and Tamilnadu were formed Tiruttani was in the undivided Madras presidency. Tiruttani is known for its shrine of Subrahmanya, a son of Śiva, from whom the great musician and saint Muthuswami Dikshithar, it is said, received inspiration.

Radhakrishnan was born on September 5, 1888, in this small town into a Telugu-speaking family, the second son of Sarvepalli Veeraswami and Seetamma. Veeraswami had lived in Tiruttani since he was ten years old. His father, Sitaramayya, and mother Kondamma, had left the family home in Sarvepalli in Nellore district (Andhra Pradesh) in the early nineteenth century, and had settled down in Tiruttani. The family belonged to the sect of *Brahmins* known as *Prāngnādu Niyogis* who lived on the eastern sea coast of the Nellore region. South Indian Telugu-speaking *Brahmins* are traditionally divided into two sects—*Vaidikis* and *Niyogis*. Customarily those who belong to the former studied the Vedas, Śāstras and rituals, and often became scholars, teachers, poets and *purohits* (domestic priests), leading lives of simplicity, austerity and piety. On the other hand, traditionally *Niyogis* took up civil, judicial or revenue service, under the rulers. During the British period in Andhra, hereditary village accountants (*Karaṇams*) were mostly *Niyogis*.[1]

Veeraswami worked in the tahsildar's office and his financial position was not good, to say the least. The economic condition of the family worsened with the passage of time as three more sons and a daughter were added to it. On Veeraswami's meager salary, eight mouths had to be fed. But this in no way dampened the religious fervour and faith of the parents. Consequently, the atmosphere in the house was religious; the Hindu rituals and customs were performed with regularity and devotion. The general religious atmosphere prevalent in Tiruttani, particularly the

1

adherence of his parents to the mores of Hinduism, left a deep and lasting impression on the mind of young Radhakrishnan. His whole attitude to life and philosophy was molded by it. As he recalled later, "My approach to the problems of philosophy from the angle of religion, as distinct from that of science, was determined by my early training. I was not able to confine philosophy to logic and epistemology."[2]

Radhakrishnan's family background, coupled with his early demonstrated aptitude for learning, took him in gradual stages to school and college. Like most of the children of the upper castes in those days, Radhakrishnan was sent to a local primary school in Tiruttani at the age of five. His father did not want him to learn English, at that time a prerequisite for secular success in India, and instead desired him to learn Sanskrit. But due to pressure from relatives and family friends he had to agree to Radhakrishnan's learning English and joining a missionary school. So, after his primary school education in Allamaram School he was sent to the Lutheran Mission High School at Tirupati to complete his secondary school education. At Tirupati, surcharged with religious activity throughout the year, the reigning deity is Lord Venkateśwara (a form of Vishnu).

After completing his secondary school education, he joined the Voorhes College at Vellore to take a pre-Bachelor of Arts, two year arts course, pass an examination and become a fellow of arts (F.A.). While he was doing his F.A., when he was fifteen he married his cousin Sivakamamma, aged ten, the daughter of T. Chenchuramiah who was, at the time, the station master of Tirupati railway station. Marriages between cross cousins and maternal uncles and nieces are in accordance with the South Indian Hindu tradition. Great authorities like Kumārila approved of this custom. Radhakrishnan must have had his wife in mind when in 1937 he wrote: "I have often been reminded in later years of Hegel's saying that a man has made up his account with his life when he has work that suits him and a wife whom he loves."[3]

Madras Christian College

After completing his F.A., Radhakrishnan joined Madras Christian College, Madras, for his higher studies, that is, to acquire his Bachelor of Arts and Master of Arts degrees. Like any other seventeen year old student in India, Radhakrishnan was undecided and unclear about the subjects he should study in college. But unlike the case of many others, he himself was enabled to choose the subject to be studied in depth by a coincidence. The decision, as later life proved, was a happy and fruitful one. One of his cousins who had been studying in the same college and was a few years senior to him, made him a gift of his old books: Stout's *Psychology*, Welton's *Logic* and Mackenzie's *Ethics*. When Radhakrishnan finished reading these books there was no wavering in his mind. The course to be pursued had been irrevocably decided for him, and his vocation in life determined. He chose philosophy as the main subject of his studies. As he recalled much later, "The subject of philosophy which I happened to take up by sheer accident has been of considerable help to me in giving me a goal to work for."[4] On this he further reflected thus:

> To all appearance this is a mere accident. But when I look at the series of accidents that have shaped my life, I am persuaded that there is more in this life than meets the eye. Life is not a mere chain of physical causes and effects. Chance seems to form the surface, but deep down other forces are at work. If the universe is a living one, if it is spiritually alive, nothing in it is merely accidental. "The moving finger writes and having writ moves on."[5]

Radhakrishnan was a serious, precocious and promising student. His memory was, and continued to be throughout his life, phenomenal. His intellectual curiosity was insatiable and remained so till the end. He read voraciously and the amount of time he devoted to his studies every day was prodigious. He had an urge to know more and more and in detail.

His upbringing in an orthodox Brahmin family and training in missionary schools inculcated in him an unflinching faith in God. As he claimed, "I had that enormous faith. From the time I became conscious of myself, there was this profound faith in the Divine sovereignty of God, Who is the Creator of the world, the Ruler of nations, the Inspirer of all that is true and beautiful. That faith never deserted me through thick and thin, and even today it is that which sustains me in varied actions which I am called upon to undertake . . . "[6] He prayed regularly to God to bestow upon him His choicest blessings and worked late into the night quite often. As he asserted later, "If I can boast of anything it is that as a student I tried to do my best and I aimed at doing my best."[7]

The Department of Philosophy at Madras Christian College, headed by Principal William Skinner and consisting of William Meston and Alfred Hogg (1875-1954) and others, very soon recognized the talents and potential of their zealous pupil. Though each one of them exercised some

influence in molding his thoughts and in helping him to realize his potential, for Radhakrishnan, Alfred Hogg was "my distinguished teacher."[8]
Hogg, according to him, "was a very distinguished theologian,"[9] "one of
the greatest Christian thinkers we had in India," and "a thinker of great
penetration in theological matters,"[10] who "was undoubtedly one of the
greatest Christian teachers of his generation," and who "left a permanent
mark on the minds of those who came under his influence."[11] As the later
works of Radhakrishnan show, Hogg's attitude to philosophy in general,
combined with Hogg's personal philosophy and teaching left a lasting
imprint on the mind of their author. In view of this, it may be necessary
to give an account of Hogg's life and thought.

Professor Alfred Hogg

Professor Hogg was a student of the idealist philosopher Andrew
Seth Pringle-Pattison (1856-1931) at the University of Edinburgh. In his
study of philosophy he was strongly influenced by the individualistic
idealism of Pattison, which when applied to religion led to unorthodox
and undogmatic theism. After getting his honors degree, Hogg undertook
theological studies and became influenced by Alrecht Ritschl and his
School of Theology. As a result, he found that Jesus Christ alone gave
meaning to history and that he alone was the guarantee that this world is
not merely a mechanical process.

After the completion of his training in theology, and having synthe-
sized Pattison's idealism and Ritschlian theology, Hogg arrived in India as
a lay education missionary of the United Presbyterian Church of Scot-
land and joined the Department of Philosophy at Madras Christian College in early 1903, approximately two years before Radhakrishnan joined
the college. In his lectures, articles and books he did not present any rigid
doctrine as a Christian, nor did he impose the *Bible* as an infallible authority. He accepted the fundamental Ritschlian principle—"Jesus Himself is the sole final revelation of God, being *literally* God manifest in the
flesh," and that revelation consists in "the over mastering and authoritative demand which Jesus makes on the hearts which He has compelled to
submit to Him." From these principles he concluded that Christian faith
means to dwell on what Jesus did and said in His life and death, to surrender to Him and to acknowledge His all sufficient and all conquering Lord-
ship. The task of theology, he said, is to elaborate in increasingly improved formulations, the nature of the absolute authority with which

Lord Jesus impresses Himself upon the individual's heart.[12] The exacting task of a philosopher, on the other hand, is "dragging into the light of full consciousness every inherited and unconscious presupposition and letting none pass muster until it had been examined and found legitimate." Philosophy, according to him, seeks "to achieve an integration of personality, by detecting and responding to the One that exists through the many, the harmony that resolves the discords, the infinite that makes the finite possible, and bestows on it its degree of worthiness."[13] The underlying assumption of this view of philosophy is the postulate that there exists such a harmonious unity, and it can be discovered. For Hogg this postulate was provided by Jesus and could be discovered by anyone who had faith in Him.

Though a sincere missionary, Hogg dismissed the attitude of many of his colleagues that all those who are not Christians are damned, and that Christianity is the only rational religion. He recognized that the practice of finding and seeking which is predominant throughout the history of religion in India is not a vain quest, and that Christianity would not be acceptable, nor would be of any relevance to the Hindu mind until it provided a challenge to it. Since Christianity in the form in which it was presented offered no challenge to the Hindu mind, he suggested that to conquer India, old doctrines of Christianity which have no relevance in the Indian context must be replaced by new ones which are relevant, and closer to the Indian situation and Indian thought. This synthesis, he thought, would give rise to what he called Indian Christian theology. In order to succeed, the new doctrine must create conditions under which the Hindu can be made to feel that Christianity has solutions to real problems. This presentation in turn would arouse in his mind the awareness of problems for which Christianity alone has solutions. He was firmly of the opinion that the main contribution which foreign missionaries could make to the emergence of Indian Christian theology was to lay emphasis on points of fundamental contact between Christianity and Hinduism, starting from the points of agreement, but concentrating on and describing in detail the fundamental differences.

With this aim in mind Hogg studied Hinduism. It was during the period 1904-1909 which coincided with Radhakrishnan's stay in the college that Hogg made a comparative study of Hinduism and Christianity, and wrote a number of articles in the *Madras Christian College Magazine*. A collection of these articles was published in 1909 as a book, *Karma and Redemption*.[14] It is regarded as "one of the most powerful and original works of Christian theology to come out of the missionary enterprise."[15]

This anthology affirms "that the innermost faith of all religions which are still, at any time, worthy of the name must be one and the same,"[16] with the reservation that "the divergences between the intellectual beliefs by which man preserves this common spirit of faith" is "nevertheless an immensely important matter."[17] The inner faith which is common to all living and healthy religions, and is a sign of their vitality, is the "assurance that the supreme Reality is humanly satisfying," or as Christian apostles put it "God is light and in Him there is no darkness at all."[18] But this faith of religion in God as a Being which is 'wholly light,' 'perfectly good' and 'totally satisfying,' he argued, is shattered when they find a world which is full of evil, and undeserved calamity. So they try to think about Him and His relation to the world in an alternative way which shows the sorrows (sufferings) in the world to be in the final analysis blessings in disguise which will ultimately make life satisfying again. Unless they think so, they cannot have trust in God. "Such a way of thinking is a religious belief, a belief about God, rendering possible faith or trust *in* God."[19]

Faith, Hogg contended, is distinct from belief. Faith is trust in God, living a relationship with Him, a desire for intelligent fellowship with Him. Beliefs, on the other hand, are intellectual expressions in which the implications and consequences of faith are expressed and also by means of which faith is sought to be projected, perpetuated and communicated. When both faith and belief do not change, but remain the same throughout, and when they cease to explain life and its problems, but are still adhered to, then they become superstitions. Beliefs by which people or races learn to protect their faith in God differ, depending upon their problems.

Hogg found the Hindu belief in the theory of *Karma* and the way of release, which is "real gospel" to a Hindu, helping him in a trustful surrender of his will to the Supreme Being, to be "strange and rather dismal." It is strange, he argued, because though *Karma* theory may be true it can neither be demonstrated nor has an analogy in nature. Rather, this theory is contradicted by the theory of evolution, it robs history of its meaning, frustrates the will to serve and interrupts natural law. But it is positive in that it provides a logical theory of punishment and offers to explain inequalities, and assumes that never can the deserts of sin become infinite. He analyzed the Hindu theory of *Karma*, and tried to show that it presents a moral dilemma. According to him, if *Karma* is a just system based on exact requital of deeds, then the desire of a truly spiritual Hindu to break and escape from a system based upon merit and demerit cannot be fully moral, and if the desire to escape from *Karma* is moral then the system on which *Karma* is based, namely, that on the principle of merit and demerit, is nonmoral, or immoral. He found the *Karma* theory "dismal" for, he thought, it is based on the assumption that the purpose of the universe is judicial and not moral and the formation of the divine providence is to requite. On the other hand, according to Christianity, God's purpose in creating the universe is not to dispense judgment but to educate man into a likeness of Himself, and the function of the divine providence is to reveal the character of God to men in such a way as to win their love, their service and their invitation. God's dealings with men are not measured by their deserts.

Hogg thought that "the feeling of the weariness of life and the unjustifiableness of unmerited suffering" from which he believed the Hindu mind suffers can be mitigated if it reinterprets the law of *Karma* in a Christian sense, that is, if it recognizes that the purpose of the universe is moral. It is to offer to every soul the eternal "boon of fellowship with God in the voluntary service of absolute good." God is love, and though the world is sinful, love can nevertheless express itself in it. The world is subject not merely to the *Kārmic* law but also the law of salvation. According to the second law if there is sin in the world God is compelled by his moral nature to enter into it, to incarnate Himself to abolish sinfulness. Hogg advocated this view of incarnation rather than the traditional Hindu view of terrestrial reincarnation. According to him, the perfect example of incarnation is provided by Jesus Christ whose message is centered on the establishment of the Kingdom of God which shows itself in "redemption from evils of soul, body and circumstances." In such a kingdom, the source of power and His plenitude, which frees us from *real* evil of every kind, is available to all, on the condition of absolute trust.

Hogg compared and contrasted the Hindu ideal with the Christian ideal, and advocated the supremacy of the latter over the former. Whereas "Hinduism offers to save man from the world which is thought of as incurably finite and unsatisfactory, Christianity offers to save the world from itself—to save all that is precious in our world order from all in it that makes for decay and consumption."[20] He supported the view that while the Hindu ideal is the salvation of the individual soul, Christianity believes that God is *intent* on rescuing from evil not merely the human soul, but the whole of human life in its concrete unity. The objective of

Jesus Christ is to rescue the entire creation from bondage, limitations and decay, and men ought to share in this task as Jesus commanded all men to do. These ideas of philosophy, faith and universal redemption had a considerable role in shaping Radhakrishnan's thinking.

Influence on Radhakrishnan

The Christian atmosphere in the Madras Christian College had both a positive and negative effect on the mind of young Radhakrishnan. It strengthened his religious outlook, and provided him an opportunity to acquaint himself with the teachings of the *New Testament*, as well as to acquire a knowledge of European philosophy, especially of Plato, Plotinus, Kant, Hegel, Bradley and Bergson. Besides, his European teachers introduced him to Western literary classics. This exposure to European philosophy and literature had much influence on his *worldview* as well as his philosophical outlook. On the other hand, he had to listen to his teachers' criticism of Indian thought, religion, and tradition, which ruffled the beliefs and practices deeply rooted in his Hindu mind. But unlike other students who were either swayed by such criticism, or were indifferent to it, his "pride as a Hindu, developed by the enterprise and eloquence of Swami Vivekananda was deeply hurt by the treatment accorded to Hinduism"[21] by his teachers. He was also taken aback by such criticism of Hindu thought and was "somewhat annoyed that truly religious people—as many Christian missionaries undoubtedly were—could treat as subjects for derision, doctrines that others held in deepest reverence."[22] As he reminisced later, "The challenge of Christian critics impelled me to make a study of Hinduism and find out what is living and what is dead in it. The spirit of the times, in which India, so to say, was turning in its sleep, strengthened this resolve."[23] This challenge became his life's mission. In order to give a befitting reply to his teachers and to avenge this sense of hurt Radhakrishnan surveyed the literature on Hinduism then available. Later in his life, especially during his stay in Madras Presidency College, he "studied the classics of Hinduism, the *Upaniṣads*, the *Bhagavadgītā* and the commentaries on the *Brahama Sūtra* by the chief ācāryas, Śaṅkara, Rāmānuja, Mādhva, Nimbārka and others, the Dialogues of the Buddha as well as the scholastic works of Hinduism, Buddhism, and Jainism."[24] Credit goes to his teachers at the Madras Christian College for awakening him from his "dogmatic slumber"—a state in which he was unreflectively following the dictates of populist Hinduism.

As he recalled later, "A critical study of Hindu ideas was thus forced upon me. . . . The need for philosophy arises when faith in tradition is shaken."[25]

As part of his M.A. course, Radhakrishnan wrote a dissertation on the *Ethics of Vedānta*, when he was just twenty. It shows that even as a student he was dissatisfied with the generally prevalent exposition of Advaita philosophy. In it he attempted a reply to the criticism leveled by his teachers, that Hinduism in general and Advaita Vedānta in particular, provide no firm basis for practical conduct. He endeavored to show that the Hindu religion was a rational way of living, with a positive ethical content, and that though essentially concerned with the inner life, it had "to express itself in reasonable thought, fruitful action and right social institutions."[26] He argued that philosophy in India, particularly Advaita philosophy "is not an abstract study remote from the life of man."[27] He further maintained that "the civilization of India is an effort to embody philosophical wisdom in social life."[28] Replying to the criticism that Hinduism in general, and Vedānta in particular relegate the world to unreality, and, therefore, there is no place in it for ethics, he contended:

> The world has no existence in the absolute sense of the term. It has no existence in the sense of "unchangeable," "immovable," "infinite" and "uncaused." Such is the meaning which the Hindu philosophers attribute to the expression *"Jagan Mithya"* though it has given rise to many misconceptions which are unwarranted and which a systematic study of the *Vedānta* doctrine would have saved. "Māyā" is just a name which is given to the world to designate its relativity.[29]

Comparing *Vedānta* ethics with the Kantian primarily, and quoting a number of Western thinkers and writers—Aristotle, Epicurus, Voltaire, Byron, Johnson, Müller, Wordsworth, Deussen, Lange, Hegel and Bailie—he maintained: "The *Vedāntic* explanation is the practical recognition of a positive fact that we are all bound up together as sharers of the same eternal life and children of the same immortal bliss."[30] He concluded that "Ignorance is the cause and knowledge the cure of the moral imperfection."[31]

Replying to the criticism that Vedānta ethics is "rigoristic," Radhakrishnan argued that it is not impractical. To the criticism that Vedānta ethics teaches "the 'I' should not find a place in any act of moral goodness"[32] necessarily implying that one must content oneself with an ascetic life, or that action should be completely motiveless, he replied that all that Vedānta ethics teaches is that action is inevitable and the only motives prohibited in the system "are the egoistic motives of affection and aversion and not any and every motive whatsoever."[33]

Hogg commented on this dissertation of Radhakrishnan: "The thesis . . . shows a remarkable understanding of the main aspects of the philosophical problem, a capacity for handling easily a complex argument, besides more than the average mastery of good English."[34]

This enterprise of Radhakrishnan to try to interpret Indian philosophy to Westerners in an idiom and language that was understood by them, and to defend the Advaitic (non-dualistic) thought in the tradition of Śaṅkara, and as expounded in the lectures, talks and writings of Swami Vivekananda, was to endure throughout his life. His dissertation was published in the same year he wrote it, i.e. 1908. As Radhakrishnan was just twenty years old then, seeing his name on the title page of the book, he later wrote, excited him a great deal.[35] In 1937 he commented: "when I look back upon the juvenile and rhetorical production, I am ashamed that I ever wrote it."[36] In the 1950s stating that the question of the relation of metaphysics and ethics had been with him from his student days, Radhakrishnan mentioned that a "somewhat jejune reply" to the criticism that Indian philosophy, especially the Vedānta variety of it, is nonethical, was contained in his 1908 thesis.[37]

To sustain himself economically, Radhakrishnan tutored throughout his stay in college, students who were junior to him by a couple of years and needed some additional personal help outside the college. One such student was E.L. Ethiraj, who later became a leading member of the Madras bar and established a women's college with his munificent donation. At no stage did he let his own poverty be an insurmountable impediment in the way of his achievements. He always upheld the view that it did not matter whether you were born with a silver spoon or a wooden spoon in your mouth, what mattered was what you swill with it. In his later life he took pride in narrating to his colleagues the earlier days when he struggled with his poverty.[38]

II.

Teacher at Madras and Rajahmundry

Teaching and Scholarly Work at Madras Presidency College

The year 1909 marked an important year in Radhakrishnan's life. He passed his M.A. in this year, though the degree was awarded at the convocation of 1911. It was also in the same year that the first child of Radhakrishnan was born. In April he entered the Madras Provincial Education Service and began his teaching career. He was first appointed to the vacant post of Malayalam master at Presidency College, Madras, the scale of pay of Rs. sixty to eighty per month, but his actual teaching was in the Department of Mental and Moral Sciences. In the college he lectured to the intermediate, B.A., B.A.(Hons) and M.A. classes.

In Presidency College, Dr. Sathianathan was the professor of philosophy. Radhakrishnan was asked to teach deductive logic and psychology. No specific accommodation in the college building was allotted to the Department of Philosophy. One who was a student at that time has recorded that in those days one could often see the fair-complexioned, tall, slim, bespectacled figure of Radhakrishnan with a big head, broad forehead, aquiline nose, a keen yet serene face, a pair of eyes that showed no fret or wavering, wearing a long white coat, a white turban and a dhoti moving with a shy and yet brisk gait through the corridors of the college.[1] Most of the students hardly noticed him. But those who were attending his classes were, it seems, highly impressed by his deep knowledge of philosophy, phenomenal memory, a rare gift of expounding even the most abstract and abstruse philosophical doctrines in terms simple and intelligible to all the class, and by the impressive and eloquent way in which he lectured. He used to give his lectures standing. According to another account, as sentences leaving unforgettable impressions flowed from him with felicitious ease, in a seried march one upon the other, the left hand shaped into a fist, but soon disappearing into the side pocket of his long coat, contracting and relaxing in unison with the flow of words.[2]

11

He used to come to the class in his academic gown. As a matter of routine, for a class of fifty minutes duration, Radhakrishnan used to come to his class twenty minutes late and finish his lecture ten minutes before the scheduled time. Yet, in those twenty minutes, it has been said, he gave a brilliant exposition, unsurpassed in brevity and clarity.[3] Whatever he taught, none failed to grasp. The impact of his short lectures was so great that the words that he used, like "In this connection, Bosanquet incidentally remarks . . ." rang in the ears of his students even fifty years later.[4] Students, it is said, adored him in a manner in which they adored none else, and though he never spoke a harsh word, a strict discipline was maintained in his classes.

The accounts referred to in the last two paragraphs were written after Radhakrishnan became important in Indian public life; these and such others are likely to be encomiastic.

Many of his students, his old classmates and school friends used to come to meet him at his residence in Madras seeking his help. He always met them with warmth and a smile, and had a kind word to say to each one of them, and if he could be of any help, even at the cost of his own convenience, he would never disappoint them.

Since those days, his appearance, dress, mannerisms, easy accessibility, and readiness to help did not change throughout his life, irrespective of the offices he held. What underwent radical change were his personal traits. According to a veracious source, Radhakrishnan in his twenties was a "bohemian" and temperamental, not very disciplined, and prone to occasional outbursts of anger, but in later life he became free from all these tendencies and attained serenity and equipoise.[5]

After working for some time in the Presidency College, in 1910, he had to undergo the training course in the Teacher's College, Saidpet, for the licentiate in teaching (L.T.) in order to qualify for a permanent post of assistant professor. Here, keeping in view the fact that Radhakrishnan had been teaching courses in psychology in the Presidency College, the professor who taught psychology exempted him from attending his classes. So, for preparing for the psychology part of the L.T. examination, he had to study on his own. Interestingly, most of the L.T. students, who were regularly attending the lectures in psychology, felt that they were not adequately prepared to take the examination. So they requested Radhakrishnan to deliver a few informal lectures on psychology. Initially, Radhakrishnan, modest as he was, declined, but when the professor himself persuaded him to supplement his lectures, he gave a series of twelve lectures. The lectures, which reflected his excellent grasp of the subject, were listened to in pin-drop silence by his classmates, all of whom were senior to him in age. Later in 1912, these lectures were published as *Essentials of Psychology*, by Oxford University Press, London. They have been republished in 1989.

Soon after Radhakrishnan completed the L.T. course in 1911, he was given a permanent appointment and promoted to the post of assistant professor of mental and moral sciences on a salary of Rs. 100 per month. Having secured a permanent post, Radhakrishnan intensified his study of the classical texts of Hinduism and Indian philosophy and started writing articles and research papers with an aim to interpret these to Western readers. He wanted to convey to them the nuances of Hindu thought and Indian philosophy in the idiom and terminology of Western philosophy which they understood. He was such a prolific writer that before he turned twenty-seven he had already contributed a number of essays reflecting his diversity of interests, on such wide ranging themes as "Karma and Free Will," "Nature and Convention in Greek Ethics," "The Ethics of the Bhagvadgītā and Kant," "Bergson's Idea of God," "Morality and Religion in Education," "A View from India on the [World] War I." These appeared in journals of international repute, such as *The Monist, The Quest, Mind, Journal of Philosophy* and *The International Journal of Ethics*. The purpose of most of these contributions in his own words was to establish "the ethical character of the Hindu religion," and to prove that:

> Philosophy in India is not an abstract study remote from the life of man. It is intimately woven into the texture of human existence. The civilization in India is an effort to embody philosophical wisdom in social life. . . . Spiritual values are realized on earth through the empiric means of family love, of love and friendship, of loyalty and reverence. To the truly religious, all life is a sacrament. Modern attempts to improve the general condition of the community, to transform society so that hope and happiness might be brought within the reach of the needy and the downtrodden, are not inconsistent with the Hindu religion but are demanded by it.[6]

His essay "A View from India on the [World] War-I," written between 1914-1918 shows that he was not just thinking about abstract philosophical problems, but also reacting to contemporary social and political events. The essay reflects his readiness, sense of duty and courage to let the world know what he thought was the Indian reaction to World War I. His second on this subject was not allowed to be published by the censor.

His article "The Ethics of the Bhagvadgītā and Kant" which was published in *The International Journal of Ethics* in July 1911 attracted the attention of Bal Gangadhar Tilak (1856-1920), who symbolized for the youth of that time burning patriotism, rare courage, indomitable will and dedication to India's freedom. Tilak was at that time in Mandalay prison where he was writing his now famous commentary on *Gītā*. He requested N.C. Kelkar to get a reprint of the article from Radhakrishnan. After reading the article Tilak returned it to Radhakrishnan with his marginal notes. Tilak was so impressed by the article that he made a mention of it along with Radhakrishnan's name in the preface to his *Gītārahasya*. Radhakrishnan was overjoyed to know this and rightly so, for the recognition had come from one of the most revered national leaders and scholars of the time. In his letter of November 4, 1915, to Tilak he wrote, "The recognition of my humble work in the field of Indian philosophy, at the hands of one so very able and learned like yourself has encouraged me a good deal."

Despite the fact that he was producing such a large number of high quality research papers in addition to teaching, he was not always immersed in books. He socialized and met friends frequently. Among his close friends of those days were Professor T.K. Doraiswami Aiyar and Sri Alladi Krishnaswamy Aiyar. The three met quite often and shared many jokes and interesting remarks.

Gandhi-Radhakrishnan Encounter

It was in 1915 soon after Mahatma Gandhi (1869-1948) had returned from South Africa, that Radhakrishnan met him for the first time in the house of G.A. Natesan, a mutual friend. Gandhi at that time was an emerging leader of the Congress political party, and an advocate of mass participation in Indian politics. The meeting, as Radhakrishnan reported to Pyarelal, was "bad." He described the meeting in his own words as follows:

> Gandhiji said to me: "Don't drink milk, which is the essence of beef."
> I replied: "In that case we are all cannibals. For we drink our mother's milk, which is the essence of human flesh."
> The conversation then turned to medical relief.
> Gandhiji said: "Thousands of births take place in the jungle. They do not need any medical attention."
> I said: "Thousands die in the jungle too."

"How do you know?"

"How do you know?"

Natesan intervened and said to Gandhiji: "Don't you know he is a professor of logic."[7]

Later they were to meet a number of times, but we will refer to two significant meetings at Wardha in chapter nine and at Delhi in chapter ten.

Teaching at Rajahmundry and Publication of First Major Work

In 1916, Radhakrishnan was promoted to professor and placed in the provincial grade and posted to the Government Arts College, Rajahmundry (Andhra Pradesh). Here too, he was able to impress the students with his depth of knowledge, characteristic style and mastery of the art of clear exposition. According to available reports, he soon became popular among the students as "the most wonderful lecturer" and "an inspiring and beloved teacher." His unassuming and friendly mannerisms won the hearts of fellow teachers, students and neighbors alike. As K. Iswara Dutt, the son of one of his friends and his next door neighbor, recalls:

> How extraordinarily simple he was and how unusual! I still remember vividly how, clad in the simplest style, he used to sit at his residence on a mat spread in the verandah overlooking the road, with a kind word to every passer-by, big or small, greeting him. I also remember how he used to stop two of my little sisters going to school, and make them sing, himself keeping time to encourage them. It was characteristic of this man of great learning that he did not discourage youngsters from talking to him even in faulty English, in their innocence. One of my fondest recollections was an exhibition of my youthful audacity when, as a student of Intermediate, I thrust into his hands an essay of mine on Ruskin! There was no sense of condescension on his part in going through it, like the typical schoolmaster, with a smile occasionally playing on his lips. He did not send me away either without an encouraging word or serious advice. I was told the language "be simple, direct and pointed."[8]

Radhakrishnan stayed in Rajahmundry until 1918. The days spent here, as he himself said, were the happiest and most fulfilling years of his life. It was during these years that he worked on the manuscript of his book *The Philosophy of Rabindra Nath Tagore* which was published in 1918. With it Radhakrishnan made a *debut* as a serious writer on philosophy. The book is a brilliant and lucid summary of much that is vital in Tagore. Radhakrishnan viewed Tagore (1861-1941) not only as a historic link in the long chain of India's cultural, traditional and intellectual evolution, but also as a prophet of the Indian renaissance heralded by Raja Ram Mohan Roy. Describing Tagore's philosophy he says, "Tagore's supreme spirit is not an abstract entity residing at a safe distance from the world, but is the concrete, dynamic life at the center of things, giving rise to the roar of the wind and the surf of the sea . . . Rabindranath's is a wholeness of vision which cannot tolerate any absolute divisions."[9]

The book reflects the deep influence that Tagore had on the mind of Radhakrishnan. While expounding and evaluating the poet's inspired lines, he to some extent worked out and presented his own world view. As a critic says, "In this book Radhakrishnan was unwittingly rehearsing his own future flights in the domain of international literature."[10] After reading the book Rabinbdranath Tagore wrote to him:

> Though my criticism of a book that concerns me may not be seriously accepted, I can say that it has surpassed my expectation. The earnestness of your endeavour and your penetration have amazed me, and I am thankful to you for the literary grace of its language which is so beautifully free from all technical jargon and a mere display of scholarship.[11]

However, much later Radhakrishnan, reflecting upon the quality of the book, thought it to be full of "all the faults of immature youth" though "it secured on the whole a friendly reception."[12]

Later in the same year when he met Rabindranath Tagore, the poet admired the young philosopher's deep insight and the literary grace of his exposition, and complimented him for his "marvelous gift of speech and originality of thoughts."

III.

Professor at Mysore

Teaching at Mysore and Publication of Second Major Work

Mysore University was established in 1916. Radhakrishnan, who had by this time established himself as a distinguished scholar and teacher, was offered the professorship in Indian philosophy in the Maharaja's College—a constituent college of Mysore University—which he accepted and joined in July, 1918. While at Mysore University, he was promoted to the imperial grade by the Madras government. Radhakumud Mukerjee, K.T. Shah and A.R. Wadia joined the college as professors around the same time. All of them became close friends, not knowing at that time that they were destined to be members of Parliament in free India. The other well-known teachers of Mysore University in those days were C.R. Reddy, N.S. Subba Rao, M. Hiriyanna, Mahamahopadhayaya Lakshim-puram Srinivasa Acharya, and a few others. The Maharaja of Mysore and his Diwan (prime minister) M. Visvesvarayya were responsible for attracting all these men to the university and making it a reputed center of learning soon after it was established.

Mysore University thus provided an excellent environment in which scholarship could flourish. As Radhakrishnan recalled later, "In Mysore, I found the impetus for learning . . . which the authorities fostered."[1] He exploited the available opportunities to the optimum. It was during his Mysore days that he published a series of articles in *Mind* in which he, after examining Bergson's philosophy, attempted to prove that he was an absolutist and wrote his second book *The Reign of Religion in Contemporary Philosophy*, which was published in 1920. It enhanced his reputation further. In this book Radhakrishnan made a serious attempt to grapple with Western thought. The book was favorably reviewed "by men of established reputation in philosophy like J.H. Muirhead, J.S. Mackenzie and J.E.C. McTaggart, among others." Reminiscing about the book Radhakrishnan wrote, "It had a very warm reception. . . . The book was used by students in metaphysics not only in Indian universities, but in several British and American ones, and I became known as a writer of philosophy."[2] The impact that the book made on philosophers all over the world can be gauged from the fact that Professor Hinman chose for his presidential address to the American Philosophical Association, the theme, "Two Representative Idealists, Bosanquet and Radhakrishnan."

The aim of the book was to show that Western philosophers, not withstanding their claims to the contrary, were nonetheless influenced by their theological beliefs and that theistic religion continued to dominate philosophy even in modern times, resulting in a return of prejudice against absolutism. In it he mentioned that truth can be apprehended through reason and logic, that what cannot be demonstrated does not exist, and that philosophy is an effort to understand reality intellectually. He upheld the view that the business of philosophy is not to give us a faith or a viewpoint, but an attempt to organize intellectually all human experience. Philosophy, he argued, must be indifferent to religion, and should not be influenced by political reasons or emotions. Once we recognize the fact that truly philosophical reasoning proceeds solely on the basis of reason and logic, and is not influenced either by religious beliefs or by other prejudices like political, social, or cultural considerations, etc., we realize that it would result in absolute idealism. Examining the philosophies of thinkers like William James, Rudolf Eucken, James Ward, Leibnitz, and Bergson among others, he tried to show that all of them supported pluralism or pluralistic theism because of their religious presuppositions and prejudices. Without their religious commitments they would all have ended up as monists. Radhakrishnan condemned such a dominance of religion in philosophy and pleaded for the development of a philosophy in which religion is neither the basis nor the motivating force.

The militant rationalism of the book created quite a stir. While recognizing the author's intellectual ardor, philosophical vigor and dialectical skill, many critics described the book as contentious and aggressive. However, much later, Radhakrishnan himself admitted that this book was "over ambitious" and that in it he did not take into account the questions whether it was possible at all to philosophize in a vacuum, whether any thinker could consciously or unconsciously completely cast off the influence of his culture, religion, upbringing, class and milieu. For he came to recognize that even a heterodox thinker is one who thinks with as much prejudice as an orthodox thinker. The iconoclast is no more a free man than the idol worshipper. An idealist is no more independent of a tradition than a theist. Such considerations in course of time led him to abandon the views expressed in this book. Consequently, it was never reprinted.

In 1917 J.H. Muirhead, who had read Radhakrishnan's articles in *Mind*, *Monist*, *The Quest*, and *The International Journal of Ethics* and was impressed by their style as well as the depth of thought expressed in them, invited him to write a book on Indian philosophy for publication in the *Library of Philosophy* series of which he was the general editor. Accordingly, during 1917-1920, in his days at Mysore, Radhakrishnan worked on this project, and more or less completed the first draft of *Indian Philosophy*, which is generally considered to be his *magnum opus*. Considerable parts of the manuscript were read by V. Subramanya Aiyar and J.S. Mackenzie and the author "profited much by their friendly and suggestive counsel." A.B. Keith read the proofs and made "many valuable comments." In preparing the second edition of the first volume, the author was "considerably assisted" by M. Hiriyanna's suggestions, and for the second edition of the second volume he was "specially indebted" to him (Hiriyanna). For the latter Mahamahopadhyayas S. Kuppuswami Sastri and N.S. Anantakrishna Sastri "helped" him with "valuable advice" (Prefaces to the volumes).

In college, Radhakrishnan showed great regard for the scholarship and expertise of his colleagues. In deciding which subject was to be taught by whom, he did not let his personal interests and the area of his specialization interfere to the detriment of the growth of his colleagues' interests and their fields of expertise. This was evident from the fact that even though at that time he himself was working on the manuscript of *Indian Philosophy*, he, keeping in mind Hiriyanna's scholarship in Indian philosophy (based on Sanskrit sources) and having a great regard for it, requested him to teach Indian philosophy courses to B.A. and M.A. classes, while he occupied himself primarily with teaching courses in History of Western Philosophy, Ethics, History of Political Thought and Psychology.

Most of the students, particularly in Maharaja's College, Mysore, and in other institutions like Central College of Science at Bangalore, had already heard so much of Radhakrishnan's erudition, and of the methodical and attractive exposition of his subject in his lectures that for them he became one with a halo. They took every opportunity to attend his classes and listen to his lectures. His classes, as a consequence, were always packed to capacity. "His exposition," as V. Sitaramaiah, one of his students in Mysore, recorded in *My College Days* later, "was so exhaustive and nothing relevant to a topic or discussion was left out that one could even pass a higher examination by simply listening to whatever he said, or read whatever was dictated. One could understand a topic to the core, and all confusions would be cleared at the end of each hour. That clarity of thought, flourish of language, and judgement regarding issues were all his. They were final. Sometimes we felt should he not leave something to us for our study? Such was the completeness of his treatment of a subject or topic."[3]

While such were the impressions of apparently infatuated students, it appears there were a few, for whom at least, his public lectures were "funeral" because of their seriousness and lack of humour.[4]

M. Yamunacharya, yet another student of his reported, "In his classes, when he held forth the philosophies of the great thinkers of the West, it gave us a thrill to listen to him, and the profound influence these lectures had on us is ineffable but nevertheless real and true."[5] While expounding the views of a particular philosopher he appeared to be perfectly in accord with his temper and spirit. He encouraged his students to think philosophically, and choose an ideal of their own. But being a realist he would at the same time exhort his students not "to lose our foot-hold on earth while sweeping the skies."[6]

He used to meet the students of his tutorial group at his residence and talk matters over tea. This personal touch as well as "his goodness of the heart, cheerfulness, easy accessibility, the confident way in which he moved about among one and all," as Sitaramaiah gushed forth, "made everyone feel he was one's own elder to whom one could go at any time for any purpose. Without an exception he was loved and respected by all, whether one was his direct student or not. He was ideal as a teacher, ideal as an example."[7] He was in the habit of patting his students on the back and shaking hands warmly with them whenever and wherever he met them. He had nicknames for many of his students. He had such a phenomenal memory that he never forgot those nicknames later. As S. Nijalingapa, who was not his direct student but was a student of Central College of Science, Bangalore, and who used to attend his classes whenever there was an opportunity to do so, recalled "Even today whenever he sees them [his students] he pats them affectionately on the back, calls them by nicknames, and it is a wonder how he remembers quite a large number of them even after a lapse of about forty years."[8]

Radhakrishnan was popular not only among students but also among teachers for his unassuming simple habits, the characteristic patience with which he listened to everyone, and his sparkling wit and humour. He never had any physical exercise, nor did he indulge in any form of recreation. He did all his reading, writing, dictating and talking to visitors, while in bed. A.R. Wadia, who was his close friend and neighbor, had to his credit the distinction of drawing him out occasionally for a stroll or a game of bridge. Wadia narrated the following two episodes as instances of his wit and sense of humour: "One of our colleagues was known to be rather pompous and fastidious and needless to say he was very unpopular with us. When Radhakrishnan was asked by a member of the Mysore government what his relationship with that colleague was, pat came the reply: 'Correct but not cordial'. Another of our colleagues had been a director of a bank. The bank had failed and it was a common joke with Radhakrishnan to say: 'The bank failed, but X has become rich'. It was a patent case of libel if taken seriously, but he said it so light-heartedly and jovially that even the victim of his joke could not help laughing with the rest of us."[9]

IV.

From Mysore to Calcutta

Asutosh Mookerjee and the University of Calcutta

The University of Calcutta was the first teaching university set up in India after Lord Curzon passed the Universities Act of 1904. Before that, like all other universities in India, it was also an examining and affiliating university. Sir Asutosh Mookerjee (1864-1924) was its vice-chancellor from March 31, 1906 to March 30, 1914 when the university was under the central government, and again from April 1921 to 1923, when the university was under the Bengal government. During the period 1917-1921, he was the president of the Postgraduate Councils in the Faculty of Science and the Faculty of Arts. He was associated with the university for a period of seventeen years as a member of the syndicate.*

His aim was to make Calcutta University a temple of learning to which students, not only from all over India but from all over the continent, would flock, attracted by its excellence in instruction and facilities for research. He wanted it to develop into a cosmopolitan and not a provincial university. The university, he hoped, would realize its motto "Advancement of Learning," and place India on the research map of the world. Keeping this in mind, he appointed the best available scholars as professors, irrespective of the region, class or caste they belonged to. He had a rare insight in spotting talent. Though he invited senior persons, who had already made a mark in their respective fields of study to join the University, his faith and trust were pinned mainly on the youth, and he picked out the brilliant ones from among the relatively fresh graduates, who were then unknown to fame, but had the hidden potential of realizing the glorious future that lay before them. He was the man who detected the genius in C.V. Raman, S.K. Mitter, S.N. Bose, M.N. Saha, H.C. Ray Chowdhury, D.R. Bhandarkar, Ganesh Prasad, Manoharlal, Khuda Baksh and many others, who were at that time unknown and brought them to teach at Calcutta University. When one looks at the list of professors

---

*Board of Trustees

22

whom Mookerjee selected, it seems as if he unconsciously had an eye on national integration too.

Asutosh Mookerjee had a high sense of self-esteem and courage to defy, when necessary, the government and act according to his convictions. When Lord Lytton offered him another term as vice-chancellor on the condition that he would not work against the government or seek aid from any agencies to defeat the government's bill on education, he declined the offer. He wrote explaining to Lytton that according to the traditions of the high office, a vice-chancellor was not expected to adapt himself to a government's views and wishes, and that he could not be a subservient vice-chancellor always prepared to carry out mandates of the government and act as a spy on the senate. He valued the autonomy of the university so much that when the government, in 1922, announced a grant of Rs. 250,000 to the university subject to eight conditions, he asked the senate to reject it. He said, "We shall not be a part of the Secretariat."

The fact that Asutosh was ready to face the government on issues which he thought were right was amply demonstrated in June 1913 when he introduced postgraduate teaching in International Law and in Arabic. He invited, among others, Abdul Rasul, K.P. Jayaswal and Dr. Suhrawardy to deliver special lectures to students. The names of the special lectures were duly approved by the syndicate of Calcutta University. The government vetoed their appointment on the ground that it considered them to be undesirable as they were taking a prominent part in the political movement. Mookerjee wrote a strong letter to the government against this decision as it overruled the recommendation of the senate. He had the matter rediscussed in the senate which resolved that the government should re-examine its decision on the unqualified blanket ban on the appointment by universities of persons engaged in the freedom struggle, as this adversely affected the interest of education by depriving universities of the services of competent persons in many instances. There were threats from the government to stop or reduce financial assistance to the university; a committee was appointed to assess postgraduate teaching in Calcutta; and a commission was set up to enquire into the conditions and prospects of the University of Calcutta. But nothing could deter Mookerjee from appointing as lecturers the persons whose names had been approved by the syndicate.

According to Mookerjee, "A university designed for the service of a nation in all possible phases of development cannot be restricted to a narrow or chosen teaching. It cannot be treated either as a great scholastic sanctuary or as a glorified teaching institute." He was of the opinion that a truly national university must necessarily provide opportunities for teaching and learning, even of those subjects which had a limited scope of employment, and, consequently attracted few students. "If we do not do so," according to him, "we will have none to advance the boundary of human knowledge except chemists and blacksmiths."[1] In accordance with his views, he introduced M.A. courses in Indian languages and promoted the study of Pali, Tibetology, Sanskrit and Buddhist studies. He appointed professors in each of these subjects in the university.

This somewhat detailed account of Asutosh Mookerjee's outstanding contribution to university development has been given, because that provided the pattern for Radhakrishnan when the latter had to nurture universities.

King George V Professorship

In 1911-1912, when the capital was transferred from Calcutta to Delhi, Mookerjee persuaded the then Chancellor Lord Hardinge to endow two professorships in Calcutta University, in commemoration of the visit of King-Emperor George V and Queen-Empress Mary to India to attend the Delhi Durbar. They were to be called the King George V Professor of Mental and Moral Philosophy, and the Hardinge Professor of Higher Mathematics. At the annual convocation of the university in 1912, Lord Hardinge announced a recurring grant of Rs.65,000 to the university for the purpose of advanced teaching. The governor-general in council, on the recommendation of the syndicate and the senate of the university, approved the former chair to be called the King George V Professorship of Mental and Moral Philosophy. This decision was governed by two major considerations: (1) There was no provision at that time for the teaching of this important branch of knowledge up to M.A. standard in any college in Calcutta, except in the Scottish Church College where, too, the arrangements were going to be unfavorably affected by the impending retirement of Professor Stephen who was then teaching this course, and (2) Mental and Moral Philosophy had always had great attraction for Indian students, and many significant papers had been written by the graduates of Calcutta University on themes in this field. It was hoped that the establishment of a chair in this subject would stimulate higher study and research on lines likely to prove fruitful. The senate also resolved that the salary of the professor would be fixed at Rs.12,000 per annum.

Later, on May 11, 1929, the senate also made the following rules, to be applicable to the holders of the chair:

1. The professor shall devote himself to original study and research in mental and moral philosophy with a view to extending the bounds of knowledge.
2. The professor shall stimulate and guide advanced study and research by advanced students in the University of Calcutta.
3. The professor shall undertake regular teaching work in the postgraduate classes and shall ordinarily deliver not less than four lectures in his subject every week for the benefit of M.A. students of the Postgraduate Department of the University.
4. The professor shall be subject to such instructions and rules regarding leave, residence and retirement as may be decided by the university as applicable to professors.

Brojendra Nath Seal, whose scholarship was encyclopaedic, became the first King George V Professor of Mental and Moral Philosophy in 1913. He continued in this position until 1920, when he accepted the invitation of the enlightened Maharaja of Mysore to be the vice-chancellor of Mysore University. A successor for him had to be found.

Invitation from Calcutta

Radhakrishnan's *The Philosophy of Rabindranath Tagore* and *The Reign of Religion in Contemporary Philosophy* had made him popular among the *bhadra lok** of Bengal. Because of his varied interests, Asutosh Mookerjee had read with appreciation these works as well as some articles of their author. So he at once thought of Radhakrishnan as a possible successor to Seal. While he was staying in Madras with his friend Sir P.S. Sivaswami Aiyar, on his way to Mysore where he was going to deliver the first convocation address of Mysore University, Mookerjee expressed a wish to meet Radhakrishnan. But Radhakrishnan was not available in Madras at that time. Nevertheless, it was conveyed to Radhakrishnan that Mookerjee would like him to apply for the King George V Professorship of Mental and Moral Philosophy. With some hesitation Radhakrishnan sent his application for it. The university senate appointed a special committee consisting of Mookerjee, himself,

---

* English educated class

Sir Nilratan Sircar, George Howells, Henry Stephen and W.W. Hanell to consider the applications received for this professorship. The committee met on November 15, 1920. Among the applicants were a few very senior and well-known professors of philosophy. After due consideration, the committee recommended that S. Radhakrishnan, M.A., be appointed to the chair. The recommendation was accepted by the senate and the syndicate, and approved by the Government of India.

Most people were surprised when this appointment was announced. They openly criticized it, for they felt that the choice overlooked and ignored the claims of senior, established and reputed philosophers. They were also perplexed at the choice of a young man of about thirty from the South as the successor to Seal, the doyen of Indian philosophers. But within a short time after Radhakrishnan joined, a number of unprejudiced critics were silenced when they became aware of his scholarship and teaching ability. The march of events soon made them see their mistaken outlook and reaffirmed their faith in the sound vision of Asutosh Mookerjee.

When Radhakrishnan received the news of his selection, he hesitated to accept the appointment for he felt that he was too young and unworthy to succeed so eminent a philosopher as Brojendra Nath Seal. C.R. Reddy, his senior in the Madras Christian College and his colleague in Mysore University, who was one of his admirers and valued friends, had to force him to accept it. As he reminisced later, "I had literally to bundle him out of Mysore."[2] He argued with Radhakrishnan and convinced him that his going to Calcutta "was indeed an export that meant for the South more than elephants laden with gold, and camels bearing precious stones and rare spices, could ever fetch."[3] Radhakrishnan reluctantly accepted the Calcutta appointment and resigned from the Maharaja College, Mysore, in February 1921.

Farewell to Mysore

The news of his resignation spread like wild fire among the students and the teachers in the college and in other institutions of Mysore and Bangalore. The reverence and esteem with which Radhakrishnan had come to be regarded by most of them was evident in the spontaneous expression of an intense feeling of separation they felt on hearing the news. They wanted him not to leave Mysore and wished that the authorities of Mysore University would persuade him to stay on by increasing his salary. But it was not so much a question of an increase in salary as that of prestige, because while Mysore's was an ordinary professorship, Calcutta, one of the oldest and most prestigious universities in India, offered the lavishly endowed and glamorous chair named after the king-emperor. The latter was more or less like a regius professorship at an English university. Parties to bid farewell to Radhakrishnan followed one after the other. V. Sitaramaiah effusively recorded later in his *My College Days*: "If there was an occasion for any student in Mysore to go mad, it was found in this instance. If one could say, students reached their *turīya* level of madness at the feeling of separation from their ideal teacher. They felt forlorn and orphaned and found it extremely difficult to part his company."

On the day of their professor's leaving Mysore for Calcutta, the students brought a horse-drawn coach—but without the horses. It was decorated with flowers to give it the look of a chariot. They insisted on Radhakrishnan's sitting in it on his way to the railway station. The coach was dragged by the students themselves—each one of them vying with the others to grab an opportunity to either pull it from the front, or to push it from behind—all along the five-kilometer-long road from the Maharaja's College to the railway station. Many distinguished citizens of Mysore and teachers of the university marched along with it. The station was packed with Radhakrishnan's students and admirers. The railway carriage by which he was scheduled to travel to Bangalore was also decorated with flowers. The students filled up every inch of the compartment and crowded onto the footboard as well.

M. Yamunacharya, one of the students present on the occasion rapturously recalled this incident thus:

> The train was about to steam off, our beloved teacher stood at the door of the compartment. We were all in tears. The great professor wept too. It was a sweet and sad parting. He held out his hand to bless us. We were grateful for his grace. Our eyes were wet and our throats were parched. We could hardly summon up the capacity to cry full throated "Radhakrishnan-ki-jai," which however we did. So he was borne away by the train and he was out of sight, leaving behind a trail of glory and the gleam of a sweet vision which is an abiding possession with us.[4]

V.

Professor at Calcutta

Teaching and Further Study

With Radhakrishnan's arrival in Calcutta, where he resided on Harish Mukherjee Road, began one of the most eventful periods of his life. His occupancy of the King George V Chair helped him to get national recognition of his talents, which gradually led to their international recognition. His sojourn at Calcutta was the most productive period of his intellectual life. It was also here that his first son and last child (named Gopal) was born in 1923. By then he was already the father of five daughters, named Padmavati, Rukmini, Sunila, Sundari and Shakuntala.

The Department of Philosophy at Calcutta University consisted of such eminent philosophers as Krishnachandra Bhattacharya, Surendranath Dasgupta, Bholanath Ray, and Nalinikanta Brahma. It provided its members an excellent atmosphere to work. In addition to teaching, Radhakrishnan seriously set about giving finishing touches to his *Indian Philosophy*, Volume I, and began to study some original Sanskrit philosophical texts, and when necessary and possible, taking the help of Sanskrit *pandits* with traditional training. He was teaching Modern European Philosophy covering the period from Bacon to Kant.

In Calcutta, too, Radhakrishnan's reputation as a teacher par excellence very soon spread beyond philosophy classes, and students from other departments like psychology, economics, and Sanskrit, were tempted to attend his classes. Most of them admired his lucid and terse treatment of the topics under discussion. Though many of them were impressed by his scholarship and fluency, some felt that he was not a "serious teacher." As one of them recalled, "He had a lot of fireworks of phrases. When, however, we tried to sum up his lectures, we often fumbled for some substance." To some of the students oriented towards Marxism, Radhakrishnan's jokes about Marx being a prophet and Marxism being a new religion "appeared to be stale." They found his claims about 'Indian Spiritualism' or about 'Advaita Vedānta' representing the highest synthesis of wisdom etc. etc., too tall, and, so, these claims "did not have much impact" on their minds.[1]

The Magnum Opus Appears

In 1923 Radhakrishnan's monumental work *Indian Philosophy*, Volume I, was published in the *Library of Philosophy* edited by Muirhead and published by George Allen and Unwin, London. The second volume of the same book was published four years later, in 1927 by the same publishers. Its publication made him internationally known, for it fulfilled a long-felt need for the presentation of the ideas and doctrines of Indian philosophy in such a manner that people in the West or scholars nurtured and trained in the Western philosophical tradition could understand them. The already existing works like those of Garbe and Max Müller had stimulated their appetite for more detailed expositions. This new work by an Indian, who had a first-hand knowledge of ancient and medieval Indian works along with a good knowledge of Western philosophy, in addition to a mastery over the English language, was hailed all over the world. In this book he made it clear by expounding in modern philosophical idiom all the schools of Indian thought with sympathy and reverence, that they had an indisputable claim to be called philosophy even in the Western sense of the term. He attempted to show that though Indian philosophy aimed at more than mere speculative understanding, it, on that account, did not lose the right to be philosophy. Though the book was not a treatise on comparative philosophy, because of his extensive knowledge of Western philosophy, his exposition of Indian ideas and doctrines inevitably resulted in a comparative presentation throughout. This, according to some, added considerably to the value of the work. In addition to discussing Indian philosophies in the light of Western philosophies, he critically and creatively evaluated them from the standpoint of absolute idealism.

On March 31, 1936, at Madras, a meeting was organized to felicitate him. He took that opportunity to describe the task he had set for himself in this book, thus:

My endeavour in my book was not so much to chronicle as to interpret. Critics will find a lot of mistakes, so many follies, in all those volumes, but my main attempt was to render the vibration of life, to reveal the movement of mind, to unfold the forces of India's mind in the profound and secret space of men's nature. I wanted to make out that Indian thought was not to be treated as something strange, quaint and antiquated. I wanted to establish that India's answers to the questions which are enjoying the attention of the world today have also their effective contribution to make to the world's spiritual awakening. That was my main interest. It may not be an accurate history, it may not be a perfectly satisfactory kind of this or that. My main idea was to bring about a fresh breath of life in Indian philosophy by reconstructing the atmosphere of philosophising and by tracing the path on which the ideas moved in Indian philosophy.[2]

He claimed to have adopted what he called "the right method" of interpreting the Indian "thinkers at their best, in the light of what they say in their moments of clearest insight." He did not start with the prejudice that he belonged to the modern generation and therefore must be right and these ancients had "faults and passions" that he did not share. As a result of this humility and sympathetic attitude, he was able to penetrate into the thoughts of the ancients and show that "Ancient Indians do not belong to a different species from ourselves. We find from an actual study of their views that they ask questions and find answers analogous in their diversity to some of the more important currents in modern thought."[3]

Radhakrishnan's *Indian Philosophy* is a classic for it not only presents the principal religio-philosophical doctrines and systems of India in a detailed manner, but has also a stylistic excellence which has resulted in uplifting a historico-analytical philosophic work to the level of creative literature. Conger describing the volumes wrote:

His work compared to other available histories of Indian thought and introductions to it, stands somewhat in the relation of a lifelike painting to a photograph. Radhakrishnan's painting shows not merely the face and the form of its subject, Indian thought; it is touched up and and set off by a play of lights and shadows from the West.[4]

The impact of the book was tremendous. It resulted in the revivification of philosophical thought in Indian universities. It helped to put Indian philosophy in its rightful place on the philosophical map of the world. An immediate consequence of the publication of the book was that Radhakrishnan was invited to write a piece on Indian philosophy for the fourteenth edition of the *Encyclopaedia Britannica*. Until its thirteenth edition, this encyclopaedia did not have any entry in it under the head 'Indian Philosophy'. Within India, the book was also responsible for drawing attention to non-Hindu, and especially the great Buddhist, systems of thought.

Overcoming the Calumny

There were quite a large number of university men as well as other intellectuals in Bengal who resented Radhakrishnan's appointment to the most important chair of philosophy in India. They felt that there were already others in the philosophy department of Calcutta University who were superior to him in teaching experience, and that one of them ought to have been appointed to that chair. It is difficult to believe that none of them had a conscious or unconscious prejudice against him, as he was a non-Bengali transplanted to a reputed, old university in Calcutta from a new university in the South. *The Modern Review* became the main forum for the criticism of his works as well as for publishing allegations against his intellectual integrity. This tirade against Radhakrishnan started within three weeks after he joined Calcutta University and continued for more than eight or nine years. To quote Radhakrishnan, in the pages of this journal he was accused of: "faulty English, ignorance of Bengali, lack of Sanskrit learning, imperfect acquaintance with Western philosophy and careless and inadequate references."[5] Although his *Indian Philosophy* was never sent to that journal for review, the book was most unfavorably reviewed in it, and letters pointing out mistakes in language, as well as expositions of theories and concepts in the book were published in it. But Radhakrishnan did not "feel called upon even once to reply to these criticisms" for as he said: "I respect the rights of reviewers to hold any opinion they please regarding works which are public property."[6]

More serious and unfortunate were the allegations made by Jadunath Sinha in a letter which appeared in *The Modern Review*, January, 1929. In 1922 Sinha had submitted a thesis on "Indian Psychology of Perception" for the Premchand Roychand studentship of Calcutta University. While he got the studentship in that year, he submitted further instalments of the thesis in the next three years. The whole thesis was examined by Professors Radhakrishnan and K.C. Bhattacharya. In the letter mentioned he alleged that "numerous passages" from his thesis were "bodily incorporated" in Radhakrishnan's *Indian Philosophy*, Volume II, published in 1927, and that "certain chapters" of his thesis were summarized without even changing his language. Radhakrishnan, Sinha wrote, "obviously wanted to pass them off as his own" as he did not acknowledge their source. Sinha also stated that some portions of his thesis which were "freely borrowed without acknowledgment" by Radhakrishnan, had already appeared in print before the publication of the latter's book. Sinha gave forty instances of what he termed "unacknowledged borrowings." In the next issue of the same journal another letter of Sinha was published citing seventy more such instances.

Unable to remain silent when, in his words, "not merely his intelligence and scholarship were challenged, but his honor and character were questioned," Radhakrishnan attempted to show the baselessness of Sinha's allegations, in his letters published in *The Modern Review*, February and March 1929. His main argument was as follows: Anyone writing on classical Indian philosophy has to use the same texts. It is meaningless for anyone who uses a few extracts from them to believe that everyone else "who follows him is indebted to him in a special sense." (Letter of February 1929.) "When two or more writers deal with the same texts, they are bound to use some common words, and characteristic expressions which do not warrant any inference of 'borrowing'." (Letter of March 1929.) His "versions," Radhakrishnan claimed, are "not close translations, but brief summaries. . . .based on the texts and not on any standard sketches of them. . . . The partial resemblance inevitable on account of the identity of texts considered" between certain passages in Sinha's thesis and those in Radhakrishnan's book could not be due to "unacknowledged borrowing," especially, since the former's attempt was a "literal translation" and the latter's "an exposition of thought" having "an eye on the texts all through." Radhakrishnan denied that he borrowed either Sinha's "ideas," or "language," because in the thesis there was "not a single idea" of Sinha's own, and Sinha used other translations, claimed them as his own and complained that Radhakrishnan was indebted to him (op.cit.). Radhakrishnan pointed out nine instances of what he called Sinha's "almost *verbatim* reproductions of Ganganath Jha's English translation" of a text. (Letter of February 1929.) Finally, Radhakrishnan also pointed out that the manuscript of his book was sent to the publishers in 1924, but was published in 1927 as its General Editor Muirhead was away in America. He signed the preface in 1926, after receiving the final proofs and index.

Radhakrishnan also pointed out that before he had even read Sinha's thesis, he had lectured to classes on many of the topics discussed in Volume II of his *Indian Philosophy*, and that it was "not at all impossible that some of the material contained in it might have found currency" before its publication. (Letter of February 1929.) Some of the most eminent scholars of the time like Kuppuswami Sastri, Ganganath Jha and Nalini Ganguli confirmed that Radhakrishnan had not only worked on Hindu epistemological theories as far back as 1922, but had also distributed his notes on these among his students and colleagues and discussed these with them, and that they contained translations of some textual passages with his comments on them. Radhakrishnan incorporated these notes with minor changes in his *Indian Philosophy*, Volume II. It was, thus, quite possible for Sinha or anyone else to have had access to Radhakrishnan's notes through his students. These scholars also declared that almost all the passages in dispute were quotations or translations from Sanskrit sources, on which no one could have a special claim. They opined that anyone with some knowledge of Sanskrit, and if necessary, with the help of a pandit could have made those translations.

Sinha filed a case against Radhakrishnan in the high court of Calcutta for infringement of copyright, and the latter, in turn, filed a libel suit against the former. Scholars like those mentioned earlier, and others rallied in support of Radhakrishnan, expressing readiness to give evidence in his favor in the court. In a communication to the court, Muirhead stated that the material in dispute was sent to him in 1924, and that the delay in publication was due to his being away in USA. On the other hand, Brojendra Nath Seal "earnestly requested" that he might be kept out of the case. At last, in May 1933 the suits were settled by a decree of compromise in the court of Phanibhushan Chakraborty, then acting, and later chief justice of Bengal. "While the terms of settlement were not disclosed, it was stated that all the allegations made in the pleadings and in the columns of the *Modern Review* were withdrawn."[7]

Today, to any fair-minded person this episode in Radhakrishnan's life would appear incredible, but jealousy and provincialism in combination could have done even worse. What is to be admired is the poise and sanity Radhakrishnan displayed throughout this period and the way he was able to come out victorious without any rancor or malice towards all those who maligned him.

VI.

Committee Work at Home and Lecturing Abroad

Involvement in Committees and Councils

At the beginning of his career in Calcutta, most of Radhakrishnan's time was spent in teaching and in secluded study. He did not take any interest in the administration or day-to-day functioning of the university. Asutosh Mookerjee, recognizing his talents, advised him to interest himself in outside affairs and take an active part in the executive and deliberative bodies, like the University's Board of Higher Studies, the Executive Committee of the Council of Post Graduate Teaching in Arts, Free Studentships and Stipend Awards Committee, and the Research Fellowship and Research Scholarship Awards Committee. Following Mookerjee's advice Radhakrishnan started participating in these in a noninterfering, yet vigilant and constructive way. He was not swayed or misguided by self-seeking, or power-mongering groups or individuals. He judged the facts of each case on merit with an alert and detached mind. Other members of various boards and committees of the university were charmed and captivated by his perception of the problems involved, and the tact and judgement with which he dealt with them. His persuasive eloquence won his adversaries to his side. He intervened in the deliberations of the academic and administrative committees to prevent injustice to the students, teachers and workers of the university. One such incident is narrated by Sukumar Sen in his memoir "The Brilliant Professor":

> In the twenties and early thirties the doctor's degree in the University was not as common as now and the award of the Premchand Roychand Studentship (PRS) was the most coveted academic distinction, even more coveted than Ph.D. or D.Sc., for which there is no age bar. The award was made on the merits of a thesis submitted, and the Board consisted of the examiners. As the University did not pay any travelling allowance, the examiners from outside Calcutta did not attend the meeting of the Board. The incident I am speaking about concerns a meeting of the PRS Board. The

thesis that had the best recommendation had been examined by a Bombay Professor and he was not present at the meeting. Some of the members present raised the objection that the writer of the recommended thesis could not be awarded the studentship as it was a complete work, there being nothing left to be done during the two years he would enjoy the studentship. The Board was about to decide against the writer of the best recommended thesis when Professor Radhakrishnan suggested that in the application the candidate had perhaps given suggestions for his future work. The application was then read and the Board was satisfied. The award went to the best recommended candidate.[1]

As a recognition of his administrative abilities, Radhakrishnan was unanimously elected president of the Post Graduate Council in Arts in the years 1927 and 1928, and again in 1930, after the death of Sir Asutosh Mookerjee in 1924. His appointment to the office was hailed by *Calcutta Review* (Vol. 24) in the following words: "His breadth of view, his deep loyalty to the institution, his faithfulness towards his colleagues in the postgraduate department and his organizing capacity will, we trust, prove useful in the discharge of the onerous duties entrusted to him by the suffrage of his fellow teachers."

Organizational Work

His organizing ability was not limited to university administration, but extended to the establishment and development of national organizations. Since the beginning of the twentieth century, a need was felt by the teachers and students of philosophy in the country to have a national forum for the promotion of philosophy. The controversies and interest generated by the publication of Radhakrishnan's *Indian Philosophy* rekindled a desire to have a platform where teachers and students of philosophy could present and discuss their research findings. Some leading philosophers of the country approached Radhakrishnan to take the initiative to establish such a national forum. Radhakrishnan, in cooperation with them, struggled for a number of years and was finally able to overcome all obstacles, financial and bureaucratic in establishing it. The result was the Indian Philosophical Congress, which was established in 1925, and held its first session in Calcutta in December of the same year. This session was presided over by Rabindranath Tagore. At this meeting, besides the normal exchange of ideas, the congress also adopted its constitution and elected Professor Radhakrishnan as its chairman. The grateful and appreciative community of philosophy teachers and students elected him as the general president for the Third Indian Philosophical Congress which was held from December 19-22, 1927 at Bombay University. Since its inception the congress has been meeting annually under the auspices of some Indian university or the other. It honored Radhakrishnan by electing him the general president for the Silver Jubilee Session held in Calcutta in 1952. It celebrated its Golden Jubilee in 1975, by hosting an international conference of philosophers at New Delhi. In 1985 its Diamond Jubilee celebration session was inaugurated by Rajiv Gandhi, the prime minister of India at Hyderabad. Successive generations of philosophy students and teachers should be ever grateful to Radhakrishnan for being instrumental in founding the Indian Philosophical Congress.

In 1925 Radhakrishnan was involved in making Hinduism palatable to Christians. He was devising ways and means through which he could achieve and propagate such an understanding. So preoccupied was he with this pursuit that when invited to express his views at a Calcutta Missionary Conference held that year, he said, "Hinduism is attempting to slough off its superstitions and purify itself, and there is no greater mission for you than to help in this process. Your task is not so much to make Christians of Hindus, as to purify or Christianize (if that term is more acceptable to you) Hinduism."[2] This is what he did in his subsequent lectures and writings.

Goes West to Lecture

By 1926 his books and articles on Indian philosophy and allied themes had made Indian philosophy more intelligible to the bulk of Western scholars. Radhakrishnan consequently came to be recognized as the foremost academic spokesman for Indian philosophy as well as Hinduism. The universities in Europe and America, which wished to organize lectures on these subjects began to invite him. So far Indians had been going to the universities in the West to learn and listen to lectures of Western scholars and not to teach or give lectures to them. The turning of the tables was significant considering that at that time the West knew very little about Indian thought. It symbolized the recognition of India as a civilization which had a philosophic heritage of her own. It is also noteworthy that one who had never received an education in the West was chosen to expound and interpret Indian philosophy to Western university audiences.

Radhakrishnan was invited to give lectures in various forums in the UK. He was elected as the Upton Lecturer at Manchester College, Oxford, for the year 1926. This invitation to deliver the Upton Lectures on Philosophy of Religion placed him in the category of eminent thinkers who had delivered these lectures in the previous years; conspicuous among whom were Dean Inge, Estlin Carpenter, L.P. Jacks and Miss Evelyn Underhill. The British Institute of Philosophical Studies invited him to deliver a series of four lectures during the months of May and June the same year. This invitation, too, symbolized the recognition of Radhakrishnan as a renowned scholar, as the lectures were originally scheduled to be delivered by Dean Inge. He was also invited to the Aristotelian Society of Cambridge University to address one of its meetings.

Across the Atlantic, in the USA, the University of Chicago elected him as the Haskell Lecturer in Comparative Religion for the year 1926. He was invited by universities all over the USA to deliver lectures on Hinduism and modern philosophical tendencies. Prominent among these were the universities of Yale, Harvard, Princeton and Columbia and theological institutions like the Union Theological Seminary of New York and the Pacific School of Religion, California.

Radhakrishnan accepted all these invitations. Calcutta University facilitated his travel, by electing him a member of a delegation, which comprised, besides him, Sir Jagdish Chandra Bose and Professor Heramba Chandra Maitra, and Bidhan Chandra Ray, to attend the World Conference of the Universities of the British Empire which was to be held in London on July 12 and 13, 1926. He was also chosen to represent Calcutta University at the Sixth International Congress of Philosophy which was to be held from September 13 to 17 at Harvard University. Before he set sail for London, his close friend and admirer, C.R. Reddy (1880-1951) advised him, "Look here, my friend, when you go abroad, put on your turban. At any rate, avoid the hat. You will understand the spirit of my observation when I tell you what I once put to an American audience, 'All the courtesies I have received here, I owe not to the Christian nature of your country but to the Turkish nature of my head dress'."[3] Radhakrishnan seems to have followed this advice during most of his foreign visits.

At Manchester College, Oxford, Radhakrishnan delivered the Upton Lectures. They consisted of four lectures on "The Hindu View of Life," delivered without a scrap of a note to assist him. Each of the lectures was of one hour duration. The arguments presented by him were reinforced with references and quotations from various sources ranging over extensive philosophical and religious literature—both Indian and Western. The impact of his eloquence, language and scholarship was such that the number of the audience which was about a hundred on the first day—half of them being teachers—trebled on the second day, and for the last two lectures the organizers had to arrange for bigger halls. His phrases and epigrams like "when the wick is ablaze at the tip, the whole lamp is said to be burning," "in liberation a man becomes his own masterpiece," "we cannot put our souls into uniforms," "the last part of life's road is to be worked in single file," became very popular with the audience, and they were noticed using them in their conversations and writings, time and again.

Radhakrishnan's main objective in his lectures was to show, primarily to the Western and Christian audience, and secondarily to Indians—who influenced by their Western training were criticizing and undermining the depth of their own tradition, culture and religion—that Hinduism is not a rigid set of doctrines, or imperatives fixed once and for all, but a way of life. It is characterized by tolerance and amplitude of vision. He made it clear to his audience that the Hindu thinker readily admits the validity of several points of view other than his own, and considers them worthy of acceptance. Hinduism seeks unity of religions not in common creed but in common quest. He boasted that "half the world moves on foundations which Hinduism supplied." He dealt in these lectures with religious experience and religious conflicts, and after analyzing them, proved that any great religion is a blend of both constants and variables. The core of any religion is the mystical which time cannot weaken, nor modernity render superfluous, but the peripheral factors of a religion like the encrustation of dogmas, the load of rituals, the draperies of custom sometimes call for change and do undergo a change, without in any manner affecting the potency and effectiveness of the core. The answers to the questions relating to the peripheral features of religion need to be formulated and reformulated in terms of contemporaneous urgency. Raja Ram Mohan Roy and Swami Vivekananda had done so earlier. They had restated what they felt was of abiding significance in their times in the Hindu thought. Even before them, from time to time, Hinduism had been interpreted and reinterpreted to accommodate and explain the phenomena of that particular time.

Radhakrishnan said that in these lectures he was, in the true spirit of Hinduism, looking upon his ancient faith from a new angle, and was attempting a new enunciation with special reference to the needs of a more complex and mobile social order. Hinduism, he insisted, must be moralized and reinterpreted so as to provide contemporary life with a moral meaning and moral values. For instance, he stated and analyzed interpretations of the Hindu notions of *varṇāśrama dharma*, *Saṁsāra* and *Karma* and in a pragmatic way concluded that though there was much merit in these notions when they were propounded and established as a system, yet in the contemporary situation they were neither satisfactory nor adequate; he went on to say that adherence to these in the present day world may even be dangerous. By taking up such concepts and analyzing them, he proved to the audience that Hinduism is not static but dynamic. He convincingly argued and established that historically Hinduism was an evolving, progressive and dynamic movement and that at no stage should it be taken as complete or as a finished set of beliefs and doctrines. He tried to prove that Hinduism cannot be regarded as "either pessimistic or fatalistc. The law of *Karma* affirms the implicit presence of the past in the present. When we unconsciously or mechanically follow the impulses of the past, we are not exercising our freedom. But we are free when our personal subject becomes the ruling centre."[4]

To make his theory palatable and acceptable to the orthodox Western Christian audience Radhakrishnan adopted an ambivalent attitude, combining defence with attack. He defined Vedānta and the Hindu view of life as something distinctive and unique, at the same time insinuating its affinity with Western thought and the Christian way of life. The tactics he adopted to make a good case for Hinduism were threefold. One, he admitted that all is not well with Hinduism; two, he read as much Christianity as possible into Hindu ideas and ideals; and three, when that was impossible, he constructed the best possible apology he could and proceeded to point out the failings of Christian civilization and the strong points of Hinduism. For example, he analyzed the notion of caste system in Hinduism and argued that "caste places all beings on a common level ... it is democracy." He concluded that the principle of the caste system, if properly used, can be a leading principle of social ethics for humanity at large, and can offer to the world a solution to the problems arising out of racial prejudice, narrow nationalism and class warfare. This flexible attitude, as expected, was successful and his argument was attentively listened to, and seriously appreciated and accepted by a wider section of the audience than it would have been if he had adopted a rigid attitude. The result was that many Christians after listening to his lectures said "If that is Hinduism, we are Hindus too."

After fulfilling all his commitments in the UK Radhakrishnan went to the USA. He delivered the Haskell Lectures at the University of Chicago and lectured in other universities and institutions. He read papers on "The Role of Philosophy in the History of Civilization" and "The Doctrine of Māyā: Some Problems" at the Sixth International Congress of Philosophy held at Harvard University in September 1926. Though reactions to his competence as a philosopher varied from "scholarly philosopher" to that he "sounded more like a preacher who had a message than a pure philosopher," his audience marveled at his mastery of the subject and the elegant and spontaneous manner of his speaking wherever he went. That he took the reactions of the audience in America in his stride is clear from the following episode he narrated later to an Indian audience in Madras. After one of his lectures an American asked him, "If India has a saving message as you have said, why does she not save herself?" His ready reply was: "The great Jesus was born to save others and not Himself."[5] As the content of his Haskell Lectures was more or less the same as that of his Upton Lectures, they were not published separately but assimilated in *The Hindu View of Life*.

So satisfied was Radhakrishnan with his first ever lecture tour abroad that he wrote after a score of years and several trips to various continents, "I have the most pleasant recollections of it. The very warm reception which I had in Oxford and Cambridge, in Harvard and Princeton, in Yale and Chicago, and many other places, is fixed in my mind."[6]

VII.

Acclaim Within and Outside India, Knighthood

A Popular Lecture at Madras

After his successful lecture tour of the UK and USA, a triumphant Radhakrishnan returned to India with international renown. On his return, Presidency College, Madras, where he had started his career and taught from 1909 to 1918, invited him to address the students. His popularity was such that the English lecture hall of the college, where the lecture was scheduled to be held overflowed with students—many were standing in the aisles and many others sat on the floor—much before the lecture was to begin. And yet not all could be accommodated, nor was there any other hall in the college which could contain the frenzied crowd of young men who had voluntarily gathered there to listen to him. The college authorities realizing the difficulty of accommodating the growing crowd, arranged the lecture out in the open, on the Marina beach, opposite the college. Just as he was to start lecturing, C.V. Raman joined him on the dais. For the audience it was a unique experience of having two great contemporary Indians together on the same platform before them. For Radhakrishnan, also, addressing such a large gathering was altogether a new experience, accustomed as he was to addressing only selected academic audiences. Slightly taken aback by the excitement of students, characteristic of political gatherings, he prefaced his lecture with the striking observation, "When philosophy becomes so popular, it makes matters suspicious."[1] Certainly it was not the popularity of the subject, but the charisma of the speaker which drew the crowd. It is recounted that the crowd hypnotized by his tones modulated to near perfection and magical phrasing, and bemused by the anecdotes that he narrated, listened to him captivated, in utter silence during the entire lecture.

Life and Work in India

Back in Calcutta, Radhakrishnan started taking greater interest in developing philosophical studies in the university by making the philosophy department active and more dynamic. With the help of his colleagues he began to organize meetings of the Philosophical Society every Thursday afternoon in which both students and teachers presented papers on a variety of themes in branches of philosophy and held discussions. With a view to developing interdisciplinary studies, to which he attached great importance, he started the Arts Faculty Club with the help of his friends like S.P. Mookerjee, B.K. Mullick and T.K. Doraiswami. One of its functions was to organize a seminar every Friday afternoon in which a student or a teacher pursuing any discipline in the arts faculty presented a paper, which was discussed by the gathered scholars. The club also invited reputed scholars from India, as well as abroad, to deliver lectures in their area of specialization. Sometimes, when the audience could not understand some expert speaker, either due to the abstruseness of the subject or because of the style of presentation, Radhakrishnan used to summarize the lecture in about ten minutes, in a short, crisp and lucid way, to the satisfaction of both the audience and the speaker. His summary revealed his sharp and keen intellect which could isolate the essential elements from the mass of details and focus on them.

Whenever guest speakers came, he would invariably invite them and members of the club to a meal at his home. Occasionally he would also entertain at his house participants of conferences in philosophy and other subjects. On such occasions the atmosphere in his house used to be very informal. The guests sat on the floor and ate from plantain leaves in true South Indian fashion. As a host Radhakrishnan made everyone feel at home, by talking to everyone in an intimate way, patting everyone on the cheek or head, and putting his hand on the shoulders of the person he was talking to. He would show deep concern in matters relating to the personal lives of his guests. No matter of detail was too small for him. During the meal, the conversations were bright and humorous without ever becoming either heavy or pedantic. One could also hear gossip about the members of the university, or matters relating to the city or the nation, in various languages—English, Tamil, Telugu, Hindi, Bengali and Marathi.

In view of his popularity, his eminence as a scholar and his active involvement in the affairs of the university and affiliated colleges, he was elected president of All Bengal College and the University Teachers Association. Delivering his presidential address to the Second Annual Conference of the Association on April 3, 1927, he criticized the government for its educational policy, and emphasized the need for educational reforms. Considering the political environment in the country, his speech was a bold and patriotic attempt to remind the British government of their duty to impart a meaningful and purposeful education which would aim at generating creative thinkers, and not just produce clerks to carry on the dictates of the alien rulers.

In the same year, Andhra University which was established in 1926, had its first convocation on December 5 at Waltair. Its vice-chancellor, C.R. Reddy, invited Radhakrishnan to deliver the convocation address. Radhakrishnan accepted the invitation and delivered an address on "Universities and National Life," the first of the many convocation addresses that he was to give in times to come. He was also awarded the first of his many honorary doctorates in this convocation. Lord Goschin, the chancellor of the university presided over the convocation function.

During this period of his stay in Calcutta, a lot of Radhakrishnan's time was taken up by the affairs of various committees and other administrative bodies of Calcutta University. He had also agreed to be a paper-setter, as well as an examiner, in Telugu for matriculation, intermediate level in arts and science, and B.A. of Calcutta University. This was obviously because of his love for Telugu and his keenness to promote the language.

His philosophical pursuits continued as before. He completed two small monographs: *The Religion We Need* and *Kālki—or the Future of Civilization*, which were published in 1928 and 1929 respectively. *Kālki*, consisting of about seventy pages, was a modified version of his Harvard lecture delivered in 1926. In this book he contended that the predominant concept of a purely technological civilization necessarily gives rise to the idea of uniformity. He asserted that due to technological advancement "though humanity has assumed a uniform outer body, it is still without a single animating spirit. The world is not of one mind." So, he argued that this incongruity between the outer and the inner has resulted in the utter failure of man to adapt himself intellectually, socially and ethically to his new environment, brought about by the scientific and technological changes, in which distance is eliminated and enormous power and wealth are placed in man's hands. This in turn, he said, resulted in constant strife and unhappiness for man. He traced the genesis of the present crisis of civilization in "the loosening hold of ethical and spiritual ideals."[2] But he asserted that there was no cause for despair as "nothing is inevitable in human affairs except peace."[3] He suggested that to bring about peace to man, the idea of uniformity must be replaced by the idea of harmony. Radhakrishnan made some very penetrating and astute observations about the dangers of mechanism, which are as valid today as they were at the time of writing the book. In this book he tried to establish that true harmony could only be of the spirit and it can be achieved only on the basis of an idealist philosophy.

England Invites Again

Radhakrishnan's earlier lectures in UK were so successful, and had left such an imprint on the minds of the listeners and the organizers that he was invited to take the post vacated by Principal J. Estlin Carpenter in Manchester College, Oxford, in 1929-1930. This invitation gave him an opportunity to lecture on Comparative Religion. In addition to these lectures Principal Jacks of Manchester College also requested him to give sermons at the college. He was also invited to deliver the Jowett Lectures for the year 1930.

Hibbert Lectures and His Most Original Work

Radhakrishnan was also invited by the organizers to deliver the Hibbert Lectures on "An Idealistic Philosophy of Life" at the University of Manchester and at the University College, London, for the year 1929. He shared the distinction of being a Hibbert Lecturer with such eminent men as Renan, Pfleiderer, Dean Inge and Rabindranath Tagore (who was elected as a Hibbert Lecturer for 1928, but owing to failing health was unable to deliver the lectures). The theme that he chose for his lectures was "An Idealist View of Life."

Radhakrishnan delivered the Hibbert Lectures in Manchester University in December 1929, and in London University in January 1930. He did so with poise and calm, self-possessed and statuesque, without making any theatrical gestures or attempt to play upon the emotions of the audience through subtle inflections of the voice. His words which flowed steadily and equably had a glow of intellectual passion, which had a direct appeal to the audience's intellect rather than emotions. In these lectures he further developed the comparative method adopted in his *In-*

dian Philosophy. He constructively applied this technique to state more forcefully his ideals, his faith and his judgement of the contemporary situation, and to propound a system of philosophy, giving expression to his personal conviction. He justified his philosophy by a reasoned analysis of the entire idealist tradition of East and West.

Making an appraisal of his contribution in these lectures, Radhakrishnan wrote "these lectures state my views on some of the ultimate problems of philosophy. They take into account the changes in the intellectual climate of the world, the crisis through which religion and social life are passing."[4] The lectures, which received much appreciation from the audience and the press, when published in 1932 as *An Idealist View of Life* received very favorable reviews in philosophical journals. A revised second edition of it came out in 1937.

The impression he made on the audience was summed up in the following words by the vice-chancellor of London University who was present on that occasion:

> It is true that in these days people are full of doubts and fears, but you have shown how these can be done away with. You have filled us with courage and hope for the future. It has been a good thing for our students to hear you. We have all wondered at the way in which you have spoken on this difficult subject. But we have also wondered at the mastery of a language which is not your mother tongue. India has always been the home of religion and philosophy, and it has been a great pleasure to us to hear a great Indian teacher on these subjects.[5]

Bertrand Russell who had attended the lectures in London came to Radhakrishnan after the lectures and told him that he had never heard philosophy better expounded than in those lectures. H.N. Spalding who had also listened to the lectures in London was so fascinated by their content and Radhakrishnan's personality and scholarship, that he decided to found a chair at Oxford for Eastern religions and ethics. The chair finally established in 1936 was offered to Radhakrishnan.

Other Lectures and Sermons in England

The Upton Lectures were delivered by Radhakrishnan on October 22, 1929 at Manchester College, Oxford; and the Jowett Lectures on the theme "East and West in Religion" on March 18, 1930 at the Mary Ward Settlement, London. He delivered sermons in the Chapel of Manchester

College, Oxford, in November 1929 and on June 8, 1930. The theme of the first was "Chaos and Creation" and that of the second was "Revolution through Suffering."

The sermon on "Revolution through Suffering" reflected the patriotism of Radhakrishnan. The timing of the sermon coincided with Mahatma Gandhi's launching of the freedom movement in India with full fervor, which was presaged by such portentous events as the celebrated raid of the Bengali revolutionary terrorists on the British armory in Chittagong. Radhakrishnan showed his reaction to the freedom movement at that stage, by choosing for his sermon *Ezekiel,* chapter 21, verse 26 which reads: "I will overturn, I will overturn, overturn it, and it shall be no more until he comes whose right it is and I will give it to him." In his sermon he said:

> So long as India is a dependency and not a dominion, Great Britain cannot complain if Italy and Germany wish to take their share in what the Britisher in other moods called the white man's burden. She has no moral authority to question Japan's adventures in the Far East or Italy's in Africa. Things are never settled until they are settled right. If we go behind the give and take of politics to the ultimate question of right and wrong, we see that the instability of the world is due to the outrage on the moral law in which powerful nations are acquiescing. It is time we restore the supremacy of law and organise the world for an enduring peace.[6]

On this sermon, an Oxford daily commented: "Though the Indian preacher had the marvelous power to weave a magic web of thought, imagination, and language, the real greatness of his sermon resides in some indefinable spiritual quality which asserts attention, moves the heart, and lifts us into an ampler air."

He was invited by the inmates of the Indian Students Hostel, London, to address them, in February 1930. Radhakrishnan used this opportunity to talk to them on "The Responsibility of the Intellectuals." While the first two lectures and the two sermons were published in *East and West in Religion,* in 1933, the last was published in *Freedom and Culture* in 1936. Commenting upon his experience of delivering lectures and sermons, Radhakrishnan wrote, "It was a great experience for me to preach from Christian pulpits in Oxford and Birmingham, in Manchester and Liverpool. It heartened me to know that my addresses were liked by Christian audiences."[7]

Nationalist Ideas and Their Impact

The subtle way in which he expressed his solidarity with the free-dom movement in India right in London, the home of the alien imperial rulers of India, was remarkable and reflected his courage and patriotism. The deep and lasting impression that the sermon made on the minds of the British and others who were present was summarized by Hiren Muk-erjee, who was present at one of the sermons in the following words, "the glory of his words which lit up the hoary thought of our stricken India used to be balm to our soul."[8]

A similar outburst of patriotism is found in the preface which he wrote on August 26, 1929, to D. Balaramakrishnayya's book *Mānava Jīvitamu*: "Swaraj is the national and legitimate birthright of every peo-ple." One's admiration for Radhakrishnan's open sympathy and support for the national freedom movement increases when one recalls that at that time he, by virtue of being a member of the Indian Educational Service, was a government servant, with a large family to support and no private source of income.

When Radhakrishnan was abroad lecturing to foreign audiences, many Indian students, who were studying for various degrees in the uni-versities there used to meet him to get their doubts resolved and to dis-cuss their problems. During his stay in Oxford, when he was delivering the Hibbert Lectures, Jayaprakash Narayan (1902-1979) who was re-turning to India after completing his studies in the USA, met him in his room. Jayaprakash Narayan like many of his compatriots had learned to turn to Radhakrishnan's works not only for knowledge but also for boost-ing his morale. For him, "meeting him [Radhakrishnan] in person was an event." Later, when in prison in India, Jayaprakash Narayan read Radha-krishnan's books. According to Narayan, "There was hardly a serious-minded freedom fighter in prison, in the thirties or forties who did not go through his [Radhakrishnan's] volumes on *Indian Philosophy . . . the Hindu View of Life* etc."[9]

In Sri Lanka

On his way back to India, Radhakrishnan delivered a lecture on "The Message of the Buddha" in Colombo in Sri Lanka. In this lecture he interpreted the message of Buddha not as nihilism, as it is generally thought to be, but as the finest type of applied metaphysics and as the most remarkable form of ethical idealism. K.P.S. Menon, who was at that time the official representative of India and was present at the lecture, recorded his reaction in the following words:

> Never before or since have I heard such a lecture. For exactly one hour he spoke without a single note in his hand and held his audience spell-bound. The speech was a harmonious whole, comparable to a great work of art—it had unity, symmetry and balance. Of the hundreds of lectures to which I have listened in different parts of the world two have left an indelible impression on my mind. One was Radhakrishnan's speech in Colombo; the other was W.B. Yeats' speech at Oxford on "My Generation in Poetry."
>
> It is difficult to think of two speeches, or for that matter of two speakers, so different from each other. Yeats was sentimental and emotional, Radhakrishnan, analytic and reflective; Yeats had a mobile face and indulged in dramatic gestures; Radhakrishnan was almost statuesque, except for his dishevelled hair, flying under the fan. One felt that the serenity of the Buddha could not have been conveyed more seriously, by a more serene individual.[10]

Convocation Address: The Punjab Incident

Back home, he delivered at the Mysore University the convocation address on October 10, 1930 on "Education and Nationalism," and the Third Krisnarajendra Silver Jubilee Lecture. From the South he moved via Calcutta to the Northwest to deliver the convocation address on "Training and Leadership" on December 23, 1930, at the Punjab University. Sir Geoffrey Montmorency the governor of Punjab and chancellor of the university, presided over the function. As the governor and Radhakrishnan were leaving the hall after the convocation, a young student walked up to them, bowed to Radhakrishnan, and after greeting him with a 'namaste', pulled out a revolver and shot the governor, wounding him. The incident showed the reverence Indian revolutionaries had for Radhakrishnan, despite the fact that he was in the good books of the British government. In those days it was very rare for anyone to be respected by the revolutionaries while enjoying the favor of the government.

Aids Journals

At that time, as in his later life, Radhakrishnan was a connoisseur of literature and the fine arts. He encouraged and patronized all those who were struggling against all odds to maintain institutions which mirrored the awakening of the nation's soul. He not only helped them spiritually but also managed material assistance through his contacts in the government and friends, who were spread all over India. In 1929, he sponsored a cultural monthly *The New Era* which was like the *Hibbert Journal* in appearance and published articles of literary and political interest. M. Seshachalapati, who later became a judge of Andhra High Court, was its editor, and Radhakrishnan, K.T. Shah and Tarachand were on the Advisory Board. The journal had to be stopped with its thirteenth issue. Another journal *Triveni* was then in the third year of its precarious existence. It was decided that *The New Era* should be combined with *Triveni*. Radhakrishnan agreed to be on the first Advisory Board of the new *Triveni* and evinced keen interest in it. To this day *Triveni* continues to be a reputed journal, which publishes articles on literary and cultural themes and translations of poems and short stories in Indian languages.

Knighthood

The imperial power ruling India could no longer remain indifferent to Radhakrishnan's increasing international fame. The then viceroy, Lord Irwin wished to recommend him for a knighthood. Since Radhakrishnan was at that time a professor at Calcutta University, according to rules and conventions, the viceroy consulted the governor of Bengal before recommending Radhakrishnan for a knighthood. Accordingly, he asked for a confidential report from the governor of Bengal, whose unusual response was: "All police reports are against him, but I like him." Finally, when Radhakrishnan was knighted in 1931, he received many letters of congratulations. Among them was one from Sir Geoffrey Montmorency who, reminding him of the event that had happened after the Punjab University convocation in Lahore, wrote: "It is rare for a man to receive, at once an honor from the king, and the homage of a revolutionary." But then Radhakrishnan was a rare person.

Andhra Mahāsabhā

Throughout his stay at Calcutta University, Radhakrishnan kept himself in touch with happenings in the Telugu-speaking areas of Madras presidency, where at that time a movement was afoot for asserting the identity of Andhra culture. The rights and the progress of Telugu-speaking people, some of their leaders believed, were endangered by other linguistic groups in the Madras presidency. So, the Andhra Mahāsabhā was established and at its annual sessions speeches on the glorious history of Andhra, the greatness of Telugu literature, the contemporary underdevelopment of Andhra and the sad plight of Telugu-speaking people were made, and resolutions were passed for the formation of a separate Andhra province made up of the Telugu-speaking districts of Madras presidency. Radhakrishnan was elected as president of Andhra Mahāsabhā. He presided over its session in 1928 at Nandyal (Kurnool District, Andhra Pradesh).[11] By availing himself of such opportunities he was always remembered in Andhra as one belonging to it, though away in Bengal, and with his ability to speak Tamil, his friendship with intellectuals in Madras and his frequent sojourns there, he was in close contact with the Tamils and was reckoned as one of them. On the other hand, his works and speeches on classical Indian thought and culture, and his book on Tagore etc., made clear his allegiance to India's unity in diversity. It is no wonder that such a man was called from Madras to Mysore, from there to Calcutta and, then, from there to Waltair (Visakhapatnam) to head a new university.

VIII.

Vice-Chancellorship at Andhra and Membership of League Committee

Andhra University and C.R. Reddy

Andhra University was established in 1926 as not just another affiliating and examining university, but also as a teaching and residential university. A well-known intellectual, publicist and brilliant speaker of South India, C.R. Reddy, who was for sometime a professor in Maharaja's College, Mysore, and also head of the Education Department of Mysore State, was appointed its first vice-chancellor. By then he had left Mysore, joined politics and become a legislator. Radhakrishnan was his colleague in Maharaja's College, and the two had become friends there. On October 11, 1921, from his home in Chittore (now in Andhra Pradesh, then in the Madras presidency) Reddy had written to Radhakrishnan, "If Andhra University comes in, we shall have to kidnap you from Calcutta." One does not know whether Reddy had in mind, while writing that letter, the vice-chancellorship or a professorship for Radhakrishnan.

Radhakrishnan Gets Involved

Before Reddy completed his first term as vice-chancellor, there were persons in the university senate who believed he was not on the best of terms with the provincial government and that he was planning to take up politics again. They at any rate preferred to have Radhakrishnan as the head of Andhra University. The reasons for this were obvious. Radhakrishnan was from Andhra, and had by then become internationally famous, was a great spokesman of Hinduism and a Brahmin too. In the senate of Andhra University the majority were Brahmins, a number of whom were either liberals or favorably inclined towards the Congress party. Reddy, as his very name indicates, was a non-Brahmin. Undoubtedly a patriot, he was sometimes with the Justice party and also, sometimes in favor of the Congress party and its freedom movement. A lover of

Telugu literature, he was a distinguished and pioneering literary critic in Telugu and one of its best prose writers. Reddy's was a highly critical mind with a satirical streak. Utterly secular, probably an agnostic much of his life, and somewhat iconoclastic, he could not be an absolute admirer or an unquestioning follower of any individual, tradition, culture or political party. It might be said, with some justification, that on the whole he preferred the Telugu translation of the *Mahābhārata*, the popular Telugu version of the *Rāmāyaṇa*, and Telugu poets like Vemana who were social critics, to the Sanskritic-Brahmanical tradition, thought and literature. He was an almost autocratic and extremely competent administrator, and a strict disciplinarian, usually aloof and aristocratic in attitude, and often sarcastic in speech and devastating in repartee. Obviously, he was very different from Radhakrishnan. By the late 1920s Radhakrishnan's fame had spread worldwide, whereas Reddy's was only regional. Moreover, Radhakrishnan was favorably inclined to the movement which worked for the self-assertion and self-expression of the Telugu-speaking people in the Madras presidency, who felt that they were being dominated by another linguistic group. Radhakrishnan had also presided over a session of Andhra Mahāsabhā, the ultimate objective of which was formation of an Andhra province out of the Telugu-speaking areas of the Madras presidency. So, it was not surprising that a good number of senators of Andhra University were wistful about Radhakrishnan becoming the vice-chancellor of their university. Some of them must have spoken or written to him extending their support if he were to agree to offer himself as a candidate for the vice-chancellorship, which had been an elected post in that university for several decades since its inception.

Consequently, on December 24, 1927, Radhakrishnan wrote Reddy a personal confidential letter in his own hand: "I am asked by a number of people about the Andhra vice-chancellorship. Let me tell you that I do not want to think of it so long as your services are available for it. They tell me that you are thinking of politics. Hope you will concentrate on the level of the university." On December 29, 1927, Reddy replied to it from Bangalore: "I am glad to know that people are already arranging for my academic funeral and installation of a worthy successor! Believe me when I say it would be a great pleasure to me to see you take up the task after me. So far as my present plans go, I intend to continue in my present work until at least a good start has been given to the teaching side of the university and the transfer of some, at least, of the government colleges is actually made and the goods delivered." But Reddy, while appreciating what he termed

Radhakrishnan's "good feelings" towards him and thanking him for the same, had made it clear that if he (Radhakrishnan) thought he had a "good chance" there was "absolutely no reason" why he should refrain for his (Reddy's) sake. He also stated that he was deeply touched by the tone of Radhakrishnan's letter and that it was "very kind" of the latter to have taken him into his (Radhakrishnan's) confidence "on the delicate subject."

Reddy at once wrote to C.V. Raman, who was also a member of the senate, apprising him of the situation in Andhra University, making clear his intention to continue as vice-chancellor and, as such, to contest the ensuing election and solicited Raman's support. On February 20, 1928, Raman replied to Reddy expressing his disapproval of political methods used in the election of a vice-chancellorship, and assured him (Reddy) that he would attend the senate meeting and vote for him (Reddy). After Radhakrishnan himself had received Reddy's reply, and had been shown by Raman the letter he got from Reddy, he made it clear to Raman and everyone else that he "stood out in order to leave Reddy a clear field." In the election that took place on March 9, 1928, the senate elected Reddy as vice-chancellor for a second term of three years. But on December 20, 1930, Reddy resigned from this high office in protest against the government's repression of the Satyagraha movement launched by Gandhi in 1930. An acting vice-chancellor was appointed and elections for the post were announced.

Radhakrishnan Becomes a Candidate for Vice-Chancellorship

Persuaded by some of his friends and admirers in the senate and outside, and perhaps privately assured of support by the provincial government, Radhakrishnan became one of the candidates for this office. His nomination was proposed and seconded by a number of prominent senators belonging to different castes, as well as by a British missionary educator. There were two other candidates: Diwan Bahadur Sir R. Venkataratnam Naidu and V. Ramachandra Rao. Naidu was then one of the foremost educators of South India.[1] He was a Brahmo Samajist, and a man of high ethical integrity, who was zealously devoted to social reform, education of women and the poor, and for whom teaching was a vocation. His was a life of unselfish dedication to ideals. His name was also proposed by a number of important senators, among whom were men of different castes and convictions. Rao belonged to Rajahmundry.

Gets Elected

The senate met on March 6, 1931, under the acting vice-chancellor's chairmanship. In the meeting, with the chair's permission, Rao withdrew his candidature. Sixty-two senate members were present and voting was by secret ballot. Thirty-three voted for Radhakrishnan, and twenty-eight for Naidu; while one vote was declared invalid. Radhakrishnan was declared elected. Though the majority of the members present were Brahmins, the voting was not based on caste alignments. All the government officials voted for Radhakrishnan. When informed of his having been elected, Radhakrishnan in his letter of March 25, 1931, conveyed to the university syndicate his acceptance and informed them that he would assume the office on October 1, 1931. The syndicate after considering his letter, felt that the university could not afford to be without a regular vice-chancellor any longer and hence asked him to join not later than the end of April 1931. Accordingly, Radhakrishnan had to take over the vice-chancellorship on May 1, 1931. He was then forty-three years old.

As Vice-Chancellor

In February, 1934 at the expiration of his first term as vice-chancellor, nominations were invited for the ensuing election for vice-chancellor. In response only one nomination, that of Radhakrishnan, was received. As such, he was unanimously elected for another term of three years beginning May 1, 1934. However, as we shall see he did not complete his second term.

In Reddy's time the syndicate and the senate had accepted in their meetings of November 19, 1927, the recommendation of their experts' committee to start a University College of Arts and Sciences. In this college honors and postgraduate courses would be organized in such a way that students would be "more guided than taught," and "initiated into the processes of investigation" so that "a taste and capacity for research" would develop in them. But, as the location of the university could not be settled before 1930 (when the legislature decided that it should be in Waltair), nothing was done. As soon as this was settled, Reddy appointed a committee to decide the details of how the teaching should be organized. In its meetings in February and March 1931, this committee's recommendations were accepted by the university senate. It was decided to start honors courses in history and Telugu from the academic year 1931, and a University College of Arts and an Institute of Applied Sciences from 1932, and, funds permitting, to start some other honors courses in arts and sciences from 1932.

At this stage Radhakrishnan became the executive and academic head of Andhra University. It had no buildings of its own, its office was in some rooms of a hotel, its classrooms were in a Zamindar's house, and the vice-chancellor's lodge was another rented building nearby. Within two months of assuming charge, the new vice-chancellor rented the best available buildings, recruited six teachers and had honors courses in history and Telugu started by July 1, 1931. Thus, the University College of Arts came into existence. In the next academic year departments of philosophy, mathematics, economics, politics and foreign languages, which immediately began honors and postgraduate courses were added. Moreover, in the same year with an honorary professor (C.V. Raman) and four lecturers, the University College of Science and Technology was established. In 1933 honors courses in technology began, and in 1934 courses in commerce were started.

Reddy's plan was that the university would affiliate with all the colleges in the Telugu-speaking districts of the Madras presidency, which were until then affiliated only with Madras University. Its University College had facilities only for honors and postgraduate courses and research courses leading to doctoral degrees. The courses leading to pass course degrees were to be confined to affiliated colleges dispersed over various districts. Only students with proven merit would be admitted to the courses offered in the University College. Those taking an honors course were required to spend a year more than those taking a pass course, and appear for an examination which was much more rigorous than that of pass course. A person with an honors degree was to be entitled to a master's degree a year later on payment of a prescribed fee (as at Oxbridge). Radhakrishnan could make this plan a reality in a remarkably short time. This was an achievement.

Following the example of Asutosh Mookerjee, Radhakrishnan did his best to recruit the faculty purely on merit, irrespective of regional, linguistic and caste considerations. Like Mookerjee he aimed at appointing personnel who demonstrated promise of quality, a cosmopolitan outlook and a critical academic strength that sustained spontaneous growth. Wherever he went he was always on the lookout for talented young men and whenever he found one he would invite him to join Andhra University. Persons like Ludwig Wolff, Sir J.C. Coyajee, V.K.R.V.

Rao, Hiren Mukerjee, Saileswar Sen, Humayun Kabir and T. R. Seshadri were brought by him to Andhra University from different parts of India. At the same time, brilliant scientists and scholars from Andhra like S. Bhagwantam, K. Rangadhama Rao, M. Venkatarangaiah, V.S. Krishna and P.T. Raju, were also appointed and encouraged. Many of them later rose to high positions in Indian academic and public life. His ignoring the regional, class and caste considerations in the selection of faculty was not liked by some politicians and other senators who had regional feelings. They questioned him in the senate meetings for not giving preferential treatment to Andhras, scheduled castes, scheduled tribes and backward classes. They even launched a propaganda campaign that Radhakrishnan was against Andhras and Brahmins. But Radhakrishnan stood firm. He replied to his critics in unequivocal terms, "We cannot but be overcareful in the selection of professors. No other consideration should weigh with us in the appointment of professors than academic achievement and original work; for where there is no zeal for research, there is no zest for teaching."[2]

Radhakrishnan selected the courses to be taught in the university, chose competent faculty members and supervised over the organization and teaching of the selected courses. He solved the problem of raising buildings for the university in a remarkably short time, by selecting and appointing an engineer in whom he placed complete trust, and allowing him freedom in the planning and execution of the construction of buildings. As a result, within one year, even before the second academic year could begin, the spacious buildings to house the arts departments were ready for use. Consequently different departments were shifted to them from the rented buildings. Students were also provided with hostel accommodations. By the time the first batch of students reached their final year, that is, two years after the construction activity began, the buildings for the departments of arts, sciences and technology, laboratories, library and hostels for students were ready for use. They were immediately put to use. The buildings were not only functional, but also aesthetically pleasing. The university complex presented a picturesque view, ranged tier upon tier, with a commanding view of the Bay of Bengal on two sides, a range of undulating hills behind, with the imposing hills of the Dolphin's Nose and Rishi Konda overlooking on either side. Consequently, the campus became not only a beautiful place for scholars, scientists and students, but also a place of attraction for the citizens of Visakhapatnam and other visitors.

Radhakrishnan used his penchant for making friends, and his understanding of the human mind to considerable advantage for the development of the university. A scholar, poet and patron of learning, Vikrama Deva Varma, the Maharaja of Jeypore (now in Orissa) was a friend and admirer of Radhakrishnan. The latter successfully impressed upon the Maharaja the need for promoting scientific and technological studies and research. This resulted in the Maharaja giving an initial donation of Rs. 50,000 for the year 1933-1934, and Rs. 75,000 for the year 1934-1935 to start the teaching of the sciences and a promise to pay a munificent grant of Rs. one lakh every year till such a time as he, or his heirs, might pay a capital sum of Rs. fifteen lakhs to meet the recurring expenditure on the College of Science and Technology. Radhakrishnan reciprocated this gesture of the Maharaja by naming after him the College of Science and Technology. The Maharaja continued to give the grant throughout his lifetime.[3]

In 1935 the Indian Medical Council conveyed to the university that it would not recognize the medical degrees of Andhra University because of inadequate facilities and training in the Medical College and hospital at Visakhapatnam, unless the facilities were improved so as to raise their standards to meet specific requirements. The implementation of the Medical Council's recommendations involved an expenditure of Rs. four to five lakhs. So, Radhakrishnan requested the Madras government to provide the financial assistance necessary for this. But the government expressed its inability to do so. Thereupon Radhakrishnan went to Madras and pleaded with the governor and the member in charge for an urgent grant. But it did not yield any result. Disappointed, he returned to Visakhapatnam. Due to a persistent threat from the Indian Medical Council that it would not recognize the medical degrees awarded by Andhra University, he visited Madras again, met the governor, the minister and the member in charge of finance and tried to impress upon them the need for an immediate grant to bring about improvements in the Medical College and hospital. Once again his request fell on deaf ears. Then, while taking leave of the governor, the member for finance and the minister, Radhakrishnan told them to their face, "This will be the epitaph: W(governor) and P(minister) founded the Medical College, Visakhapatnam, and E(governor) and B(minister) demolished it."[4] The next day a communication was received from the Madras government that the amount necessary for this purpose had been sanctioned. Thus, by his boldness and by exerting psychological pressure on the three functionaries of the government he saved the Medical College of Andhra University from imminent closure.[5]

Radhakrishnan used his contacts in the government not only to the advantage of the university, but also for helping and protecting teachers and his other colleagues. The year 1931 in which he assumed the office of the vice-chancellor, was the year immediately following the second phase of Mahatma Gandhi's civil disobedience movement. The period from 1931-1936, the years of his vice-chancellorship, marked years of turmoil and political tension in the country. The government was highly suspicious of teachers in the university who were habitual wearers of khadi and sympathized with the Indian National Congress. Among the teachers appointed in Andhra University, there were a few who were suspected by the government on these grounds. But Radhakrishnan dealt wlth the government's opposition to their appointment in the university, with courage and tact. Without exception, he stood by the teachers in the university, whom he regarded as colleagues and never as subordinates, to safeguard their academic freedom, and to protect the autonomy of the university. Hiren Mukerjee, whom Radhakrishnan had appointed as a teacher in the university, was a staunch Communist. He made it a point to air his views in the classes and other forums, and to support and advocate a socialistic pattern of society for India. This irked many in the university. They frowned at his propensity towards what they called "dangerous thoughts," and were ready to physically assault him. But Radhakrishnan saved him from public wrath by saying that such "thoughts" were welcome as they "stirred the soil" in the minds of the youth. To pacify frayed tempers he quoted "If one is not a socialist before his twenty-fifth year, there is something wrong with his heart. And if one is a socialist after his twenty-fifth year, there is something wrong with his head," without making it clear whether he was quoting this approvingly or not.

Supports Freedom of Thought

It would not be out of place to recount here an episode in an affiliated college of Andhra University. Goparaju Ramachandra Rao[6] was a lecturer in botany in P.R. College, Kakinada from 1928. Towards the end of 1932 he contributed an article on "The Concept of God" for a student manuscript magazine *The Critic*. In this Rao maintained that while the 'concept of God' was useful, it was false and encouraged superstition and fanaticism. So, he argued, it should be discarded like every other falsehood. The college, at that time, was dominated by Brahmoism, and its authorities took exception to this advocacy of atheism and asked the writer for an explanation. He explained that he was a convinced atheist and that he had expressed his views. Thereupon, in 1933 the college dispensed with his services for spreading atheism among students after giving him due notice of three months. A number of people considered this as unjustified. Radhakrishnan, too, felt this and stated that a teacher should not be penalized for his views, so long as he was a good teacher and did his duty. From all accounts Ramachandra Rao was a good, sincere and respected teacher.

The management and principal of Hindu College, Masulipatnam (Machilipatnam), sympathized with Rao, but botany was not a subject of study in the college. On Radhakrishnan's suggestion, they applied to the university for permission to introduce teaching of botany in the college. The university appointed Dr. Ekambaram of Madras University as a one-man commission to inspect the college and report whether such permission could be given. Dr. Ekambaram was a friend of Ramachandra Rao. He gave a favorable report, which the university accepted, and the college was permitted to start the teaching of botany. The college established a Department of Botany and appointed Ramachandra Rao as lecturer in it. Thus, after one year, in 1934 he was again appointed a lecturer in a college affiliated with Andhra University, mainly because of Radhakrishnan's interest in upholding freedom of thinking.[7]

Relations with Teachers

Radhakrishnan's wit saved people in embarrassing situations. Ludwig Wolff, a German Jew refugee whom Radhakrishnan had appointed as the principal of University College of Science, was not very articulate in English. His inaugural lecture was being attended among others, by the vice-chancellor, registrar, principal of Arts College, teachers and students. Wolff wanted to apologize to Radhakrishnan for something. But inadvertently he said, "I hope the vice-chancellor will apologize to me." After the lecture Radhakrishnan good humoredly said, "I apologise to Dr. Wolff for our laboratories as they may not be up to his standards."[8] This protective attitude of Radhakrishnan was extended to all teachers including those who opposed him in the meetings of the syndicate or the senate.

Any teacher could meet him at any time. He never stood on formalities for appointments or "permissions." He would talk to the teachers and other staff like members of his family, and never was there any occasion when he was rude or discourteous to teachers or workers. He had confidence in the men appointed by him in the university and gave secondary importance to material results. His faith in teachers followed from the conviction that with well-qualified and sincere men at the helm of affairs, good results would automatically come forth. Teachers in turn reposed faith in him. B. Sundra Rama Rao, one of the teachers at the university, records the response of the teachers towards him, "We automatically felt that our destinies were in excellent hands and we revelled in the majesty and grandeur of his eloquence."[9] This familial atmosphere resulted in a harmonious academic community in the university. There were no pro- or anti-vice-chancellor groups in Andhra University in Radhakrishnan's time.[10]

As Chairman

In the administrative bodies of the university which he chaired, he judged issues on intrinsic merit and never on the basis of external considerations, like whether a proposal came from a friend or a foe. Before coming to the meetings, he would go through the agenda, weigh the pros and cons of the matter involved and come to his own conclusions. He upheld the principle that "A vice-chancellor can manage his syndicate if he has thought things out, and knows his own mind." As a result, he could push through the long agendas of the meetings of the various bodies of the university in practically no time. This in no way meant that he did not allow discussion and debate on the issues involved or acted dictatorially. On the contrary, he encouraged debate and discussion, but he saved time by putting a definite stop to all unnecessary and irrelevant discussion without offending anyone, in a pleasant and persuasive manner. He had enough resilience to meet difficult situations as and when they arose, without having to sacrifice the essentials.

Vice-Chancellor-Teacher

Despite his deep involvement in the administrative and developmental activities of the university, Radhakrishnan could not resist the temptation of taking classes in the Philosophy Department, which had started functioning from the academic year 1932. He got himself designated as honorary professor in the department, whereas Dr. Saileswar

Sen was the reader and head. His other colleagues in the department were Humayun Kabir, P.T. Raju and T.A. Purushottam. The number of students in the Department of Philosophy used to be 8-to-10 per class. His daughter Suseela was also a student in one of the batches that he taught.

All through his stay at Andhra University, he regularly taught the honors classes in the Philosophy Department. He taught Contemporary Philosophy (Bergson's *Creative Evolution* was the text) and Logic (Bradley's *Principles of Logic* was the text). He used to take courses for two hours a week. But, since his stay in Waltair was uncertain, due to his other preoccupations other teachers were also doing these courses independently. P. T. Raju used to teach Logic, and T.A. Purushottam taught Bergson. Radhakrishnan usually took his classes in the last period of the day, which was in the afternoon on Wednesdays and Fridays. In a period of fifty minutes duration he used to lecture for about 30-to-35 minutes. His characteristic style kept the students spellbound. Initially, some senior teachers of the university, like J.C. Coyajee (economics), M.V.N. Subba Rao (English), G.V. Rao (history), and others used to gather outside his classroom, and stand in the verandah by the side of the windows to listen to his lectures. Radhakrishnan came to know of their presence when he noticed the students stealthily staring at them. This, he realized, was distracting the attention of the students. So he requested the teachers to go away and not distract the students by their presence. He actually lectured twenty to twenty-five minutes and dictated the contents of his lecture for the benefit of weaker students for about ten to fifteen minutes. In the rest of the period, for about fifteen to twenty minutes he used to have chit-chat with the students about happenings in the hostels and the university. This gave him feedback on the policies he adopted and the decisions he made regarding the development of the university, which in turn helped him improve the functioning of the university.

For the teaching work that he was doing, he drew the allowance specified for such work by the university. Some teachers in the philosophy and other departments used to comment in private that he undertook teaching for the sake of the allowance and not for the love of it. Such a comment found support in the fact that due to financial difficulties the government had imposed a 10 percent cut on the salaries of all university teachers and administrators. The allowance for teaching that he drew more than compensated for the cut, allowing him to get as much as his full salary, whereas all others drew 10 percent less than their actual salary.[11] This contention gained further ground from the fact that he was very scrupulous in marking the students' attendance in his lectures, which was not the case when he taught in other universities. All this was reinforced when towards the end of his stay in Andhra University Radhakrishnan read out in his class the letter offering him the Spalding Professorship in Eastern Religions and Ethics at Oxford, and asked the students "Do you advise me to accept the offer?" And, he added: "I am tired of talking and talking and talking."[12]

Administration

To see that everything was in order, Radhakrishnan used to regularly inspect colleges and hostels. If he found anything amiss, or if something irregular was brought to his notice, he would take stern action to set it right, irrespective of whether students or teachers were responsible for it. On one occasion he found written on the blackboard in a classroom of the science college, "Mr. Govinda Krishnaiah has absconded without engaging the class." Radhakrishnan ordered Govinda Krishnaiah, who was a lecturer, to meet him in his office the next day. When Krishnaiah met him, Radhakrishnan told him that he would either have to take his work seriously or leave the university at the earliest convenience. Even before the academic year ended Krishnaiah resigned from the university and joined Burma Shell as an executive. On another occasion he noticed that the majority (eight out of twelve) of the B. Sc. (hons) chemistry students had been boycotting Dr. T.R. Seshadri's classes continuously for two weeks. On investigation, he found that as at that time there was an agitation for a separate Andhra province, this boycott was for the reason that Seshadri was a Tamilian. Radhakrishnan sent for the students and asked them whether they had any complaint against Seshadri's teaching. When the students did not reply and remained silent, he warned them that severe action amounting to their suspension would be taken if they did not attend the classes from the next day. Students, knowing that Radhakrishnan would not hesitate to put his warning into action, withdrew their boycott and started attending Seshadri's classes regularly.[13]

Whenever he visited the colleges, he made it a point to visit their libraries too. He took keen interest in the development of libraries, as he firmly believed that a library is the heart of a university. It was because of this interest of his that the Andhra University library developed very fast during his time. At the time of his joining the university, the library had less than 7,000 books in it, with no qualified librarian to head it. By the end of his tenure it had over 23,000 books, and was subscribing to over 200 periodicals, journals and newspapers, with a qualified librarian to look after its acquisitions and development.

Radhakrishnan also used to visit hostels from time to time, to see that they were being maintained properly. He would usually visit the hostels in the evening, while out for a walk with his teenaged son. He did not hesitate to reprimand any student whose behavior was found to be such as to disturb others in the hostel, and would take prompt action to replace or replenish anything that he found missing or lacking. On one such visit, when the students had left for their homes during the Dussehra holidays, he found that due to oversight at the time of construction, windowbars had not been provided for even in the ground floor rooms of a hostel. Without going through the routine administrative sanctions he ordered that those windows be provided with bars without delay. By the time the students came back from holidays they found that all ground floor windows had been fitted with iron bar frames. On another such visit, he found a student, Narasimhananda Panda singing an Oriya song loudly in his room. He waited for a minute in front of the closed door of the room. As the singing became louder and louder, he knocked at the door. Panda continued to sing as he opened the door of the room without realizing that he was facing the vice-chancellor. Radhakrishnan kept his cool and in his suave manner said, "You seem to be a little excited. But you must realize that you may be disturbing other students." Thus, without being rude or harsh Radhakrishnan could maintain discipline in the hostels and command respect from the students.[14]

To give the residents of the hostels a feeling of being members of a family he would on occasions sit with them on the floor and eat with them. But as soon as the students started smoking after dinner to give them freedom to talk and joke with one another, he would leave jovially remarking "a lot of belching chimneys all around me."[15]

Introduces Intercaste Dining in Hostels

Radhakrishnan always encouraged innovative efforts to improve and enrich the life of the students in the university, not necessarily through rules and regulations, but through debate and persuasion. In those days it was common to make boarding arrangements in the hostels on the basis of castes or communities to which the students belonged, so that there were separate kitchens and dining halls for Brahmins, non-Brahmins, Muslims and Christians. On October 3, 1931, in a meeting of the senate, P.V. Narayana, the warden of the hostels put forward a resolution to have common dining arrangements for the students belonging to different communities and castes so that a feeling of brotherhood could be fostered. While expressing his sympathy with the objective of the resolution and assuring him that every possible facility would be provided to encourage and develop a system of intercommunal and intercaste dining, Radhakrishnan objected to such legislation being passed by the senate. Consequently, after some discussion the member saw the wisdom of Radhakrishnan's view that such an arrangement if forced through legislation or compulsion might backfire, and withdrew the resolution. Later, Radhakrishnan after discussing the matter with the students, with their consent, did away with the segregation in dining arrangements. Thus a revolution was brought about silently without any resentment from any quarter and the hostels acquired a cosmopolitan character, fostering a feeling of oneness among the students of different creeds and castes.

Medium of Instruction

Radhakrishnan also realized the importance of teaching and learning in one's mother tongue rather than in English. As a first step in this direction he engaged experts to write matriculation and intermediate level textbooks in Telugu. He also appointed a committee consisting of competent scholars from the departments of science and technology to compile glossaries in Telugu for different science subjects. Once the Telugu textbooks were ready, he made it compulsory for Telugu students to write their matriculation examination in Telugu. But with the deep insight that he had (he could think much ahead of his time), he soon realized that students were not as yet prepared for this change and that it could also pose problems, if it were adopted compulsorily. Consequently, though some wrote their matriculation examination in Telugu, a majority of them preferred to write them in English and sought his permission to do so, which he gave.

Women, Extension Work, Sports

Likewise, realizing how important it was to educate women, Radhakrishnan wanted to open a university college for women, and also provide a hostel for them. To attract girls to join the university he announced a 50 percent fee concession for them, and also exempted them from compulsory attendance. The minimum number of students required to open a hostel was eight. But at that time even such a small number of girl students, who desired to stay in a hostel, were not available and he had to drop the idea. However, he left it to the discretion of the principals of colleges to admit girls.

Radhakrishnan realized much before many in India did, that universities, unless involved in the development of the areas in and around their place of location would soon become ivory towers producing intellectual snobs cut off from their socio-cultural milieu and white elephants for the society at large. He prepared a blueprint for utilizing the services of the university teachers, research fellows, scholars and students for rural upliftment and reconstruction. The scheme, much later came to be called the National Service Scheme in free India and was adopted with partial success in most of the universities.

Radhakrishnan also recognized the importance of games in a university. He employed a full time physical instructor and games coach with the result that the university did very well on the games front by winning many prizes and trophies in state and national level sports competitions and other events.

Maintains Proprieties

Though Radhakrishnan was ready to change what he thought was not right, and brought about a revolution both in the academic and cultural life of the university, he was a stickler for etiquette. This was made amply clear by two incidents that took place in the university. He had organized a lunch in honor of Lord Erskine, the governor of Madras and the chancellor of the university who had come to Waltair to attend the Annual Convocation of the university in December, 1935. He had invited about twenty-five other guests. The Maharaja of Vizianagaram whose estate had been taken over by the Court of Wards of the Madras government on the plea that it was ill managed was one of them. At that time on behalf of the Maharaja Radhakrishnan was negotiating with the governor to have the estate returned to the former. But when the Maharaja started nibbling at the food items while they were being served, even before the chief guest had started eating, and later left the lunch abruptly without the customary apology, Radhakrishnan took serious note of this and from that day onwards stopped negotiating for the return of the Maharaja's estate.[16]

A second incident relates to a meeting of the Literary Association over which Radhakrishnan was presiding and in which the Maharaja of Jeypore, Sir Vikram Deo Verma, was the chief guest. The hall was packed to capacity and the students had squeezed themselves in the doorways and on the windowsills. The Maharani of Vizianagaram had also come to attend the meeting but as all the entry points to the hall were blocked, she could not find a way to get into the hall. Radhakrishnan saw her from the dais and lashed out at the discourtesy and incivility of the students in not giving way to a cultured lady like the Rani who was trying to enter the hall, and ordered them to make way for her. It is reported that the students did so without even a murmur of protest. On the contrary, some students were heard saying "Serves us right."[17]

In one of the senate meetings an amusing incident occurred. Pamula- pati Vekataranksishnaiah Chowdary in his speech repeatedly referred to Sir C.V. Raman, who was also a member and was present there, as "the knight from Bangalore." Raman was irked by this and said excitedly, "Mr. Vice Chancellor, the Honorable Member is insulting His Majesty's gov- ernment which conferred that title on me." Chowdary replied, "If I don't call the Honorable Member a knight, it will be a greater insult to His Majesty's government." Radhakrishnan from the chair said, "Mr. Pamul- apati is right. Sit down, Raman," to the amusement of the house.[18]

Another incident relates to the farewell function organized for Lanka Sundaram, a lecturer in politics, on his resigning his post at the univer- sity. The fact of the situation was that if Lanka had not himself resigned, he might have been asked to resign, as he was not taking his job seriously. Lanka at the end of his farewell speech, said, "Ten years ago I was a clerk in the university office. Ten months ago I became a lecturer here, who knows what I will be ten years hence?" Radhakrishnan in his concluding remarks said, without mincing any words, "We should not allow our frustrations in life to disturb our equanimity."[19]

Other Preoccupations

In 1931 the government nominated Radhakrishnan as a member of the International Committee on Intellectual Cooperation of the League of Nations. He had to attend meetings of this body in Geneva every year. As vice-chancellor he could attend annual meetings of Congress of the Em- pire Universities, of the Inter-University Board of India and as a founding member, the annual meetings of the Indian Philosophical Congress. He did not usually miss any of them. Moreover, because of his reputation as a scholar and speaker, he was often in demand as convocation orator from several Indian universities.

Convocation Addresses

On December 5, 1931, he delivered the convocation address at Lucknow University on "The Spirit of Youth." He astounded the audience when he reproduced extempore word by word without deviating, even by a comma, the fourteen page address printed and circulated to the audience in advance. The speech was not just a mnemonic feat; the ideas it expressed were equally electrifying. The audience was exhilarated when without mincing words he said: "We repress our natural sympathy with those who suffer because it does not pay us. An acceptance of large scale injustice is the price we pay for our comforts. We applaud an aberration which denies human rights to millions of our kith and kin and to our lasting shame, we confound it with religion."[20]

Public Homage to Gandhi

He gave a bigger surprise to his audience at the Annual Convocation of Allahabad University on November 13, 1934. This time the theme of his address was "Democracy and Dictatorship." In the course of it Radhakrishnan eulogized Gandhiji in these words: "Gandhi's appeal will be written not only by the side of the utterances of the great national leaders like Pericles and Cicero, or Washington and Lincoln, but also of the great religious reformers, as that of one of the immortal voices of the human race in all that relates to the highest efforts of men and nations."[21] The governor of Uttar Pradesh, Malcolm Hailey, who was presiding over the function as the chancellor of the university, was upset by the general tone of the speech, and turned red with rage on hearing these words. But Radhakrishnan, ignoring his indignation, continued with his speech.

Eyes Without Sight, Brains Without Soul and Science Without Philosophy

Radhakrishnan attended the sessions of the Indian Philosophical Congress held in 1931, 1932 and 1933 at Patna, Mysore and Poona respectively. He was also the general president of its 1932 session. The 1934 session of the Congress was held at Andhra University. While welcoming the delegates, as the chairman of the organizing committee, he said:

> Oscar Wilde has a great short story which reads thus: Christ came to a white plain from purple city and as he passed through the first street, he heard voices overhead and saw a young man lying drunk on a windowsill and said: "Why do you waste your soul in drunkenness?" He said, "Lord I was a leper and you healed me; what else can I do?" A little further through the town he saw a young man following a harlot and said: "Why do you dissolve your soul in debauchery?" and the young man answered: "Lord I was blind and you healed me; what else can I do?" At last in the middle of the city he saw an old man crouching weeping upon the ground and when he asked him why he wept, the old man answered: "Lord I was dead and you raised me to life, what else can I do?" Here the story ends. If Jesus should visit us today and find that we are comfort-minded and have taken to worship of the most monstrous illusions like militant nationalism and are pouring molten steel into the veins of innocent youth that it may be used to undreamed of heights in mutual destruction and ask: "Why do you indulge, after so many centuries of civilization, in human sacrifices on this colossal scale?" our answer would be: "Lord you gave us eyes but no sight; you gave us brains but no soul; you gave us science but no philosophy."[22]

League of Nations, The Committee on International Intellectual Cooperation

The Committee on International Intellectual Cooperation was constituted by the League of Nations on the suggestion of M. Hymans, the representative of Belgium on the League's Commission at the Peace Conference, and at the instance of Senator Lafontaine of USA. The primary, aim of the Committee was to make concerted effort to create an atmosphere favorable to mutual understanding among nations, to their mutual benefit, and to make the intellectuals in every country take an active interest in promoting the objective of the league. The committee sought ways of making intellectuals everywhere effective agents for advancing peace and intellectual cooperation. The committee also aimed at rapprochement among men of different nations, holding different views and convictions, so as to establish some harmony, some order in intellectual work, and some kind of unity of mankind. The underlying idea was to create an international mind by the widening and sharing of interests. It was also a goal of the committee to secure, for intellectuals all over the world, a reasonable degree of comfort, such as that they had enjoyed before the first world war. So, it planned to propose international action for fixing the pay and status of teachers; protecting the copyright of authors; deciding the modalities of the loan of manuscripts and museum exhibits and settling the question of equivalence of examinations. In short, its main task was to carry out a complete and comprehensive enquiry into various aspects of the intellectual life of that time. The committee dealt with the following problems: (1) university relations; (2) science and bibliography; (3) arts and letters; (4) intellectual rights; (5) instruction of youth in the aims of the league; (6) interchange of teaching staff. It pursued these problems with these aims: (1) to develop the exchange of ideas and to effect personal contacts between intellectual workers of all countries; (2) to encourage and promote cooperation between institutions doing work of an intellectual character; (3) to facilitate the spread of a knowledge of the literary, artistic and scientific efforts of different nations; and (4) to study jointly certain major problems of international bearing.

The committee was comprised of a carefully selected group of fifteen very distinguished thinkers of the time, including great scientists and scholars like Madame Curie, Albert Einstein, Henri Bergson, and Gilbert Murray. The guiding principle for nomination to the committee was to choose representatives of the principal branches of intellectual activity, who at the same time were representatives not only of nationalities, but also of principal groups of culture. The members of the committee were also members of the governing body of the International Institute of Intellectual Cooperation, Paris, whose main task was to carry out the decisions and recommendations of the committee, and to promote intellectual cooperation by organizing intellectual work throughout the world. Radhakrishnan's nomination to the committee meant recognition of him as a leading intellectual of the time. Membership of the committee enabled him to contribute towards the possible solution of some vital problems of post-war education and its reorganization. He attended the meetings of the committee held in Geneva in July every year from 1931-1935. In each of these years he delivered speeches outlining his own proposals for intellectual cooperation and reacting to those of others. Two of the recurring themes in them were a plea for a better understanding of the ancient wisdom of India as preserved in its intellectual traditions and its contemporary educational problems. He maintained that the weakening of religion and religious ideas had deprived peace of one of its main props. If the league, he pleaded, had to succeed in establishing peace, and in creating values fostering peace to be handed down to succeeding generations, it had to find a substitute for religion. In his opinion art and poetry were most suitable to take the place of religion, as in these the genius of a nation finds expression. He suggested that the talents in these fields from all over the globe should be enlisted to propagate the values of peace. For this he put forward the examples of Maxim Gorky and Rabindranath Tagore.

In Radhakrishnan's opinion the aim of the league to establish an international mind could be achieved only if the conditions were conducive for it. The most important condition, he felt, was establishment of justice and equality among all nations, which would be possible only if countries suffering from political subjugation were emancipated. Without a substantial improvement in the political and material conditions of all countries, he argued, no effective participation in intellectual cooperation was possible. He stressed that if countries like India were to effectively participate in international intellectual cooperation, their colonial status must first end.

Development of an international mind, Radhakrishnan pointed out, was not an easy task as it imposed on all the duty of loyalty to the human community, making it obligatory for all to try to exert moral pressure on all those who were exploiting other peoples. Asians, he said, were by training, temperament and conviction pacifist. But their present condition, their material means, and their moral disgust with their subjugation was making them wonder whether pacifism was a mistake and militarism the right thing. Before they were compelled to change their attitude in this respect, he felt the League of Nations ought to try and enforce justice and equality among all nations, small and great, backward and advanced. According to him, only the right kind of education and enlightenment would give rise to a new habit of thought replacing the existing one obsessed by war. The right type of education was not merely intellectual education in religion, economics, law and art. He declared: "The education we want is a constructive process, a fundamental recreation of the human mind directed not merely in the interest of the nation and state but for the welfare of the human community. . . . Let us teach the rising generation the love of humanity and the greatness of peace. Let us impress on them the unity of mankind and the duty we owe to humanity as a whole."[23]

To handle the situation effectively he suggested that (1) the leadership of the world should be with its educators, who alone could propagate a movement of ideas which were more the causes than the effects of public action, and (2) such leadership should not fall into the hands of politicians who were full of greed, jealousy, hatred, suspicion and narrow nationalism. "We have to change," he said, "the present political arrangements, which are far behind our economic actualities and scientific facts. The world has become one physically. . . . It is an era of the dictatorship of high finance. Our professionals, our profiteers, our financial leaders are all for perpetuating the present conditions, although we are on the edge of a volcano. The development of world unity and of a world culture which will express itself in a world citizenship is our only hope."[24] He strongly felt that world unity could only be achieved if we set about changing the mind of the youth, and that if we failed to do so civilization itself would not survive. The only hope of human survival, he emphasized, was in the development of an international mind.

He suggested that an education commission should be set up to study the problems of education in India and China, as in both these nations the old education methods had been abandoned and the new system had not yet proved quite satisfactory.

Radhakrishnan was not in favor of forming one single committee on intellectual cooperation for the whole of India. Instead he recommended that a central committee functioning as a coordinating body, with four subcommittees, each one representing the intellectual activity in the Southern, Northern, Eastern and Western parts of the country, should be formed. The committee, he suggested, should be entirely nonofficial in character, and should have representatives of the cultural life of the regions. The committee may be provided with state subsidies and, if necessary, may have one or two state representatives as well. He made these suggestions because he believed that the best way to arouse interest among Indian intellectuals and to bring them together for the league's work of intellectual cooperation was complete decentralization and minimal or no official interference in the functioning of the committees so formed. On Radhakrishnan's suggestion the Inter-University Board of India was treated as a National Commission and it carried on, at least partially, the functions of a National Commission.

Radhakrishnan's association with the committee on International Intercultural Cooperation gave him an opportunity to acquire an intimate acquaintance with the domineering structure of European civilization. Working with the best minds of the West, he became aware of the exact position of his age-old civilization *vis à vis* its chief modern antagonist, Western civilization. But very soon during the deliberations of the committee he realized that the league had a double face—one for the

Westerners whose culture and civilization was its main object to protect and further, and the other for non-Westerners who were expected to be thankful to the committee for what had been generally done for them. The membership of Radhakrishnan, as well as of other Asians, was generally considered by the Westerners as a gracious gesture to Asians. It was seen as a great chance given to people from backward civilizations to collaborate with Westerners in order to implant advanced Western civilization in backward nations. Radhakrishnan, with his sensitivity and deep sense of pride in Indian civilization, was hurt by such an attitude. But unlike others Radhakrishnan did not sulk; instead, he took it as a challenge and repudiated the claim that Western culture was the most advanced. He stood up as a protagonist of Asian culture, and boldly criticized the Western claim when it overstepped its limits. He did not do so by dogmatic assertions, but through arguments. For the first time, in an international forum the dogmatic assertion of the superiority of Western culture was challenged by an Asian, and the Westerners given a chance to rethink and revise their evaluation of civilizations. His association with the league, therefore, gave him an opportunity to give a concrete shape to what was hitherto an abstract faith, or an academic belief. It laid the foundations for the formulation of his political ideas and political philosophy into a living political principle.[25]

At Andhra University

The annual foreign sojourns of Radhakrishnan meant his yearly absence for a period of eight weeks (from the third week of June to the third week of August) from the university. When he was away, syndicate members who were friendly with him and regarded him highly were made acting vice-chancellors. In 1931, 1932 and 1934 T. S. Tirumurti, in 1933 J.C. Coyajee, and in 1935 O. Pulla Reddy acted in his place, and generally followed the policies laid down by him.

Some senators, however, questioned in senate meetings the propriety of the vice-chancellor's long absence from the university to attend meetings abroad. They felt that the university did not gain anything from his attending such meetings. To this Radhakrishnan replied that the university's gain in a matter like this could not be precisely defined. Moreover, as the members of the Committee on Intellectual Cooperation were chosen entirely for their individual eminence in the world of thought, he was attending its meetings in his individual capacity. If anything, his membership of this committee only enhanced the prestige of the university.[26]

Imports and Reads Communist Literature

In those days the import of communist literature into India was banned by the British government. Being a member of the League of Nations' Committee on Intellectual Cooperation, Radhakrishnan was exempted from a search of his luggage by the customs authorities. Taking advantage of this, Radhakrishnan brought communist literature into India on return from each of his visits. Voracious reader as he was, he would read much of it in no time and pass it all on to his colleagues like Hiren Mukerjee, Adhikari and others who were avowed leftists. Once they had read the books, they were sent to the university library. The result was that Andhra University Library, because of Radhakrishnan's intellectual curiosity and liberalism, found itself endowed with the best single collection of socialist and communist literature found anywhere in India. But his successor C.R. Reddy handed over all these books to the government when the latter threatened to search the university library for communist literature.

Students' Union

Whenever Radhakrishnan was in Waltair, he made it a point to attend the meetings of the Students' Union, inter-college debates, elocution contests and meetings of the Athenaeum of Waltair of which he was ex officio president. In these meetings he would never let the participants and the office bearers be overawed by his presence. He was kind and informal, and encouraged the younger generation to come forward and present their views freely and fearlessly. He listened to them with attention, just as he would listen to any eminent speaker or writer. His discussions with them were as animated as they would be with learned professors. Even if he did not agree with the youngsters' view or even if he found them too harsh and pedantic he never scorned at them or showed any disrespect. If he noticed that the student in charge, whose duty it was to propose a vote of thanks was too shy to do so, he would quietly ask him in his own language, "Will you propose a vote of thanks or shall I do it?" On being requested to do so, he would comply with his customary elan. The office bearers of students' organizations were ever grateful to him for delivering the introductory speech, the concluding speech and the vote of thanks.[27]

Visits of National Leaders and Others

Among the dignitaries who visited Andhra University during Radhakrishnan's time were not just Nobel laureates like C.V. Raman (an honorary professor and senator of Andhra University) and Rabindranath Tagore, but also freedom fighters, prominent among whom was Babu Rajendra Prasad. In those days to invite such men to a university required a lot of courage and the risk of losing the favor of the British government. But Radhakrishnan was not afraid of that; he could be friendly towards such individuals without being out of favor with the government. In 1935 Radhakrishnan invited Rajendra Prasad, who after being released from the Cuddalore jail, was passing through Waltair on his way to Calcutta. Accepting the invitation, Rajendra Prasad broke his journey at Waltair and addressed the Students' Union. Radhakrishnan made it a point to be in Waltair on that day, and presided over the meeting.

He invited Rabindranath Tagore to Andhra University to deliver Alladi Krishnaswamy lectures on December 8, 9 and 10, 1933, and again on December 2, 1934. At that time Visva-Bharati, the university founded by Tagore at Santiniketan, was in financial distress. Tagore came to the university on his second visit with a dance-drama troupe, and stayed as a guest of the Maharaja of Vizianagaram. The troupe presented two plays, one of which was *Sapamocan* directed by Tagore. For the benefit of the South Indian audience, Tagore had also included *Śiva Tāṇḍava* in the program. The dance was performed by male artists. On seeing men perform a dance, many of the students started laughing. This angered Tagore who in an imperious way ordered the play to be stopped and the curtains dropped. Radhakrishnan, who was sitting among the audience, went on to the stage and persuaded the poet to resume the play. When the play ended, Radhakrishnan closed his vote of thanks by saying, "On behalf of the audience and on my own behalf, with a sense of shame, I do apologize to the poet."[28]

Mālapalli (Harijan Hamlet)

But his inviting the freedom fighters and others to the university, which could annoy the government, did not mean that he did nothing to placate the government, when necessary. The *Mālapalli* incident is ample proof of how he tried to keep the government on his right side.

Vunnava Lakshminarayana (1877-1958) was a barrister-at-law of Guntur (Andhra), who became a staunch nationalist, freedom-fighter and Gandhian. He was also a scholar, practitioner of yoga, social reformer and writer. "Śāradā Niketan" at Guntur, an institution established by him for promoting women's welfare and education, is a standing monument to him. His novel in Telugu, *Mālapalli*, was published in parts: Part I in November-December 1922, Part II in February-March 1923, and Part III on July 27, 1923. A review in the leading Telugu newspaper of the time, *Āndhra Patrika* (Jan. 25, 1923), pronounced Part I of it to be a work of great genius, an original work in language, style, and ideas, and commented that, except for *Kanyaśulkam* (a play by Gurajada Appa Rao), it was for the first time that a work of perennial value had appeared in the spoken tongue. The *Swarājya* of May 18, 1923, evaluated it thus: "a book of surpassing literary charm . . . the first genuine attempt to portray the life of the lowly *Panchama*[29] in Āndhradeśa . . . the herald of a coming social order, when no more shall any man be deemed untouchable or condemned to a virtual bondage solely because of his birth. . . . The book represented a revolution in style . . ." In a letter (November 10, 1924) to C.P. Ramaswami Iyer, then in the governor's executive council, C.R. Reddy informed them that *Mālapalli* was "one of the few works of undoubted genius in Telugu . . . a genuine work of creative art and imagination . . . written in a colloquial style." He too compared it to *Kanyaśulkam*.

As the Telugu translator to the government of Madras pointed out in his report (January 8, 1923), the book denounced most unsparingly the system of criminal settlements, police, jails, courts, etc. It "zealously preaches at some length," he added, "the principles of Bolshevism and the creed of non-cooperation." The CID Report (October 30, 1935) rightly found that it made out capitalists and bureaucrats as tyrants. The advocate general, A. Krishnaswami Iyer, described the book as follows (May 16, 1936): "Dissatisfied with the present social system and economic ordering of society," the author "thinks that the panacea for all these evils is the attainment of self-government and the reform of the existing system of administration . . . . According to him the existing economic evils in the society lend to perpetration of crime and lawless acts on the part of the poor and oppressed in society." There is no doubt *Mālapalli* sought to show some sort of harmonization of *Swarājya* (self-rule) with *Samatā* (equalitarianism), and of Gandhism with communism, was possible and desirable.

It was not surprising that on May 14, 1923 the government declared the first two parts of the book forfeited since, in its opinion, it contained seditious matter, and on August 8, 1923 the third part met with the same fate. Apparently on the representations of men like C.R. Reddy, and after some correspondence with the author, as the government had men like C.P. Ramaswami Iyer at the helm, in March 1928 the government first permitted publication of a revised edition of the book with the objectionable passages expunged, and later in November 1928 permitted sale of its available copies after the removal of objectionable portions from them and rebinding them. In August-September 1935, a revised edition of it with an additional part, part four was published.

In 1935 the Board of Studies in Telugu of Andhra University prescribed *Mālapalli* as a nondetailed textbook for the B.A. examination, and this was approved by the Academic Council presided over by the vice-chancellor. This was announced in the gazette of January 8, 1935. Men belonging to the Justice Party which was in power then (like K.V. Reddy) thought that as the whole book was "nothing but communistic propaganda," prescribing it as a textbook was simply outrageous and irresponsible (January 16, 1936). On February 7, 1936, the chief secretary to the government wrote to the vice-chancellor of Andhra University, drawing the latter's attention to "the objectionable character" of certain passages in the books and informing him of the government's intention to proscribe it. On February 14, 1936, the registrar of the university explained to the government that the revised edition of *Mālapalli* was prescribed by the Board of Studies and approved by the Academic Council, and informed it that as the university's attention was drawn to "the objectionable character" of certain passages and to the government's intention to proscribe it, the university had "removed" it from the list of textbooks. It was substituted by K. Veeresilingam Pantulu's (1848-1919) *Sweeyacharitramu* (autobiography). Veeresilingam was a pioneer of modern Telugu literature and a social reformer; the government had conferred on him the title of Rao Bahadur.[30]

In the March 1936 meeting of the Academic Council, Radhakrishnan, the vice-chancellor, requested the council to confirm his action in "cancelling" *Mālapalli* as a textbook and replacing it with Veeresilingam's book. A couple of members of the council asked for the reasons for this action. One of them specifically asked wherein lay the "unsuitability" of the replaced book, and commented that what was done was detrimental to academic interest and was a great injustice to the author. In reply

Radhakrishnan told the members that he had as much respect for the great novel and its distinguished author as anyone else, and requested the council not to press him for the reasons of his action, as their disclosure, he stated, would not be either in the interests of the students or of the author. He was informed of its "unsuitability," he added, only after it was proscribed, and then he had to use the emergency powers he had as vice-chancellor for acting as he did. After this the council ratified his action.[31]

On July 14, 1937 the government of Madras, then headed by C. Rajagopalachari (1878-1972), removed the ban on *Mālapalli.*

Family Life

Radhakrishnan's family had moved to Waltair when he was elected the vice-chancellor of Andhra University and lived on the Upper Panchavati beach. Some time later Radhakrishnan built his own house in Maylapore, Madras, and the family moved there and he divided his time between Waltair and Madras. However, he made it a point to be in Waltair whenever a VIP visited the university. Probably his wife did not return to Waltair, and never again lived with him in Calcutta, Banaras, or Delhi. She did not go to Oxford or Moscow. He and she were together only whenever he visited Madras.

Contribution to University Development

Radhakrishnan gave equal weightage to teaching and advanced research in the university. He believed that research was the basis of efficient teaching. So, he never hesitated to give grants for research projects. Credit goes to him for creating in the university an atmosphere which was peaceful and highly conducive to academic work. He appreciated and encouraged the teachers who excelled in their academic pursuits. With a predisposition favoring innovation and experimentation, a capacity to take the right decisions quickly and firmly, and a resoluteness to implement decisions, he made Andhra University rapidly progress within a short span of five years and establish for itself a secure place in the Indian academic world. Recognizing his contribution to the development of the university, the senate in its meeting of March 30, 1935, elected him as a life member. While proposing that Radhakrishnan be elected, O. Pulla Reddy said, "The name of Radhakrishnan as a professor of philosophy has reached the very ends of the world. There was not a single endowed lecture to which he had not been invited. He had the unique honor and distinction of being a lecturer in Comparative Religion in the University of Oxford. High pandits like Professor Gilbert Murray and Dean Inge had a great admiration for him. In regard to his contribution to the advancement of the Andhra University it was a matter of common knowledge that the infant university had grown to its full stature under his watchful care and guidance. The magnificent pile of buildings would bear testimony to the truth of this statement. His contribution to literature and philosophy were known to every one, and they were prized by the world as treasures of great value. In honoring him, the university would be honoring itself."[32]

Scholarly Work

During his vice-chancellorship Radhakrishnan, while doing full justice to the administrative, developmental and teaching work in the university, found time to give several convocation addresses and scholarly lectures both in India and abroad, and keep up his scholarly productivity in every other way. During this period, in addition to contributing research articles to renowned journals, the following books of his were published: *East and West in Religion* (1933); *Freedom & Culture* (1936) containing his university convocation and other addresses; *The Heart of Hindusthan* (1936), a collection of his speeches and lectures on Indian religions and philosophy. He also co-edited with Professor J.H. Muirhead a volume on *Contemporary Indian Philosophy* (1936).

The comparative method adopted in *Indian Philosophy* and developed and applied in *An Idealist View of Life* was used with striking effect in *East and West in Religion* to make a comprehensive study of oriental and occidental values. He tried to show that the talk of the meeting of East and West was not just an ideal put forward by a few visionaries. Such meetings had actually taken place in all significant epochs in history, and the two "hemispheres of thought" had in the history of mankind borrowed from each other. He did so by proving that "religion consists in doing justice, in loving mercy, and in making our fellow creatures happy. A saint is not a stained glass image, but one who works for his fellow men and endeavours to establish a new relationship of loving kindness among them. He regards an individual's need as a sufficient claim on his generosity. We must believe in the equality of men not only in the soul, but in the flesh. It is true that we cannot fall in love with a telephone directory. Love of humanity must be defined in terms of the men and women with whom we are brought into contact."[33] Reviewing this book *The Times Literary Supplement* said: "The metaphysics of Radhakrishnan's absolute idealism represents a real forum for East and West in-so-far as it boldly confronts the problem which haunted Bradley . . . that of the relation between the absolute and the God of religious experience . . . and answers it in the form of an eschatology at which Bradley may have hinted at the denial of ultimate reality to the finite self, but which is never made fully explicit. Radhakrishnan suggests a solution of the problem which is, in essentials, derived from Indian idealism." In his article in *Contemporary Indian Philosophy* Radhakrishnan maintained that the Indian mind considers philosophy to be practical because it is conceived as having its source in men's authentic suffering and anguish. It understands philosophy as a discussion regarding human nature, its origin and its goal. He attributed the political downfall of India to the inadequacy of anaemic Hinduism.

Oxford Professorship Offered, Farewell to Andhra

In the beginning of the year 1936, Radhakrishnan was offered the newly established Oxford Chair for Eastern Religions and Ethics. He accepted it on the condition that he would spend six months in Oxford, from January to June every year, and the rest of the year from July to December in India. From all accounts the syndicate of Andhra University did not favor his being away from India for six months every year, while continuing to head it. But the University of Calcutta was agreeable to his continuing to be its King George V Professor, while being away at Oxford for six months annually as Spalding Professor. Oxford, too, agreed to this arrangement. He had come to Andhra University from Calcutta University on leave without pay and allowances until August 19, 1937. Calcutta agreed to his resuming his duties as professor from that day, while simultaneously occupying the Oxford Chair. Consequently he placed his resignation from vice-chancellorship from May 20, 1936, before the senate in its meeting of February 15, 1936. It was accepted and before it became effective C.R. Reddy was elected as his successor. Though there were other candidates for the post, Tirumal Rao and Vepa Ramesam, they were defeated in the election, because of Reddy's eminence and Radhakrishnan's support for his predecessor.

Even on the day of his farewell, Radhakrishnan bantered good naturedly with his colleagues and this indicated the friendly relations between them. On the eve of his departure from Andhra University, a group photo was taken. Sir J.C. Coyajee, principal of the Arts College, had some other engagement and therefore excused himself from being present at the time of the photograph. But just as students and teachers settled down for the photograph, and the photographer was ready to click, Coyajee came in in a hurry and said to Radhakrishnan, "I want to speak to you urgently for a minute." Radhakrishnan quipped "I won't believe you. I know you have come for the photo." All the students and teachers burst into laughter.[34]

IX.

The Spalding Professorship

The Offer

In England, H.N. Spalding, after listening to Radhakrishnan's Hibbert Lectures in 1929-1930, had begun persuading the authorities of Oxford University to establish a chair called Henry Norman Spalding Professor of Eastern Religions and Ethics. He finally succeeded in 1936, due to his philanthropy. The chair was allocated to All Souls College. The purpose of instituting the chair, according to Spalding, was to promote "mutual understanding and appreciation." In a letter dated March 8, 1935, to the vice-chancellor of Oxford University he wrote: "The principal object would be to bring home to Oxford and the West a living knowledge of the great contributions made to religion and ethics, both individual and social or political, by Eastern countries; while at the same time comparing and contrasting the ideals of the East with those of the West." He was so much under the spell of Radhakrishnan's scholarship and personality that he saw to it that the chair was offered to Radhakrishnan. Radhakrishnan accepted the offer and began preparations to set sail for England to take up the new assignment at Oxford.

Farewell at Madras, Important Speeches

A large number of farewell meetings were organized not only on the campus of Andhra University, but also in the town. But more important than these meetings was the dinner-meeting organized by the leading citizens of Madras on March 31, 1936, to honor Radhakrishnan on his appointment as Spalding Professor and to bid him farewell on the eve of his departure to England. This was held in the Freemasons' Hall, Egmore, and was attended by more than two hundred guests consisting of high officials of the government, distinguished educators and other dignitaries. In the meeting, in his after dinner speech The Rt. Hon., Mr. V.S. Srinivasa Sastri remarked that Radhakrishnan could not be said to be a philosopher in the traditional sense of the term, viz., "a person who looks nowhere round about him, but always has his gaze fixed in far-off places, preferably in the skies. We know too the proverbial philosopher amongst us who carried once some little *ghee* in a leafy cup and propounded the problem whether the cup held the *ghee* or the *ghee* held the cup, and who finally dropped both and lost his dinner and thereafter lost his reputation and that of his tribe as well. Sir S. Radhakrishnan has shown by his conduct of Andhra University that he is much more than a professor of philosophy, and that given a chance he could show rare administrative power. That university owes almost the whole of what it is today to Sir Radhakrishnan's ability of management."[1] Praising Radhakrishnan's administrative abilities Sastri "wished that Sir Radhakrishnan could be kept here and asked to run the Education Department" of the entire Madras presidency. Commenting on Radhakrishnan's appointment to the chair at Oxford, and in an indirect way silencing those of his critics who were alleging that he had got his appointment because of his contacts with the authorities at Oxford and not because of his merit, Sastri said:

> I should like some light to be thrown upon how he obtained this post. There is some mystery about it, leaving I might say in some quarters some suspicion. This Professorship of Eastern Religions and Ethics—to consult the proprieties of the day—should have been advertised for in India, Japan and China. I should like, if I were somebody in Oxford to put a question to the authorities: "was this place duly advertised in the public print of these three Eastern countries? If not, why not?" If the answer be "yes" what were the peculiar qualifications that determined the choice? I think we all know the answer. We all know that the appointment was not advertised anywhere in the East, but that with that wisdom and sense of propriety which sometimes is exhibited even by learned bodies, the right man was chosen for the right place.[2]

Sastri continued:

> I do not know whom to congratulate—the professors and students of Oxford who will have him expound Eastern philosophy and religion to them, or us here who will have our most cultured Indian to be an interpreter of our faiths and religions to the West. It seems to me that Sir S. Radhakrishnan need not be congratulated.[3]

R. Little Hailes, the then Director of Public Instruction, Madras, citing the example of Woodrow Wilson who started his career as a professor and rose to be the president of USA, prophesied that if some day India became a republic Radhakrishnan would become its president. Sir C.R.

Reddy, Radhakrishnan's predecessor as well as successor in Andhra University, hailed Radhakrishnan's appointment as the recognition of a culture, and said:

> I suppose this is the first organized invasion of Indian culture since the day of Asoka when we sent out many missionaries to far-off Syria, Tibet, China, Burma, Ceylon and other countries. Indian culture is under the spur of a new Indian nationalism. All nationalism tends to grow into imperialism of some kind or other, and our culture has now begun the invasion of European countries; and Sir S. Radhakrishnan represents our vanguard.[4]

According to him, the recognition of the merit and scholarship of Radhakrishnan was not his alone, but that of the whole of India. "In our present condition," Reddy added, "we have to treat all talent as investments of our nationalism in the world markets and we are sending out, along with the gold exports, Sir S. Radhakrishnan. I trust that the results of the second case will not be so disastrous as in the first."[5] He meant thereby that Radhakrishnan would come back to India and not be permanently lost to the West. Professor Kuppuswami Sastri, the well-known Sanskritist, and Professor A.G. Hogg, Radhakrishnan's old teacher were the others who spoke at that meeting.

In his response, Radhakrishnan attributing to luck and chance his success in life in general and his appointment to Oxford in particular, spoke as follows:

> There is something in this world to which we owe whatever good happens to us. I remember it said that when Napoleon's eagle eyes flashed across the list of names proposed for promotions in the army, he used to scribble on the margin "Is this man lucky?" Napoleon never asked the question, "Is he worthy?" I think it is my luck that at the present juncture the chair is instituted at Oxford and that I got it. It is the same luck which is responsible also for the reputation and general regard for me, and my works on Indian philosophy. I know that there are deeper students of Indian philosophy, I know that there are greater students of Sanskrit in this country, and in this very hall. I have no doubt about it; but it is my good fortune that I am able to turn at some particular moment to that particular task of bringing out my first volumes on Indian thought.[6]

Speaking about an ideal philosopher he said:

> I think a philosopher must be fearless. He must have a mind which has resilience about it, some kind of flexibility, some kind of daring adventur-

ousness; so long as you do not have it, you are not truly philosophical
students. You must be perpetual seekers of truth; you never claim that you
knew anything, but want to find out and discover. If you have got the
philosophical attitude in you, it must be your endeavour to question; take
nothing for granted, and be prepared to go to the root of the matter. I think
philosophy lives in a world of thought and aspiration, is not wedded to
beliefs and dogmas which have got a kind of mathematical rigidity about
themselves. Unless the mind is kept open, and fearless, unless you have
courage, it will not be possible for you to have a philosophical attitude.[7]

Analyzing the contemporary political situation, and the role that
intellectuals could play in it, he continued:

I do believe that it is not merely politicians who solve political problems. I
do think that whereas the relations between Great Britain and India may
not be comfortable to either side, on the plane of ideas by the play of moral
and intellectual forces, political problems may obtain a lateral approach.
You need not attack them in front. It is possible for you to develop an
atmosphere of friendliness and fellowship and trust . . . . Intellectual commerce knows no barriers and tariffs; and if it is possible for us to develop
that, other things will gradually drop off of their own.[8]

Speaking about the work that he proposed to take up in Oxford in particular and in the UK in general, Radhakrishnan concluded his speech thus:
"You may rest assured that my own work will be to directly propagate
philosophy, and indirectly to convince all that India is not a subject to be
administered but a nation seeking its soul."[9] This certainly was a brilliant
speech which must have pleased and impressed scholars, government officials and nationalists as well. With such an objective, carrying the good
wishes of his countrymen for his success, Radhakrishnan left India.

Life and Work at Oxford

At Oxford as Spalding Professor, Radhakrishnan became attached
to All Souls College, to which his professorship was allocated. All Souls
College, Oxford, occupies a special place in that university, for it does not
have undergraduates on its rolls and it elects as fellows and teachers only
those who have gained a reputation in their fields of work. As such, there
is very little regular teaching work. The fellows and teachers, therefore,
have plenty of time for their research and writing. They need spend only
a small part of their time supervising the research work of the graduate

students. The Spalding Chair was attached to the Department of Oriental Studies and not to that of theology or philosophy, and as a result did not attract many regular students.[10] Consequently, Radhakrishnan could devote himself almost solely to his own study, thinking, writing and fulfilling lecture engagements.

His inaugural lecture on October 20, 1936, was on the theme "The World's Unborn Soul." It was an exercise in synthesizing the philosophies of history and of religion. In it he traced through examples the inner travail of man through the ages, and the "adjustments" he had to make now and then in the successive epochs of history. But he rejected all "adjustments" that man had so far made as, according to him, they were all inadequate to meet the present crisis. The lecture presented a comprehensive vision of the East and West and the future of religion and humanity, without taking recourse either to the "prevalent issues" of philosophy, or to its systems. He tried to restore philosophy to its original conception of a vision of, to use Plato's terms, "The Idea of the Good."

Radhakrishnan used to deliver his statutory weekly lecture during the term on Wednesdays at 5:00 p.m. in a hall at All Souls College. The audience consisted of not more than 10-to-15 undergraduates of Oxford, a few elderly ladies from the town and one or two casual Indian students who happened to be in Oxford at that time.[11] He usually lectured on the philosophy of religion, adopting a comparative approach. The reasons for the small audiences at his lectures were not far to seek. *First*, there was no great interest in learning Indian philosophy. In fact many undergraduates and graduates did not even know of the existence of such a thing as 'Indian Philosophy'. *Second*, most of the undergraduates were too busy doing their main subjects, and had little interest in sparing any time for peripheral subjects. Nevertheless, Radhakrishnan delivered his lectures with all seriousness and made an impression on the minds of those who attended, both by his style and the content of his lectures. As a result of this he was invited to deliver lectures by a number of British organizations, and to deliver a sermon by the Unitarian Church at Oxford.

On January 19, 1937, Radhakrishnan delivered a lecture on "Progress and Spiritual Values," at the evening meeting of the British Institute of Philosophy. The theme of Sir George Birdwood Memorial Lecture delivered at the Royal Society of Arts, London, on April 30, 1937, was "Mysticism and Hindu Thought." On June 29, 1938, he delivered the Annual Henriette Hertz Trust Lecture on a Master Mind at the British Academy. He spoke on "Gautama—The Buddha" with such eloquence, lucidity and profundity that the chairman of the British Academy who was present on the occasion commented that "the inspiring lecture was not only on a Master Mind, but by a Master Mind."[12] His Lewis Fry Memorial Lecture at Bristol University on February 27 and 28, 1939 was on "The Renaissance of Religion." In one of the sermons in the Unitarian Church he spoke on charity and compassion. To illustrate the meaning of compassion he narrated the anecdote of the Buddha and a Banaras courtesan:

> Soon after attaining enlightenment, while on a visit to Banaras, the Buddha was passing through the streets. The favourite courtesan of the king, intoxicated with her wealth, beauty, and power saw him from the balcony of her palace, and when the Buddha came near her house with his begging bowl, she spat into it. He smiled and moved on. Many years later when the Buddha again returned to Banaras, he came across a diseased woman covered with sores and filth, lying at the gates of the city. She was unattended and ill-nourished. Recognizing her as the same courtesan who had spat into the Buddha's begging bowl, his disciples reminded him about that episode and requested him to ignore her. But seeing her, he wept and said to her, "Sister, what sin have I committed to see you in this condition?" He picked her up, and tended her wounds and nursed her back to health.[13]

By introducing anecdotes and stories of this sort he made his lectures illuminating and interesting. Another example may be given. Once while lecturing he found that he was dealing with the subject, mysticism, in a complex and abstract way and that he was losing the attention of the audience. So, at an appropriate juncture he referred to what he called was a belief in certain parts of the world: When God created man, the latter felt lonely and begged for a companion. God responded by creating from the energy of the wind, the heat of the sun, the coldness of ice, the resilience of quick-silver, the beauty of the butterfly and the noise of the thunder, a woman. This sudden change of mood from very serious to nonserious rejuvenated the interest of the audience in the lecture and kept them glued to their seats throughout.[14]

Besides giving these public lectures, Radhakrishnan guided an occasional senior student who would visit him in his room in All Souls College, in his research work. A good number of Indian students who studied in the universities in the UK or who happened to pass through the UK on their way to the USA or some other European country, or on their way back to India, made it a point to meet him in Oxford or in London if he happened to be there. In London, he stayed at the Hotel Imperial and he invariably treated students who came to meet him, to a lunch or a movie. For lunch he would take them either to the Kohinoor Indian Restaurant or to Shearn's Fruit Restaurant. His discussions with them ranged from the abstract and the abstruse, to their personal problems. He was ever willing to give them his personal advice, no matter on what issue they sought it. In Oxford he took the visitors to his home for a meal. His home was the Mecca for most of his friends, for it was about the only place where one could find Indian food as one got it in India, especially South Indian dishes to which some of them were accustomed. Not only in his house, but also in restaurants he treated his guests to vegetarian food, as he himself was a vegetarian and teetotaller. Even at official dinners and functions he did not drink or eat nonvegetarian food. He took pride in sticking to vegetarianism and abstention from alcohol. He believed that it created a good impression on the foreigners if Indians, who were traditionally vegetarians and teetotallers, remained so even on occasions when meat and drink were served. The foreigners, he thought, held in high esteem the Indians who upheld their own tradition and culture.[15]

Throughout his stay in Oxford Radhakrishnan did not waste any time on frivolities and exercised self-restraint. The following anecdote will bear this out. Once Dr. J.C. Ghosh, who was lecturing Indian Civil Service probationers in Oxford, addressed himself to Radhakrishnan and quipped, "Ah, professor, it's a lovely May morning, with girls in beautiful frocks, wandering in the streets, but you are a big wig and you can't accost any of them!" Radhakrishnan at once replied, "Do you think I can't go and fall in love with the next girl? I can but I won't."[16]

Radhakrishnan was highly impressed with the atmosphere of higher learning at Oxford, created by the devotion of both teachers and students to it. He dreamed of a university like a Cambridge or an Oxford in India and saw "no reason why we in India cannot set up such institutions." When political, financial and traditional obstacles to the establishment of such institutions in India were pointed out to him, he opined that there could be no serious political obstacles, and observed: "Resources can be no trouble, if only our princes can be won over. Your point about tradition is true enough but that is all the more reason to start soon. After all, time is a great factor here."[17] It is interesting that, notwithstanding his experience as a professor at Calcutta and a vice-chancellor at Andhra, Radhakrishnan should have held such a view while at Oxford.

Another Major Work

Radhakrishnan utilized most of his time in attempting a synthesis of the religio-philosophical views of the East and West. As results of this his book *Eastern Religions and Western Thought* was published in 1939. *The Times Literary Supplement* hailed it as a turning point in religion. It was an attempt to show how in the West religion and philosophy have mutually influenced each other at different times. It exposed the myth of the superiority of Western philosophy and religion, by making a comparative study of the Judaic and Christian doctrines and practices, and Greek and Roman philosophies on the one hand, and the Hindu and Buddhist doctrines and practices, on the other. After proving that East and West have been fruitfully influencing each other from very ancient times till the present, he goes on to suggest that an effort must be made to synthesize the best elements in the philosophies of East and West, especially European humanism and Eastern religion, the goal being to evolve a new living philosophy which would be more profound than either and which, therefore, would have broader spiritual vision and stronger ethical force. The book combines a trenchant criticism of the outward shams of religion, with a plea for toleration. When an admirer, N.A. Nikam, told him the book was profound, he replied, "Yes, Oxford gave me leisure and freedom from visitors."[18]

Relations with Gandhi

Perhaps Radhakrishnan first wrote on Gandhi in 1921 in an article "Gandhi and Tagore" published in the *Calcutta Review* (October 1921). His sermon on "Revolution through Suffering" at Manchester College, Oxford, in June 1930 was in praise of the Gandhian revolution. In his Allahabad University convocation address 1934, he hailed Gandhi as a great religious reformer, and his voice as an immortal voice of the human race. So, it is no wonder he built up a rapport with the Mahatma. In 1938 he met Gandhi in Sevagram at Wardha to suggest that it would be appropriate to have Subhas Chandra Bose as the president of the Tripuri session of the Indian National Congress. Gandhi replied that as Bose was not then in the best of health, it could be thought of next year. Radhakrishnan responded to this by gently saying that if Gandhi agreed to have Bose as president, his health would become all right. As is well-known, Gandhi agreed and Bose was elected.[19]

During the period 1936 to 1939 Radhakrishnan edited a felicitation volume in honor of Gandhi, which he planned to present to the Mahatma on his seventieth birthday. He got some of the world's leading minds to contribute to it. Albert Einstein, Pearl Buck, Rabindranath Tagore, et al. responded to his call and contributed their articles. The book entitled *Introduction to Mahatma Gandhi: Essays and Reflections on Gandhi's Life and Work*, was published and presented to Gandhi on October 2, 1939, his seventieth birthday. *The Times Literary Supplement* reviewing the book wrote, "One of Gandhi's successes has been in securing the devotion of a man like Radhakrishnan who, if he is less experienced in the rough and tumble of political life, has higher intellectual attainments and perhaps a finer quality of soul than Gandhi himself."

For his sustained work of synthesizing occidental and oriental idealism and his exponential efforts in creatively interpreting Indian thought, the British Academy elected Radhakrishnan its fellow in 1939. He remains the only Indian to have been honored thus.

Radhakrishnan returned to India in July 1939, after completing his assignment at Oxford for that year, without any inkling that he would be going back to Oxford only in 1944. Due to the outbreak of the Second World War, he had to apply for a leave of absence for the duration of the war.

X.

Vice-Chancellorship at Banaras

Malaviya's Search for a Successor

In August 1939 when Radhakrishnan again started teaching in Calcutta, Pandit Madan Mohan Malaviya (1861-1946), the founder of Banaras Hindu University and also its vice-chancellor since November 29, 1919, underwent medical treatment there. The ailing Malaviya had begun to feel that he should retire from the vice-chancellorship of the university, and had started looking for a person who could be elected to replace him. Having steered the university through very difficult times, he knew that the task of choosing its vice-chancellor was not an easy one. He had worked for the development of the university with a passion. Mahatma Gandhi called him the "biggest beggar," because whenever he met an Indian prince or industrialist he asked him for a donation, big or small, for his university, and almost always got a positive response.

In Malaviya's opinion to be a successful vice-chancellor of Banaras Hindu University, the eligible candidate had to fulfill at least five conditions. *First*, he should be a great Hindu. *Second*, he should be a great patriot. *Third*, he should be an internationally acknowledged intellectual. *Fourth*, he should be acquainted with the functioning of the university. *Fifth*, he should have a fund-raising capacity. Searching for someone with all these qualifications, Malaviya found that Radhakrishnan had them all. He was a great Hindu, who by his personal example, by his eloquence and by his writings had raised the Hindu religious tradition and culture to soaring heights. By championing Indian nationalism and Indians' right to self-rule, criticizing the continued suppression of freedom by the foreign government, and displaying his solidarity with Gandhi, he had established his patriotism. His international reputation by then was unquestionable. He was well-acquainted with the Banaras Hindu University as he had been its honorary professor of philosophy and, therefore, a member of its senate since 1927. He was elected to the court of the university in 1928. He was conferred the honorary degree of the doctor of laws by the university in its twenty-first convocation where he also delivered the convocation address on "Religion and Politics." As such he was aware of the problems of the university and was known well to the members of its various academic and administrative bodies. As vice-chancellor of Andhra University, he had proved his fund-raising capabilities. It has also been said that Gandhi suggested to Malaviya Radhakrishnan's name for the Banaras vice-chancellorship.

Malaviya Succeeds

So, in August 1939 while in Calcutta, Malaviya requested Radhakrishnan to meet him. When they met, Malaviya requested Radhakrishnan to accept the vice-chancellorship of the Banaras Hindu University on the same terms and conditions on which he was working at Calcutta University. At the outset Radhakrishnan declined the offer for two reasons. *First,* because he knew that Banaras Hindu University was undergoing a financial crisis, therefore, he did not want to take up any paid appointment in the university which would have added further to its financial problems. *Secondly,* he was already overworked with his assignments at Oxford and at Calcutta. But Malaviya had made up his mind and was bent upon having Radhakrishnan as the head of Banaras Hindu University. Taking his second objection first, Malaviya told Radhakrishnan that most of the work in the university was done by the pro-vice-chancellor and the heads of various departments. The vice-chancellor's work, therefore, in the main consisted only of coordination and supervision. The university's work, he said, would get done if Radhakrishnan could spend the weekends of all the months during the term from July to December at Banaras and then, of course, spend the following six months from January to June at Oxford. Turning to his first objection Malaviya suggested that Radhakrishnan should, besides the traveling and daily allowances connected with his travel, accept a token honorarium from the university. In this way he would not be putting a strain on the meager finances of the university. Radhakrishnan could not resist such an offer, and in any case it was very difficult, almost impossible, to say no to so eminent a man as Malaviya who was held in high esteem by the entire nation. Radhakrishnan agreed to be the vice-chancellor in an honorary capacity, accepting only the actual railway fare from Calcutta to Banaras and back for every visit; he declined the offer of traveling allowance, daily allowance and the token honorarium. Malaviya was gratified by this.

Election Process

After receiving Radhakrishnan's consent Malaviya resigned from the post of vice-chancellor on August 20, 1939, requesting the university to release him as soon as possible, and directed the pro-vice-chancellor to place the matter before the council for its consideration at its meeting to be held on August 26, for fixing a date for a special meeting of the university court to elect a new vice-chancellor. The council in its meeting held on August 26, decided to convene a special meeting of the court on September 17, 1939, to consider Malaviya's resignation and to elect a new vice-chancellor.

The special meeting of the court was held as scheduled, under the chairmanship of the pro-chancellor, Maharajadhiraj Dr. Sir Kameshwar Singh Bahadur of Darbhanga. In the meeting rich tributes were paid to Malaviya who was mainly responsible for establishing and developing the university. The members also commended the nomination of Radhakrishnan for the vice-chancellorship. Radhakrishnan was present in the meeting as a member of the court. Maharaja Sir Ganga Singh Bahadur of Bikaner, the chancellor of the university, who could not attend the meeting, sent a telegram as follows: "I am happy to feel in Sir Sarvepalli Radhakrishnan the university has secured as its vice-chancellor the services of one who by his academic distinction, and by his recognised achievements in upholding the cause of Hindu culture, has earned the esteem and confidence of his countrymen."[1] Maharaja Sir Hari Singh of Jammu and Kashmir sent a telegram saying, "Sir Radhakrishnan's acceptance of [the] vice-chancellorship despite his commitments, is worthy of his remarkable personality and a guarantee of the continuance of the university's vigorous life."[2] The resolution passed by the Old Students Association, Calcutta, stated, "Sir Sarvepalli occupies a unique position in the academic world and is the greatest exponent of Hindu philosophy and culture. No one could have been better fitted than he to hold the reins and guide the working of this great center of learning."[3]

The pro-chancellor while proposing that the services rendered by Pandit Madan Mohan Malaviya, and the debt of gratitude of the university to him may be put on record, spoke as follows:

We must congratulate ourselves that the mantle of this great countryman (Pandit Malaviya) of ours is going to fall on another great countryman of ours (Dr. S. Radhakrishnan) who has already attained international reputation as a profound scholar, an original thinker and an authoritative interpreter of Indian religion and philosophy. It is in the fitness of things that the control of the affairs of this university, the object of which is to create synthesis of the East and the West, should be primarily in the hands of one who has made a special study of the subject and has the vigour, enthusiasm and ability to put his precepts into practice. Again, it is remarkable that he will continue his connection with Calcutta and Oxford while discharging his duties and obligations to this university. I have every hope that by this way he will be able to establish an effective contact between the Eastern and Western civilization and cultures and with the past and the present create a future worthy of the glorious literary traditions of the ancient place.[4]

Seconding the motion Dr. A.B. Dhruva said:

The silver lining which we ... see ... before us is the appointment of a gentleman endowed with learning and scholarship to the position of vice-chancellorship of this university, and I count largely on him for the development of the subject of Hindu religion and Hindu culture which is particularly of very great importance to this university and which are one and the same thing in India and of which our friend is a great exponent.[5]

Professor M.B. Rane addressing himself to Pandit Malaviya, expressed his views on the occasion thus: "Fortunately, sir, you have been able to find as your successor a vice-chancellor who is an outstanding personality, a man of international repute, a person in whose hands you can safely leave the university. This must be a source of great comfort and satisfaction to you on your retirement."[6]

Pandit Malaviya moved the proposal for the election of Radhakrishnan in the following way: "He has long been active in the service of the motherland. He has interpreted the culture of India to the East and West as few scholars have done so far. He is a scholar of international fame. It is the good fortune of the university that it has been able to secure the services of this great scholar. I asked him to take up the appointment on the salary which he was drawing at Calcutta, but he preferred to take it up in an honorary capacity. At present he will spend three days during the week at Banaras. But I have no doubt that he will devote sufficient time to the work of the university as the need will be felt. I expect that this university will become a great centre of philosophical learning and I have no doubt that Sir Radhakrishnan's presence as vice-chancellor will contribute largely to this result. It is not surprising that the news that he has agreed to accept the office of the vice-chancellor has given satisfaction to all those who are interested in the welfare of this all-India institution."[7] The proposal, seconded by S.S. Bhatnagar, and supported by Pandit Gopi Nath Kunzru, K.M. Munshi, Iswar Saran and S.K. Maitra, was accepted unanimously.

Elected Vice-Chancellor of BHU

On being unanimously elected vice-chancellor of Banaras Hindu University for a period of three years from the date of his joining, Radhakrishnan responded thus:

In the circumstances in which I am placed, my election to the vice-chancellorship is not a fair deal to this university. But I get vacations and it will be possible for me to spend some time in this university and do the work of this university. I do not hope to be as great and distinguished a vice-chancellor as our Panditji or his predecessors but all that I desire is to do a little to further the interests of this university. In my devotion to Indian culture and its spread, I assure you I am of one mind with Panditji and many of his colleagues here. I will be a humble fellow worker with them in the shrine of learning. Mr. Pro-Chancellor, you and others who followed you have expressed their appreciation of my humble services. You have yet to see the result of my undertakings. With the Grace of God and with the blessings of Panditji I hope to do my best.[8]

After his return to Calcutta he sought the permission of the vice-chancellor to join the Banaras Hindu University as its vice-chancellor in an honorary capacity. The permission was readily granted. In his letter dated September 14, 1939, to the registrar, Calcutta University, thanking the university for permitting him to join the vice-chancellorship on a part-time basis in an honorary capacity, Radhakrishnan reiterated, "It will not be necessary for me to attend more than two days at weekends now and then in Banaras. If, however, on account of unforeseen circumstances I am obliged to spend extra time during weekends, I shall ask the university for permission. You may kindly intimate the fact to the authorities."

The vice-chancellorship of Banaras Hindu University, however, was not an easy job. Compared to Andhra University, an infant university with very few departments, Banaras Hindu University was the biggest university in the country with thirty-nine departments and 130 subjects of study. Moreover, the financial position of the university was precarious, depending mostly on year to year donations collected primarily by Malaviya. It had no consolidated fund, and the government grant, which was the only certain source of revenue, was too meager to run an institution, which had been developed to unmanageable dimensions in respect to both the number of students admitted annually and the number of departments created. There were quasi-political groups among the teaching staff as well as in the administrative bodies of the university. These

problems were further compounded by the fact that the political atmosphere in the country was turbulent, with the hopes raised and agitations
launched by the Indian National Congress. The youth of the country in
general, and a significant number of students in the universities in particular, were keen to make their contribution to India's freedom struggle by
their participation in it. The government, on its part was equally keen to
stop any uprising, particularly in a university.

With the resolve "to show the results of his undertakings" and to prove
his mettle Radhakrishnan arrived in Banaras on September 24, 1939, to
assume charge of his new office. Malaviya, the students of Banaras Hindu
University, and the prominent citizens of Banaras wanted him to deliver a
lecture on the *Gītā* to commemorate the day of his assuming the office of
vice-chancellor, to which he agreed. After formally taking over the charge
of the office from Malaviya, accompanied by Malaviya, he arrived in the
pandal, which was erected to accommodate the audience, in the Central
Hindu College quadrangle of the university, to deliver his inaugural lecture
on the *Gītā*. The teachers, students and other prominent citizens of Banaras
gave him a standing ovation. For the first time, Malaviya seated him in the
Vyāsa Peeṭha and requested him to deliver his lecture. Radhakrishnan then
gave his first public lecture as vice-chancellor of the Banaras Hindu University, keeping the audience spellbound for forty-five minutes.

The same afternoon he chaired the first meeting of the council. The
speed and quietness with which the agenda was covered, decisions taken
and the way in which the proceedings were conducted by him surprised
every member and filled them with admiration for the chairman. When
the bill for the vice-chancellor's travel from Calcutta to Banaras and back,
prepared by the office as per the university rules, was placed before him
for his signatures he put a cross on the bill and wrote on it, "Actual Rs.
Seventy Return Ticket." He refused to accept anything more than that.
The university then on its own deputed from his next trip onwards a
servant to accompany him on his journey. The trip of the servant cost the
university ten rupees, the return fare from Calcutta at that time. Thus the
weekend vice-chancellor or "commuting vice-chancellor" cost the university a total sum of Rs. eighty per trip.[9]

From his previous experience, Radhakrishnan knew that as a vice-
chancellor he had two-fold duties. *First*, to see that the standards of teaching and research were kept very high, and *secondly* to ensure that the
administration was prompt, clean and just. He also knew that he would
be able to discharge his duties well, to his own satisfaction and to that of

his colleagues and students, if and only if the university was in a sound
financial position. The first task, therefore, that he set before himself
after joining the university was to tackle its financial administration. For
this purpose he persuaded N.V. Raghavan, who had retired after serving
as accountant general in various provinces of India, to join the university
as honorary special officer, initially for a period of four months. Radhakrishnan got the appointment approved by the council in its meeting held
on October 8, 1939. N.V. Raghavan was required to report directly to the
vice-chancellor and the council on matters relating to the financial position of the university, maintenance of accounts, systems of audit and
allied matters. Subsequently, Raghavan was asked to continue for two
consecutive years. He resigned on his own on September 7, 1941.

A meeting of the court was held on December 22, 1939 within less
than two months of Radhakrishnan's joining the university. The members
of the court, and all those who had come to watch its proceedings—
students, members of the staff and others—were impressed by the dexter-
ity with which he conducted the proceedings of the meeting and the metic-
ulously prepared statement regarding the affairs of the university which
he placed before it. The statement reflected his complete understanding
and command over the problems of the university. Dr. Hriday Nath Kun-
zuru, commenting on his statement said, "I am sure everyone here will
agree with me when I say that not even Pandit Madan Mohan Malaviya
could have given a more impressive account of the achievements of the
university than what you, Sir, have given this morning."[10] And pointing
to Malaviya who was also present in the meeting he said, "Well, Sir, if I
may say so without impertinence in your presence, we feel that you have
been able to get a worthy successor."[11] In a way this statement reflected
the sentiments of all those who were present in the meeting of the court.

Work as Vice-Chancellor

As already said, the outbreak of the Second World War prevented
Radhakrishnan from visiting Oxford. So, he could devote much of his time
to the problems of the university, which were primarily economic. Though
he believed that "the real wealth of a university" has to be measured "by
the extent of the sacrificial service that has endowed it," yet realizing the
importance of financial stability for a university, he requested N.V. Raghavan to submit a report on the financial position of the university. After
carefully studying and analyzing it, Radhakrishan came to the conclusion

that deficit financing of the university was primarily due to unplanned expenditure, and he prevented this in the following way: As a long term measure, he got a rule adopted by the council according to which no activity could be undertaken by the university involving extra expenditure unless the entire recurring and nonrecurring expenditure likely to be incurred on the proposed activity was secured by special donations earmarked for the purpose.[12] A strict adherence to this rule coupled with rigorous control over expenditure resulted in closing the university's revenue account for the year 1940-1941 with a surplus of Rs.35,920. It certainly was a landmark in the history of the university which had hitherto closed its balance sheets invariably with a deficit. And to get over the prevailing overdraft of the bank he started collecting donations. By April 1941, he was able to collect about four lakhs of rupees for this purpose. By adopting these measures, a beginning was made to place the university on a firm financial footing.

Gaekwad Chair

Malaviya and other members of various administrative, financial and academic bodies of the university, were so impressed by the method and style of his functioning, that they wanted Radhakrishnan to take over the vice-chancellorship of the university as a full-time job. But he declined the request time and again, on the grounds that he did not want to overburden the already stretched university finances by accepting a paid appointment in the university. Fortunately for the university, on November 4, 1940, Maharaja Sir Pratap Singh Gaekwad of Baroda offered an endowment for establishing a chair to be called "The Sayaji Rao Chair of Indian Culture and History," and three fellowships to be called "Sayaji Rao Fellowships." They were to be established for perpetuating the memory of Maharaja Sir Sayaji Rao Gaekwad, who throughout his life had been interested in fostering the study of Indian culture, to which different races and religions— Hindu, Muslim, Christian and Parsi—have contributed and which can be said to be the greatest contribution of India to the world. The main function of the professor and fellows would be "to promote the cultural unity of India by means of scholarly publications and lectures." The endowment was gratefully accepted by the council on November 20, 1940. However, the Maharaja of Baroda agreed to the proposal of the council to call the chair instituted by him as "The Sayaji Rao Chair of Indian Civilization and Culture."

Malaviya, who was very keen to have Radhakrishnan in the university on a whole-time basis, corresponded with the Diwan of Baroda, Sir

V.T. Krishnamachari, suggesting that the new chair be offered to Radhakrishnan. As a result of this, the Maharaja of Baroda proposed that Radhakrishnan should be the Sayaji Rao Professor in Banaras Hindu University *for life*. The other terms and conditions were the same as for the George V Professorship, that is, he was allowed to retain the Spalding Professorship for the statutory period of two terms each year. However, the salary was payable during this period at half the rate. Besides this, he was also permitted to visit foreign countries and to accept casual nonrecurring engagements with or without honorarium in India or abroad. The salary for the period of such visits and assignments was payable in full. There was to be no restriction on his freedom of thought and expression relating to any matter. His obligation was that when he was in India and free from other engagements, he should reside in Banaras during the working days of the university and organize and guide postgraduate and research work in the Department of Indian Philosophy and Religion. Respecting Radhakrishnan's desire not to draw any salary from Banaras Hindu University, the Maharaja of Baroda suggested that his salary be paid directly by his government.

Resigns George V Professorship

In its meeting on February 23, 1941, the Banaras Hindu University council accepted the donor's suggestion and resolved that the normal university rules be held in abeyance as long as Radhakrishnan occupied the Gaekwad Chair. Thereupon Radhakrishnan informed the council that he would accept it from July 1, 1941. In his letter of March 20, 1941 to the authorities of Calcutta University, resigning the King George V Professorship, he expressed his sentiments as follows: "On this occasion I recall with gratitude the uniformly kind and generous treatment I have had for twenty years, i.e. since March 1921 when I first took up this appointment. I feel happy that during this period it was given to me to serve this university not only as a professor but also in several other capacities, as a member of the Executive Council, the syndicate, president of the Post Graduate Council in Arts, delegate to the Congress of the Universities of the British Empire and the International Congress of Philosophy at Harvard University. If in the course of my service here such coveted distinctions as the Hibbert Lectureship, an Oxford Chair, Fellowship of the British Academy and Fellowship of All Souls at Oxford came my way, the credit is due mainly to the facilities offered and the encouragement given to me by the university authorities from the time of the great Sir Asutosh Mooker-jee who selected me for this post in 1920." He concluded his letter thus: "I have given the best part of my life to the university of Calcutta and the service of the people of Bengal and though my official connection with them may terminate in July, I may assure you that my love for them will endure." Calcutta University accepted his resignation, and in due course in recognition it showed its high appreciation of his contribution to its academic life by conferring on him the degree of LL.D. *Honoris Causa* an emeritus professorship and in 1946 its honorary fellowship. Subsequently, it honored him by inviting him to address its centenary convocation.

Life at Banaras

Having thus become a professor at Banaras Hindu University with no teaching to do, he could function as its whole-time vice-chancellor. Cochin House, constructed with a donation from the Maharaja of Cochin, was his official residence, in which he lived alone. His family had been living in Madras since the time he built a house there. So, after leaving Andhra University, whenever he had to stay at Calcutta, he either lived in the house of his friend S.C. Majumdar or in the Great Eastern Hotel.

In Banaras he seldom went to the office, conducting most of the official work at home. His home was accessible to one and all, whether they be students, teachers, or the administrative personnel of the university. They could meet him at any time of the day without an appointment. He received them all, reclining in bed. His wooden bedstead covered with a sheet with a pillow on it was placed in the center of the room; in front of it were a few chairs and behind it a cupboard. The room was full of books of all kinds. He would meet the visitors one by one, listen to their grievances or suggestions, immediately grasp the purpose of their visit, solve their problems if possible or at least give a satisfactory reply and send them off. The visitors, almost without exception, admired the courtesy, patience and quickness with which he dealt with men and matters. They were convinced of his impartiality, as well as of his support to all those who were devoted to the pursuit of knowledge and its dissemination. Their conviction that he was a man devoted to scholarship, as well as justice and fairplay, strengthened their faith in his judgment. Even those who came determined to oppose him were won over by his charming manners, openness, and unassuming friendliness.

Only once in a while did he lecture at the Department of Indian Philosophy and Religion, but he attended all its social functions. On the other hand, whenever he was in Banaras, he made it a point to deliver a lecture on the *Gītā* every Sunday for 40-to-45 minutes. These lectures were popular and were attended not only by the students, teachers and other employees of the university, but also by many citizens of Banaras. He guided, in some sort of general way, the research of a few fellows.[13] He would meet them at the most once a month, read their writings if possible, and make suggestions. Besides this he did not participate in actual teaching in the university. The members of the department liked him for his cordial, courteous and generous behavior towards them.

Silver Jubilee of BHU, Gandhi's Visit

During his vice-chancellorship the Silver Jubilee of the university was celebrated on Vasant Panchami day, January 21, 1942. He invited a distinguished galaxy of national leaders, public men, educators, princes and administrators to participate in a special function held on that day. Prominent among those who attended were the chief guest Mahatma Gandhi, Rajendra Prasad, Jawaharlal Nehru, Govind Ballabh Pant, Syama Prasad Mookerjee, Smt. Vijayalakshmi Pandit, and Jugal Kishore Birla. In the course of his address to the special convocation held on that day, Gandhi said: "You all know very well that I have neither the physical strength nor the inclination to undertake a long journey, and yet when I received Sir Radhakrishnan's invitation to deliver an address on the occasion of the Silver Jubilee Convocation of the Banaras Hindu University, I had not the heart to decline it. . . . I, therefore, could not say 'No'. Sir Radhakrishnan's letter was a call to a pilgrimage."[14] Later, in his speech Gandhi referred to the command over the English language of Malaviya and Radhakrishnan: "Malaviyajis and Radhakrishnans are rare and thousands cannot achieve what they have done."[15]

Lauding Gandhi in his thanksgiving speech, Radhakrishnan said:

> At the time when the world is groping in the dark, he gives us faith, when we are surrounded by disillusionment, he imparts hope; when we are lost in resentment and misunderstanding he calls us back to the path of love and truth. A living symbol of nonviolence, incapable of the least ungenerous thought, with a heart so large as to encompass the whole of humanity, he is truly a man of peace and therefore the most powerful adversary to the present passion-torn, war-shattered world."[16]

On this occasion Radhakrishnan conferred the Hon. D.Litt. degree on Jawaharlal Nehru, Rajendra Prasad, some princes and other eminent persons.

University's Closure

1942 was a turbulent period in the history of the freedom movement in India, for it was the year in which Gandhi had launched the "Quit India" movement. He gave the nation the slogan "Do or die," and called upon even the students studying in the institutions conducted or controlled by the government to come out of them and asked those who were above sixteen years of age to join the *satyāgraha*. But before the *satyāgraha* could be launched, he, along with other prominent Congress (political party) leaders, was arrested and put behind bars, by the government, in a determined move to curb the movement. This angered the people and a wave of excitement, indignation, and anti-British feeling swept the country. Banaras Hindu University could not remain unaffected by this wave. The classrooms became empty and processions were formed by the students. Radhakrishnan closed the university and asked the students to vacate the hostels. But he did not allow the police to enter the campus, assuring them that university teachers and other staff would carry out the "watch" and "ward" functions in the university on their own to prevent any untoward incident and unsocial activity from taking place in the campus.

Police Enter Campus

However, the government having received confidential reports from its intelligence agencies about the political activities of some students and teachers, without giving any warning to them, ordered the police and the military to occupy the campus on August 19, 1942. Consequently, about three hundred students who could not leave the hostels earlier because of the nonavailability of trains, and were still staying in them, were thrown out with their bag and baggage. Radhakrishnan and the members of the council rightly felt indignant at this and sent a letter of protest to Lord Linlithgow, the viceroy, requesting him to order the withdrawal of the police and military from the university. Radhakrishnan sent the official letter drafted by the council along with a personal letter. In his personal letter he wrote:

I do not know to what extent our students have associated themselves with such undesirable activities (damaging railway properties). Even assuming that some of them have done so, we venture to think that our position is not much worse than what happened or is happening in other educational institutions. . . .Being a university of an all India character, supported by the princes, the people and the government of the country, any special or drastic action taken in this regard to the university will be viewed with concern by the public at large. If any member of our staff, or any of our students are found guilty of any criminal conduct, the law must certainly have its course. But any orders of the government which will in any manner restrict the normal functioning of the university, are bound to cause deep resentment, which doubtless, we are all anxious to avoid.[17]

Efforts Make Police Quit

In order to sort out the issues quickly Radhakrishnan and Gurtu, the pro-vice-chancellor, met the governor of Uttar Pradesh in Lucknow, but the governor after a frank discussion on matters relating to the university expressed his inability to give a decision as it was an all India question and needed to be discussed with the viceroy. In the meantime Radhakrishnan received a message from M.S. Aney, who was a member of the Executive Council of the university and was also a member of the Executive Council of the viceroy, that he should come to Delhi and meet the viceroy who had on his (Aney's) request agreed to meet him (Radhakrishnan). Radhakrishnan accompanied by Gurtu went to Delhi to meet the viceroy on September 9 to discuss the prevalent situation in Banaras Hindu University. After first meeting Aney they went to the viceregal lodge to meet the viceroy. But the viceroy expressed his unwillingness to see them. Indignant at this rudeness they returned to Aney's house, who, hearing about what happened, asked them to wait in his house and himself went to see the viceroy. When Aney told the latter that his refusal to meet Radhakrishnan would be rightly construed not only in India but also in England, where Radhakrishnan was held in high esteem, as an act of unmerited discourtesy, and that a report of it would sabotage the movement for enlisting the sympathies and getting the cooperation of the Indian people for the government in their war effort, the viceroy agreed to meet Radhakrishnan. Consequently, Radhakrishnan and Gurtu went and met the viceroy. In about an hour that he spent with the viceroy, Radhakrishnan apprised him of the situation in the university and persuasively pleaded with him for the withdrawal of police and military personnel from the campus and the early reopening of the university. At the end of their meeting the viceroy had a better understanding of the affairs of the university and its working.[18]

Satisfied with their meeting with the viceroy, Radhakrishnan and Gurtu returned to Banaras. Radhakrishnan continued to pursue the matter of reopening the university through correspondence and personal meetings with the governor of Uttar Pradesh, Sir Maurice Hallett. In his letter of September 14, to the governor, he distinguished between political discussion and political activity, and argued that the university is the rightful place to allow and encourage political discussion. He wrote as follows:

> It is true that our students in their unions, used to discuss political subjects, but we always exerted to promote a dispassionate examination of the conflicting views and a judicial temper. As in other universities, we have had here also the Students' Federation interested in voicing their characteristic demands. As a professor of the University of Oxford, and a fellow of All Souls College, I am aware how the Oxford Union, for example, carried with large majorities in great excitement and heat, such totally subversive propositions as "we shall not fight in any circumstances for our King and Country," and "This House has no confidence in the foreign policy of His Majesty's Government," and so forth. Every university in Great Britain has its clubs, representing widely different political views such as liberal, conservative, labour and communist. We do make a distinction between political discussions and political activities.'[19]

University Freed, Work Starts

Persuaded by Radhakrishnan's pleas, the governor finally agreed to the removal of the police guard from the university on October 24 and its reopening on October 26, 1942. Radhakrishnan thus saved the university from a *sine die* closure. The classes started from November 11 and examinations were held on time. A precious academic year of the students was saved.

Radhakrishnan received universal praise for his successful efforts leading to an early reopening of the university. Maharaja Ganga Singh, the chancellor of the university, wrote to him, "I should as chancellor like to convey to you my appreciation of the way in which you conducted these delicate and difficult negotiations and to congratulate you on their successful outcome."[20] Munshi Isvar Saran expressing the feelings of the court, in its meeting held on November 26, 1942 said, ". . .by your dignity, by your scholarship and by your experience, by your ability, and I might also add, by your position you have succeeded in these troublous times to save the university, and the rumours of which we heard so much proved to be unfounded."[21]

Reelected Vice-Chancellor

During this period of turmoil, Radhakrishnan's first term of three years as vice-chancellor was to expire on September 16, 1942. Three days before that he was unanimously elected for a second term of three years in a special meeting of the court. In that meeting proposing Radhakrishnan's name, Dr. Kanhaiyalal spoke as follows:

> The university has greatly prospered under his [Radhakrishnan's] watchful care. He has given up other lucrative engagements elsewhere and his influence has helped the university in establishing some new chairs and donations for different purposes. We require at this juncture a man of cool judgement and of calm and dispassionate outlook and in Dr. Radhakrishnan we have a man to meet those requirements.[22]

Works as Vice-Chancellor

Radhakrishnan remained aloof from campus politics throughout his stay in the university, particularly during the election of university teachers to the executive body of the senate. Even though he was approached by many prospective contestants he never favored anyone. In one of his addresses to the court on November 28, 1942 he said, "There has been loose talk about parties, official nominees, etc. I wish to say here emphatically that the officials of the unlversity have no interest in any individual or group. In this university there can be only one party, and it is the party of the university which works for the university. The officials of the university are prepared to work with any set of people because they feel that whoever comes to work for the university will keep the interests of the university higher than anything else. In this election, I may tell you, you are at liberty to vote according to your conscience."[23]

Besides concentrating on the development of the academic activities in the university and opening new courses in commerce, ayurveda, engineering and technology, Radhakrishnan also laid stress on the importance of physical education. The guiding philosophy underlying the stress that he laid on physical education was stated in his address to one of the meetings of the court in which he said, "Even our ancient *Śastras* lay considerable emphasis on the development of physical culture, as it is essential for the growth and development of both cultural and spiritual life. The means provided and the methods prescribed by the sages of India for discipline and culture of the mind and for the acquisition of knowledge are highly rational. The glory of physical education, therefore, lies not only in the development of physical perfection, but in the advancement of intellectual and spiritual life. We want to make it compulsory in the case of all university students."[24] He did indeed make it so.

Radhakrishnan knew very well that both teachers and nonteaching staff of the university form the foundation on which the superstructure of the university stands. He paid great attention to improving their service conditions. When he joined the university there were sixty-nine teachers who were getting a salary of Rs.100 or below per month; seventy-three who were receiving emoluments between Rs.100 to 150; and sixty-seven whose salary ranged between Rs.151 to 300. The number of teachers who were getting more than Rs.200 per month was just about fifty. Nearly half of the teaching staff was without any graded salary. Of the administrative and ministerial staff only twenty-three had a graded salary and the remaining 146 did not. These salaries were quite meager compared to those of other universities in the country. Radhakrishnan decided to give graded salaries to all the teachers and others on the staff. The task of fixing the grades was not an easy one, as right from the inception of the university no attempt had been made to correlate the grades with the posts, no definite plan having been adopted while fixing the salaries. The salary was fixed in an *ad hoc* manner taking into account the person who was being considered for the post. The difficulty was further compounded by the fact that designations of certain employees of the university were not clear. He overcame all these hurdles and fixed the grades of posts rather than fixing them for individuals occupying them. To improve the service conditions of the teachers and other employees, Radhakrishnan increased the university's contribution to their provident fund from 3.5 percent to 6.25 percent. As the scales of pay which had been fixed during the war were awfully inadequate in the post-war period when prices rose considerably and rapidly, he once again revised the employees scales of pay with effect from April 1, 1945.

Though the scales of pay of the class four staff were revised with effect from April 1, 1945 along with those of others, they found the increase in their scales inadequate to meet the rising cost of living. They went on a strike for six days, from November 22-27th. Though Radhakrishnan wanted to increase their salaries further, the finances of the university did not permit him to do so. Understanding this, the students and teachers cooperated with him, and the six-day strike period passed without disturbing to a great degree the functioning of the university.

Elected Vice-Chancellor a Third Time

Radhakrishnan's second term as vice-chancellor was to end on December 1, 1945. The war had enabled him to serve the university for six years without any interruption. But now with the end of the war he was obliged to go to Oxford for the period beginning January 1946 to June 1946, and every year thereafter for the same period, to discharge his duties as Spalding Professor. So he felt that he could not accept the vice-chancellorship for another term. But Malaviya refused to listen to him and earnestly pleaded with him not to sever his connection with the university. In deference to the wishes of Malaviya, Radhakrishnan agreed to his name being proposed for reelection. He was unanimously reelected vice-chancellor a third time for a further period of three years in the meeting of the court held on December 1, 1946. Immediately after his election in the third week of December 1945, Radhakrishnan left for Oxford for a period of six months, until June 1946.

On his return from Oxford, he found that the government desiring that the university should revise the scales of pay of teachers and other staff of the university to provide them financial relief had given a substantial grant to the university for this purpose. Nothing for him could have been more welcome than this. Consequently, the salaries of the teachers and other staff members were revised for the third time during his tenure as vice-chancellor effective from July 1, 1946.

Freedom Comes

As is well-known, in India around this time a number of political developments took place. The British government headed by Attlee agreed to the formulation of an interim government of India and of a constituent assembly. An interim government headed by Jawaharlal Nehru (1888-1964) was sworn in on September 2, 1946.

Malaviya's Demise

The Government of India nominated Radhakrishnan as the leader of the Indian delegation to UNESCO, the first General Conference of which was held from November 19, 1946 in the Grand Amphitheatre at the Sorbonne in Paris. He left for Europe in the last week of September 1946. While he was abroad, Madan Mohan Malaviya, the virtual founder and architect of Banaras Hindu University, passed away on November 12, 1946. This was a great loss for Radhakrishnan and the university.

Tensions in University

Malaviya was held in high esteem by all, and nobody dared to differ from him. But soon after his death voices of discontent were raised by the disgruntled, as was evident in the election of the pro-vice-chancellor, a position which had fallen vacant since January 8, 1947, due to the resignation of the incumbent Ram Behari Lal. Radhakrishnan wanted Dr. Syama Prasad Mookerjee to be elected as the pro-vice-chancellor, as he thought that this would add to the efficiency and the reputation of the university. Moreover, Syama Prasad Mookerjee was a son of Asutosh Mookerjee, a great benefactor of Radhakrishnan and maybe it was Radhakrishnan's intention to make Mookerjee his own successor when the time came. He had persuaded Mookerjee to accept the nomination for election to this post. But Madan Mohan Malaviya's son, Govind Malaviya, who perhaps was planning to succeed Radhakrishnan in due course, was interested in it. So, he was also a candidate for it, and he did not agree to withdraw from the contest, despite Radhakrishnan's and other members' requests. An election, therefore, became inevitable.

Radhakrishnan in the larger interest of the university wanted the pro-vice-chancellor's election to be unanimous. So, in the court meeting held on January 12, 1947 to elect the pro-vice-chancellor, he reasoned thus:

It is my earnest desire to avoid any kind of conflict. To elect responsible officers after a contest is not a healthy tradition. So, if we are to maintain healthy traditions in this university, the pro-vice-chancellor should be elected without any contest or opposition. It is necessary that he should be elected with practical agreement of a large majority of the staff, students and the members of the court. I find that it is not possible to have unanimous election at the present moment. The only way in which unanimity can be brought about is by the withdrawal of one candidate. If one candidate does not withdraw, then the other should withdraw. Therefore, I should be allowed to withdraw the name of Dr. S.P. Mookerjee. I am not concerned about my personal prestige. It is just dust in the balance.[25]

The members of the court were so moved by his passionate concern for harmony in the university, that they suggested a postponement of the election and asked the vice-chancellor to suggest the name of one who could be elected for the interim period. Radhakrishnan suggested the name of Dr. A.B. Mishra, who was then elected pro-vice-chancellor until the time a regular pro-vice-chancellor was elected. The decision of the court was approved by the council in its meeting held on March 30, 1947.

Finding that the atmosphere in the university had become vitiated by groupism and nepotism, Radhakrishnan did not want to continue as its vice-chancellor. He, therefore, requested the council on the same day to relieve him and elect a new vice-chancellor as soon as possible. But the council did not accept his request. Several members made it emphatically clear that "in the present stage of university's development and, in these momentous times" his guidance was needed more than ever before. He had by acts of kindness and courtesy made himself so dear to many of the teachers, students and the other staff of the university that it was impossible for them to imagine the university without him.

The next meeting of the court was held on December 13, 1947. It was the first meeting of the court in free India. In the course of his annual statement, Radhakrishnan outlined the new responsibilities of the university in free India thus:

> The tasks imposed by freedom may not be so dramatic as those demanded by the fight for freedom. But they are not less exciting. It is easy for us to assume that once the basic aim of independence is achieved, the other objectives in terms of which independence is interpreted are also achieved. Political independence is the beginning of a continuous revolution. It gives us power and opportunity but much depends on how we use that power, how we utilise that opportunity. Freedom is not a static condition. It is something dynamic and creative. We have to bring home to the masses of people the reality of freedom in terms of economic security and educational opportunity.[26]

Resignation

The election for the post of pro-vice-chancellor was also held on December 13, 1947. There was a contest between Govind Malaviya and

A.B. Mishra, the acting pro-vice-chancellor. Govind Malaviya won by just three votes. Radhakrishnan realized that he could not hope to work smoothly with the newly elected person. So, the next day he sent in his resignation to the court, and requested that it may be accepted with effect from January 16, 1948. When the news of his resignation spread in the campus, many students formed a procession shouting "We want Radhakrishnan." But no amount of pressure and persuasion could make him withdraw his resignation. The court in a special meeting held on January 11, 1948 accepted with regret his resignation. Members of the court paid glowing tributes to him for the services he had rendered to the university. Dr. Hriday Nath Kunzru in his speech, which was typical of many other speeches made on the occasion, said, "During the last eight years and more, he has guided the destinies of this university. He has done his very best to place the university on a secure footing and has raised its status in the world of scholarship. When he came here, there were many difficulties which faced him. . . . He by his tact, patience and ability of the highest order, solved those difficulties and improved the affairs of the university, to such an extent as to delight the hearts of all constituents. . . . He has during the last eight years that he has been connected with the university, collected nearly eight lakhs of rupees for the university."[27]

Amarnath Jha's was the only nomination received for the election to the office of vice-chancellor. His name was supported by Govind Malaviya. Amarnath Jha was elected for a period of ten months, the residual period of Radhakrishnan's term. Curiously, Amarnath Jha did not mention the name of Radhakrishnan even once in the speech immediately after his election.[28]

Thus ended Radhakrishnan's vice-chancellorship of Banaras Hindu University. He not only saved the university from indefinite closure during the war period, but also put it on a sound financial footing. The overdraft which was Rs.1,343,548 on April 1, 1939, the year he assumed office, was reduced to Rs.754,485 on April 1, 1947. The number of students increased during this period from 3,603 to 5,233, and several new faculties started functioning.

After attending the formal farewell function held on the evening of January 12, in the Sanskrit Mahavidyalaya Hall, Radhakrishnan left Banaras for England to resume his duties as the Spalding Professor.

Demands Freedom for India After War

During his term as vice-chancellor of Banaras Hindu University he had been invited to deliver the convocation address of the University of

Patna in 1940, Agra University in 1941, and Gurukul Kangri Vishwavid-
yalaya in 1942. In these addresses he, in unequivocal terms, criticized
British rule in India. At Patna he spoke on "Education, Politics and War."
At Agra, while speaking on "Purpose of Education," he said, "Are we to
stand up for Britain simply because we must avoid the worse alternative
of Nazi despotism? Before it is too late, I hope Britain will establish her
good faith at the bar of history, by implementing her many pledges and
declaring that India, not at some undated future but immediately after
the war, be a free and equal country in the Commonwealth of nations."[29]
In Gurukul Kangri he warned the British of the dangerous implications of
Cripp's proposals thus:

> The weakest part of Cripp's proposals, which were very satisfactory in
> other directions, was in the encouragement which they implicitly gave to
> the dismemberment of India. It will be the practical undoing of the greatest
> trust imposed on Britain, namely to develop an independent, strong and
> united India. The work of good British statesmen and administrators for
> over 150 years will be destroyed, if any such disintegration is encouraged.[30]

Visit to China

In 1944, he visited China from May 6 to 21 to deliver a series of
lectures on Indian and Chinese philosophies and religions in Chungking.
His lectures were translated from English into Chinese. In China he was
always surrounded by Chinese intellectuals and scholars. He was, as K.P.S.
Menon (at that time India's representative in China) reminisced, "at his
best in the congenial company of the intellectuals and scholars. Among
the mandarins he was himself a mandarin, among the students a student.
Here I thought, was no intellectual recluse living in the ivory tower, but a
man of the world, as at home in the company of—men and women—as in
the company of books."[31] The lectures were later published in the same
year under the title *India and China*. Besides this, during the period of his
vice-chancellorship, his following works were published: In 1945 *Is This
Peace?*, in 1947 *Religion and Society*, based on the lectures that he delivered at Calcutta and Banaras under the auspices of the Kamala Lectures
Endowment of the University of Calcutta, and in 1948 *The Bhagvadgītā*.
In addition to these, he published articles in various journals, wrote prefaces to about half a dozen books of others, and delivered lectures in
various national and international academic forums including the general
conferences of UNESCO.

Gandhi Requests Advice

This may be the right place to give an account of Radhakrishnan's meeting with Mahatma Gandhi in December 1947 at Birla House, Delhi, a few weeks before the latter's assassination. On that occasion when Radhakrishnan sought Gandhi's permission to dedicate his *Bhagavadgītā* to him, Gandhi replied: "I know you will not write anything unworthy, but before that I want to ask you something. I am your Arjuna, you are my Krishna. I am like Arjuna—*dharmasammūḍhacetah*—confused."[32] With these words Gandhi placed before Radhakrishnan his doubts regarding his theory and experiment relating to *brahmacarya* (physical and spiritual celibacy).

Gandhi held that if one achieved complete chastity in thought, speech and action and perfect control of one's libido, one would remain entirely passionless, calm and still even while sharing the same bed with a person of the opposite sex, though both might lie naked side by side. To test how far he progressed on the road to *brahmacarya* and grasp its full meaning, Gandhi who had completed seventy-three years of his life by then carried on an experiment by sharing his bed with a nineteen-year-old girl, his virtual grand-daughter. This raised a controversy and some of his followers had left him in protest. Undeterred by such protests Gandhi continued his experiment.[33]

It was about this Gandhi asked for Radhakrishnan's advice. In his reply Radhakrishnan stated that some social customs and conventions were essential for the community, and that Gandhi, as the greatest leader of the Indian people should not discard them.[34] Gandhi, of course, agreed to have Radhakrishnan's work dedicated to him.

Gandhi's saying "You are my Krishna" to Radhakrishnan, as the latter himself explained, was "a casual remark, not at all premeditated or deliberate. I mentioned the *Gītā*, and it was a spontaneous reaction on his part to use the language of the *Gītā* in order to express something that was on his mind."[35]

XI.

Participation in Public Life and Making Higher Education Relevant

Preparation for Public Life

Radhakrishnan had studied in Christian missionary institutions for twelve years (1896-1908), and "at an impressionable period" of his life (as he wrote) he became familiar with Christian teaching as well as Christian missionary criticisms of Hindu beliefs and practices. Consequently, his "pride as a Hindu roused by the enterprise and eloquence of Swami Vivekananda was deeply hurt by the treatment accorded to Hinduism in missionary institutions."[1] His M.A. thesis (1908) "was intended to be a reply to the charge that the Vedanta system had no room for ethics."[2] "That little essay," he wrote years later, "indicates the general trend of my thought."[3] Having grown up in India's long philosophical and religious tradition, he "started with a prejudice in its favor," but the criticism of Indian thought by his Christian missionary teachers, made him confess: "[it] disturbed my faith and shook the traditional props on which I leaned."[4] This led to his critical study of Indian philosophy and religion. By the time he came to write the second volume of *Indian Philosophy* (1927) he concluded that both conservatism and radicalism were "defective," and perceived "the faint promise of a great future" in the writings of Gandhi and Tagore, Aurobindo Ghosh and Bhagavan Das. About them he said, "While drawing upon the fountains of humanist idealism in India's past, they show a keen appreciation of Western thought."[5] From this it is clear that beginning with his early exposition to the influence of Vivekananda ending with his later absorption of the ideas of Gandhi, Tagore and Aurobindo, Radhakrishnan had become an ardent nationalist.

By 1927, as his Andhra University convocation address shows, he came to reject both "protection of privilege" and "universal conformity," as well as the reactionary and the radical extremes.[6] He attended the 1928 session of the Congress party at Calcutta, when he met Jawaharlal Nehru for the first time and continued to correspond with him. After he won recognition and honors in Britain and was knighted and, even more so after he became a professor at Oxford, he began to express his nationalistic ideas freely and boldly and develop contacts with nationalist leaders. For instance, in his Agra University convocation address of 1941, he declared that "Britain has not been able to mobilize—the moral forces— because she is unwilling, even in this critical hour, to apply the principles of democracy to India." In the same address he went on to condemn those who felt "no sort of longing for Indian freedom and unity," and exhorted that "we must strive for the great ideals of economic justice, social equality and political freedom."[7] Such pronouncements, his general attitude, his inviting Rajendra Prasad to Andhra University, his bringing out in 1939 a volume of essays in honor of Gandhi, open expressions of sympathy for the Indian freedom struggle, tributes to Gandhi in his convocation address, inviting him, Nehru and Rajendra Prasad to Banaras, his panegyric of the former whom he had made the chief guest in the Silver Jubilee Convocation, his conferring of honorary doctoral degrees on the latter two, and his article on Nehru "A Clean Advocate of Great Ideals" in 1949,[8] indicated to close observers that he was planning to enter active public life. His frequent visits to Europe in connection with his university work at Oxford and the League of Nations work at Geneva, meetings and interaction with some of the best minds of the West, as well as his own understanding of and reflection on the world situation, must have led him to foresee the inevitability of India becoming independent after the end of the Second World War. It is, therefore, not surprising that he prepared himself to have a significant role in free India. Persons like Khasa Subba Rau could discern this in 1946.

Subba Rau (1896-1961) was a perceptive, fearless and well-known journalist of his time. He had been Radhakrishnan's student at Presidency College, Madras, and had graduated in philosophy. He was a very active participant in the struggle for Indian independence. He was editor at different times of "Indian Express," "Swatantra," "Swarājya," etc. In July 1946 in a brief essay on Radhakrishnan, he assessed the man and his prospects thus:

Of late Sir S. Radhakrishnan has been dallying a little with politics and public life, and he would undoubtedly make an excellent politician. . . . He has all the attributes needed for a resplendent political career: economic independence, alertness of mind, an eye for the main chance, capacity for intrigue, intellectual brilliance, masterful powers of exposition, and, more than all else, the glamour of a vast international reputation."

Subba Rau thought that "the setting is ready for his assuming a place of prestige in the top ranks of political leadership," and commented: "A career—beginning with the teaching of philosophy and now involving a leap into the rough and tumble of politics, is an interesting phenomenon to watch."[9] Subba Rau's prognosis was proved correct by Radhakrishnan's subsequent career.

Entry into Public Life, Sapru Committee

In 1943 a Nonparty Conference was held in Poona. The object of the conference was to persuade the British government to relax its rigorous regime and to restore constitutional government in the provinces. It was attended by the Indian leaders who were affiliated neither with the Muslim League nor with the Congress. Radhakrishnan also participated in the conference. In the deliberations of the conference he reportedly "appeared uninvolved."[10] On November 19, 1944 the Standing Committee of the Nonparty Conference appointed a committee to examine the whole communal and minorities question from a constitutional and political point of view and suggest a constitutional method to solve the communal problem. Sir Tej Bahadur Sapru who had been a member of the Governor General's Executive Council, the Round Table Conferences, and the Joint Parliamentary Commission, was appointed its chairman. Sapru selected twenty-nine members who had never identified themselves with any political party or organization. Radhakrishnan was one of them. The committee came to be known as the Sapru Committee.

The Sapru Committee appointed a subcommittee under the chairmanship of Radhakrishnan to prepare a report on the problems of scheduled castes and aboriginal tribes. The subcommittee noted "that the religious and social disabilities to which they have been subjected have been innumerable and that the treatment these castes have received in the past cannot be defended according to modern social ideals."[11] It recommended that the members belonging to these castes be treated as equal to all before the law, be given right to education and public employment, and access to public wells, reservoirs, tanks, hostels, restaurants and parks. It also proposed that special concessions be made in the matters relating to representation in the central and provincial executive bodies, and the recruitment in all branches of service for these communities "till their economic and educational level reaches the average standard of the whole of India."[12]

The membership of the Sapru Committee was probably Radha-krishnan's first entry into politics. Eleven of the Sapru Committee members served in the Constituent Assembly. Sapru himself acted as a chief adviser to the assembly leaders from his sickbed.

Membership of the Constituent Assembly

In July 1946, when the British, due to the international situation, their own military and economic condition, and the mounting Indian freedom struggle, finally decided to leave India, a Constituent Assembly was set up to decide the constitution of independent India. It was to have as its members representatives of various Indian political parties, rulers of native states, intellectuals, experts in constitutional law and others. Radhakrishnan was one of the representatives from Uttar Pradesh. One of the other forty-two representatives from Uttar Pradesh was Nehru. The Constituent Assembly functioned as an assembly framing the constitution, and also as a legislature until the constitution was promulgated.[13] Though Radhakrishnan could not attend regularly the meetings of the Constituent Assembly, due to his participation in the UNESCO conferences, his assignment at the Oxford University, and later his preoccupation with the Education Commission, he very soon through his eloquent and provocative speeches, reflecting a thorough grasp of the problems and issues at hand, made his presence felt in it. According to Rajendra Prasad, who was its president, Radhakrishnan's "contribution to debates in the Constituent Assembly were not frequent, but whenever he did speak, his speeches were listened to with rapt attention not only for the very high level of their content, but also for their felicity of expression of which he is a master."[14]

In addition to giving him access to active politics, Radhakrishnan's membership of the Constituent Assembly gave him an opportunity to come into closer and almost daily contact with the leading political personalities of India, and to involve himself not only in the task of framing the constitution but also in the legislative processes and debates. Speaking in the meeting of the assembly on July 1, 1947, he commented on the British decision to divide India, thus: "The scheme for the division of the country is a great triumph of British political acumen. . . . Mr. Churchill who is supporting the Marshall Plan for a joint economic scheme of re-covery of Europe and who wants unification in Europe, wants disruption in India. Separation by religion is separation by history."[15]

The respect and attention that Radhakrishnan received from the members of the Constituent Assembly is indicated by the following epi-sode narrated by M.S. Aney, who represented the ruling chiefs of Deccan and South India in the assembly:

> It was on the memorable night of the 15th August, 1947. A resolution was moved by Pandit Jawaharlal Nehru to express our thanks to the British Government for the transfer of authority and also proclaiming our sense of joy at the success achieved at the end of a prolonged struggle, etc. The trend of the language used in the resolution was to assert that the achieve-ment of independence was mainly, if not exclusively, due to the patriotic efforts made by the people of India. Mr. Kamath who was then a member of the Constituent Assembly, moved some amendment to the effect that it was also due to the favour of Almighty God or something of that kind. I supported the idea underlying the amendment though not the exact wor-ding of it. After one or two speeches, Dr. Radhakrishnan made a remarka-ble speech showing how the divine hand invisibly shapes the destiny not only of individuals but also of nations. He urged that some reference to this Divine favour should be made in the resolution. After this speech, the whole house felt that some amendment was necessary. I am not quite sure whether it was at the instance of Jawaharlal Nehru or some other prominent Con-gressman, Dr. Radhakrishnan was asked to suggest a suitable amendment. He did it, and the resolution as altered by the amendment of Dr. Radha-krishnan was passed unanimously.[16]

On the historic night of August 14-15, 1947, when the whole nation was celebrating the advent of independence, hailing that momentous event, Radhakrishnan in the course of his speech in the assembly reminded free India's citizens of:

> our national faults of character, our domestic despotism, our intolerance, which have assumed the different forms of obscurantism, of narrow min-dedness, of superstitious bigotry. Our opportunities are great but let me warn you that when power outstrips ability, we will fall on evil days. We should develop competence and ability which would help us to utilise the opportunities which are now open to us. From tomorrow morning—from midnight today—we can no longer throw the blame on the British. We have to assume the responsibility ourselves for what we do. A free India will be judged by the way in which it will serve the interests of the common man in the matter of food, clothing, shelter and the social services. Unless

we destroy corruption in high places, root out every trace of nepotism, love of power, profiteering and black marketing which have spoiled the good name of this great country in recent times, we will not be able to raise the standards of efficiency in administration as well as in the production and distribution of the goods of life.[17]

Chairmanship of the University Education Commission

Soon after the newly formed government of independent India had recovered from the immediate effects of partition, and had consolidated its authority and framed a constitution, it turned its attention, among other things, to the education system in India, which was rightly perceived to be important for the economic development in particular, and crucial for the progress and upliftment of the masses in general. It appointed a University Education Commission in December 1948 consisting of some leading educators under the chairmanship of Radhakrishnan, to suggest and devise ways of making higher education in India relevant to its changing needs. Under Radhakrishnan's chairmanship the commission worked with such efficiency and speed that it was able to submit its report in August 1949. The report bore the imprint of the chairman's style of thinking, for it contained not merely suggestions and concrete proposals to give higher education a new orientation, but also outlined the principles relevant to higher education policy anywhere.

The purpose of education, the commission's report said, is "to lead us from darkness to light, to free us from every kind of domination except that of reason . . . to free us from the shackles of ignorance, prejudice and unfounded belief."[18] Laying emphasis on spiritual education, it said, "there are three types of existence, which are inter-related—the national, the social and the spiritual. (Accordingly), the content of teaching may be classified under three heads—our relation to things or nature; our relation to men or society; our relation to values or the world of spirit."[19] It emphasized the importance of interdisciplinary studies and upheld the view that "the divisions of subjects into sciences, social studies, and humanities are not exclusive. It will be wrong to assume that science is amoral or indifferent to values. Science is not to be taught as something external to man. It is one of the greatest of the creations of the human spirit. . . . Its aim is not only utility or success but the pursuit of truth."[20] The report tried to explain the terms contained in the preamble to the constitution of India, in the context of university education. According to the report, democracy is based on a belief in the inherent worth of the individual, and the dignity and value of human life, "as the development of body, mind and spirit of each individual with his specific nature," and it pleaded for "the relation of the different studies to the growth of the individual, the nature of human freedom and the need for social changes."[21] Justice was defined "as the foundation of states, which demands that we create a society which is free from the evils which it is within human power to banish."[22] It used the concept of liberty "to refer to the liberating character of all education, the need for the autonomy of the universities and for freedom of thought and expression for teachers."[23] Stating that equality should be the basis of any democratic society, it upheld the view that education should be provided to all members of the society "irrespective of race, religion, sex, occupation or economic status."[24] It urged that the idea of fraternity be treated at two levels—the national and the international. It advocated closer cooperation among colleges and universities and within universities between the teachers and the pupils, development of a residential system promoting corporate life, and a knowledge of India's culture and history for promoting fraternity at the national level. Fraternity at the international level, the report said, could be promoted through fostering among the members of the university the spirit of "one world" and acquainting them with the culture and achievements of other peoples.[25] The report recommended that though universities received grants from the government, they should be autonomous, because "State aid is not to be confused with state control over academic policies and practices." It felt that state control would certainly hamper "the pursuit and practice of truth regardless of consequences,"[26] which should be the goal of universities. It opposed the policy of reservation of quotas for admissions to different courses for various communities in the educational institutions "as that would lead to tension and spiritual damage" though it recommended "assistance to backward communities."[27]

The report of the commission was submitted to the Government of India on August 25, 1949.

XII.

Ambassador at Moscow
and Professor at Oxford

Moscow

Jawaharlal Nehru, as his works show, was deeply influenced by Marxism and the achievements of the Russian revolution. As early as 1927 he wrote "India and Russia are neighbors. India is an Asian state and the USSR is a state sprawling all over Asia and Europe. Between two such neighbors there can be amity or enmity; indifference is out of the question."[1] So, he sent his own sister Mrs. Vijayalakshmi Pandit (b. 1900) as India's first ambassador to the USSR. Despite being the Prime Minister's sister, her participation in the Indian freedom movement, her political experience (she had been a minister in the government of Uttar Pradesh) and her impressive and charming personality, she did not succeed in making the Indo-Soviet relationship more than just correct and lukewarm. The relations remained friendly, but formal, passive rather than active. Like most other ambassadors in Moscow, Mrs. Pandit was not even received by Stalin. So, she was shifted to Washington, where she proved to be a successful diplomat. Nehru spent a great deal of time and thought in selecting the successor to Mrs. Pandit. Among the names suggested to him were those of Devadas Gandhi and K.M. Panikkar.[2] Nehru had read some of the works of Radhakrishnan, had quoted them in his own, had met and heard him on several occasions and had been honored by him in Banaras Hindu University. Nehru liked and admired his brilliant interpretations of Indian thought and culture, his up-to-date knowledge of the world of ideas and of events, and his progressive views. Above all, there was no other Indian with a greater international reputation and wider contacts with intellectuals everywhere. Besides, in the League of Nations Committee and in UNESCO, his presence and speeches had made a significant impact. Hence, Nehru felt that Radhakrishnan would be the best choice as India's ambassador to the Soviet Union, and, accordingly, he was appointed on July 12, 1949.

Many eyebrows were raised at Nehru's selection, for many felt that there was no place for an idealist thinker, and a professor of comparative religion in the land of dialectical materialism. They also felt that a professional diplomat rather than a novice in diplomacy should have been appointed to this position, as only a professional could bring about the desired results. Justifying his selection, Nehru said: "This sending of Radhakrishnan to Moscow is rather an interesting experiment. I am more and more coming to the opinion that we should speak a little more the language of India in foreign countries, that is to say the language of the Indian mind. It may sound odd to others but it should make them think a little and realize that India is not just a copy of the West."[3] The Soviet Union welcomed the proposed appointment of Radhakrishnan. This was evident from the fact that the proposal's approval came within a couple of weeks after it had been communicated to Moscow. The time taken by a government to convey its readiness to have the person proposed as ambassador in its country is taken as an index of its satisfaction or dissatisfaction at the proposed appointment.

Radhakrishnan had accepted the ambassadorship on the condition that he would be allowed to retain his professorship at Oxford, which was agreed to by the government of India. In fact, work in the Indian embassy in Moscow in those days was negligible. The cold war between the super-powers, each followed by its own allies, was at its peak. In the USSR Stalin's power was supreme, and neither of the super-powers took an effective step towards detente. International relations seemed frozen. Under these circumstances the diplomats in the USSR had practically no work to do, but to wait and cool their heels in the hope that things may change. Consequently, Radhakrishnan was allowed to spend eight weeks in a year at Oxford. Soon after his selection as ambassador, after submitting the Education Commission's report Radhakrishnan resigned from the Constituent Assembly and left for Moscow.

A few weeks after his arrival in Moscow, on January 14, 1950, Radhakrishnan received a message from Kremlin that Stalin wanted to meet him the same day. He was told that Stalin could not see him earlier as Radhakrishnan had left soon after taking over as ambassador in October-November, 1949, for attending the UNESCO meetings, and in December Stalin was busy with the visit of Mao Tse-tung. This was rather unusual as Stalin met very few diplomats. As already mentioned, he never met the first Indian ambassador, and many other diplomats waited for months to have an audience with Stalin. Keeping in view Radhakrishnan's habit of going to bed early, his meeting with Stalin was fixed at 9:00 p.m. instead of at midnight, the usual time Stalin gave to diplomats and others for an audience with him. Radhakrishnan went to the Kremlin to meet Stalin along with his Minister Rajeshwar Dayal. They were received in Kremlin by the chief of protocol of the Soviet Ministry of Foreign Affairs and conducted through a maze of corridors to Stalin's office. Mr. Vyshinsky (1883-1954), the then foreign minister of the USSR, was with Stalin. Pavlov was the interpreter. The meeting lasted three hours. Throughout the meeting Radhakrishnan addressed Stalin as "Marshal," while Stalin called him "Professor," not contemptuously but with due deference to his learning and wisdom. Because of his openness, friendliness and boldness Radhakrishnan soon found himself at home with Stalin.

The first question Radhakrishnan asked Stalin was, "Mr. Chairman, Sir, why is it so difficult to meet you?" When this was translated into Russian Stalin smiled and replied, "Is it difficult to meet me? You are meeting me now." This relaxed the atmosphere in the room and they settled down for a talk about political affairs. Radhakrishnan is reported to have told Stalin that in his view Soviet Russia was two states—a police state and a welfare state, and that India would not like to have anything of the former but everything of the latter; that while the Russians were what they were because of what they had to go through, India was under no obligation to copy from Russia anything that did not suit her. Radhakrishnan later told others that at one point during their conversation he "found an excuse to put my fingers in Stalin's hair and ruffle it." However, no account of that "excuse" is available. It is said he narrated to Stalin the story of King Ashoka who after his victory in the devastating Kalinga war, renounced war and became a monk, and commented, "You have waded your way to power through force. Who knows that might happen to you also?" In response to this, Stalin smiled and said, "Yes, miracles do happen sometimes. I was in a theological seminary for five years."[4] After the meeting was over, Stalin remarked to Pavlov that Radhakrishnan "is not a narrow patriot. His heart bleeds for the suffering humanity."[5] From all accounts there is no doubt that Radhakrishnan made a favorable impression on Stalin. That Stalin took seriously whatever Radhakrishnan said about improving Indo-Soviet relations was demonstrated when the *Tass* correspondent in New Delhi, who, Radhakrishnan complained, was guilty of sending tendentious dispatches, was recalled within twenty-four hours of this meeting.[6] Later Stalin at the request of Radhakrishnan sent a shipload of wheat to India.

Radhakrishnan's lifestyle in Moscow was unusual for a diplomat. He was indifferent to the usual conventions. At official dinners, state banquets and other functions he did not partake of all the dishes that were served, but only those that were to his liking and at times did not eat at all. He seldom stayed at diplomatic parties till the usual midnight hours. Around 10 p.m., his time to go to bed, he began "to be fidgety, showing his impatience by gently tapping on the table. Then he would begin humming a śloka from the *Bhagvad Gītā*."[7] He left diplomatic parties by 10 p.m., after taking leave from the host and the hostess. In the beginning, many professional diplomats frowned at him but soon they got used to this unusual diplomat and were often heard saying, "There goes the philosopher." He, unlike most diplomats, did not make the rounds of other embassies comparing his notes with those of others on the situation in the Soviet Union. He refused to cultivate the airs, graces and poses of a professional diplomat and remained as he was before. He treated all alike: everyone, whether the highest or the lowest Soviet citizen, was just a human being with his own feelings, problems and failings and good points.[8] He continued to wear Indian dress, the only concession that he made to the climate of Moscow was the addition to it of a fur coat, a fur cap and fur boots. He seldom came to the office in the embassy and usually worked and met the embassy officials, and fellow ambassadors reclining in the bed in his bedroom surrounded by books on all sides. He hardly interfered in the day-to-day functioning of the embassy and left it totally to his Minister Gundevia, while Mrs. Gundevia played hostess at the official lunches and dinners.[9] Most of his time was spent in translating and writing commentaries on the *Upaniṣads*.

Radhakrishnan's presence in Moscow, his lifestyle there and his meeting with Stalin in which he narrated Ashoka's story, did not immediately and drastically alter the USSR's view of India. This was because Stalin, seeing the world in terms of black and white had already relegated India to the blacker half, and had allowed a number of articles to be published in the press condemning India's foreign policy and criticizing Mahatma Gandhi. For Stalin Gandhi was a traitor to the Indian people, as he helped colonialism. Leading Soviet indologists (e.g. Dyakov and Reisner) of his time pronounced that Gandhi was not a progressive leader of the national liberation movement. An article, grossly maligning Gandhi, appeared in the *Great Soviet Encyclopaedia*. Radhakrishnan remained unruffled by this misunderstanding of the history of the Indian freedom struggle, Gandhi's role in it and of free India's policies, but slowly and patiently worked towards changing the Soviet perception of India. So, though he modestly claimed that his only achievement while in Moscow was to translate the *Upaniṣads*, the seed of Indo-Soviet friendship, which later grew into a mighty tree, was sown by him. He was the first to suggest to Nehru that India should enter into a friendship treaty with the USSR. On this issue, for once, even Bajpai the then secretary general, External Affairs, who rarely approved of Radhakrishnan's ideas or his style of functioning, agreed. But the treaty could not be immediately formulated and signed, as Nehru wanted India to move cautiously without annoying the UK and the USA and watching their reactions at every step. With his elegant manners, sublime thinking, scholarly approach and sincerity of purpose, Radhakrishnan was able to contribute to some extent to a better Soviet understanding of India's domestic and foreign policies. This along with many other factors ultimately resulted in the establishment of abiding friendship and cooperation between the two countries.

It may not be out of place to recount the following incident at Radhakrishnan's farewell meeting with the foreign minister of the USSR in 1951 to give an instance of the way he functioned as a diplomat. After preliminary talk, Vyshinsky commented that he was "sure that the Ambassador was glad to escape the severe Russian winter." Radhakrishnan reported in a light vein that the Russian winter would begin when he departed and summer would return when he came back to Moscow. After this banter Radhakrishnan with a slight chuckle suddenly asked Vyshinsky, "But tell me, what is your representative doing in the Security Council? Why does he not support us on the Kashmir issue against Pakistan?" Vyshinsky was taken aback because this was supposed to be just a courtesy call without any official agenda. After he regained some composure, he "said something about India never having asked for Soviet help in the Kashmir debates in the Security Council." Radhakrishnan shot back "But that's what I am doing now, am I not?" Without stopping at that he continued "Why don't you one day fly one, two or three of your aeroplanes somewhere near Kashmir's northern borders, which touch the Soviet Union?" This remark restored Vyshinsky's good humor and he could even laugh. Four months later in the next debate in the Security Council in Paris on January 17, 1952, the permanent representative of the USSR at the United Nations strongly supported the Indian stand on Kashmir and scathingly attacked the position of the UK and USA.[10]

Moreover, Radhakrishnan on his own initiated and carried on talks with the Soviet foreign office and the US ambassador in Moscow, for finding ways to solve some world problems like the one faced in Korea. During the Korean war his advice to the USSR was not to send their forces to the battle-front lest it cause a world conflagration, and his advice was well taken, as the Soviets believed that it was disinterested.[11] So, the Indian philosopher-diplomat did contribute, in howsoever small a way, in localizing the Korean war. He is also said to have expressed his displeasure to Nehru on the Indian government's Korean policy.[12] Narrating the secret of his success and his experiences in Moscow as a diplomat, years later on June 15, 1956 at a Kremlin reception he said, "As I was not a professional diplomat, I approached my duties here in a friendly and human way and I did not find any great difficulties. I was able to explain to your leaders the fears and apprehensions of the outside world about your policies and I did not find any iron curtain of incommunicability."[13]

In 1950 India adopted the Constitution, and had its first elections based on universal adult franchise in 1951-1952. In the elections, the Congress party received a massive mandate from the people, and Nehru, its leader, became the political head of the government of India for five years.

In his writings Nehru had acknowledged the Marxist influence on his thinking. He claimed to be a socialist and assessed the establishment of socialism in the USSR in an extremely positive way after his visit to that country. So, he was baffled by the Soviet Union virtually ignoring the first Indian ambassador to Moscow and its indifference to India. Noting the Soviet reaction to Radhakrishnan's appointment as ambassador, Stalin's reception of him and his work there, Nehru was deeply impressed, and his esteem for Radhakrishnan increased. Consequently, Nehru requested him to accept the nomination to the office of vice-president of India. On getting Radhakrishnan's consent, the working committee of the Congress party in its meeting held on March 24, 1952, formally nominated him as a candidate for vice-presidency. On April 25, 1952, he left Moscow for India.

On the day of his departure, Vyshinsky, foreign minister of the Soviet Union gave a lunch in honor of Radhakrishnan. It was the first lunch ever given in honor of a departing noncommunist foreign diplomat by the Soviet authorities. At lunch the minister informed Radhakrishnan that Stalin would like to meet him. As Radhakrishnan was leaving the same day, his meeting with the Soviet leader was hurriedly arranged. At this meeting, in which Vyshinsky and Gundevia were also present, after normal mutual routine courtesies were over, in the course of conversation

Radhakrishnan stated that India had peacefully resolved the problem of its princes. Querying whether India had really done so, Stalin referred to how a Russian peasant who sees a wolf deals with it. Raising his right hand and sharply bringing it down forcibly as if it was a chopper, Stalin said, "Liquidate Mr. Ambassador" and once again acting in the same way he repeated, "Kulaks! Liquidate!" After some more conversation Radhakrishnan concluded with these words: "We have our history and tradition to guide us, and we still try to continue to follow our path of peace, and if we succeed it will be a lesson for other nations." Narrating this Gundevia reports Stalin's response thus: "We know, Mr. Ambassador, that you and Prime Minister Nehru are not our enemies."[14] Radhakrishnan reminisced later: "Stalin's face looked somewhat bloated. I patted him on the cheek and on the back. I passed my hand over his head. Stalin said: 'You are the first person to treat me as a human being and not as a monster. You are leaving us and I am sad. I want you to live long; I have not long to live.' Six months afterwards he died." Radhakrishnan wished Stalin all success in his endeavor to build up a strong state in the most natural way. The latter bade him farewell with moist eyes. Such a show of emotions by Stalin was unprecedented.[15]

Throughout his stay in Moscow, Radhakrishnan regularly received requests from scholars and writers on philosophical and religious themes to write forewords for their books, or to send them his comments and suggestions for the improvement of their manuscripts. Radhakrishnan did not disappoint anyone of them. Khushwant Singh who had sent him his translation of Sikh scriptures narrates his experience as follows: "He wrote back pointing out some errors and advised me to study Vedānta in order to understand Sikhism better. He was an affectionate *guru* and took pains to instruct people he chose to guide."[16]

Oxford

All these years, even when he was ambassador, with the exception of 1949-1950, Radhakrishnan had been annually at Oxford for a period of at least eight weeks to deliver his lectures. His lectures were regularly attended only by a few who were keen to learn Indian philosophy. With this select group of students he discussed stanza by stanza the *Bhagavadgītā*, the *Upaniṣads*, the *Dhammapada* and the *Brahamsūtras*, on which he was writing at that time. He expounded the Sanskrit terms and conveyed their meanings to them "by illustration often from our own English poetry and literature of which Radhakrishnan seemed as deeply versed as his own."[17] He would sometimes punctuate his lectures with anecdotes of his meetings with Nehru or Stalin. Most of the students, as A.J. Alston[18] recalled, regarded this kind of name-dropping as a kind of "amiable weakness" that they were privileged to assist at. They also felt that "Radhakrishnan was going to be out of his depth in public life, and that it was a pity he was not going to devote his last years to further literary productions in the academic field." Many found his lectures "more interesting than those of any other Oxford lecturer,"[19] some were inspired by his love and appreciation of Indian philosophy,[20] but the less reverent among the audience also made fun of his pronunciation and vied with each other to imitate his diction 'the cosmic yugg' or 'what may be if it must be yyis' after each of his lectures.[21] What the casual onlookers found amusing and unusual was, as A.J. Alston reminisced, that "on the occasion of the last lecture he gave before leaving for Moscow at the end of any series of lectures, he would time matters so that he walked straight out of the lecture hall into a taxi waiting at the gates of All Souls to take him on the first stage of his journey to Moscow, all arrangements having been previously made."

On January 28, 1951 the Spalding Trust came into being and helped to establish the "Union for the Study of Great Religions." It also instituted a series of books on the ethics and spiritual classics of the East to be published by Allen and Unwin. Radhakrishnan was the President of the Oxford chapter of the trust which was called "Society for the Study of Great Religions." Writing about the genesis of the trust, *The Times* of London wrote that it was conceived by Radhakrishnan, H.N. Spalding, K.J. Spalding and Canon C.E. Raven who "looking round a distracted world agreed that the military, political and economic steps being taken by governments would, even if successful, still leave a spiritual vacuum, and that aggressive atheism, the skeptical philosophies, naturalistic morals, materialism and apathy prevalent everywhere *would enlarge rather then fill it*. What was needed, they thought, was to promote ethical, philosophic, devotional and mystical education and culture through the study of the great religions, Christian and non-Christian, so far as possible, throughout the world."[22]

Though Radhakrishnan was quite popular among the students in Oxford because of his unfailing kindness, courtesy, subtle humor, dispassionateness, easy accessibility, and readiness to help and encourage them, the establishment at Oxford did not fully accept him.[23] While some at

Oxford with deep prejudice for non Christians did not like Radhakrishnan simply on account of his holding a good post and not being a Christian, some others there resented him for his strict adherence to vegetarianism and teetotalism and to his refusing to socialize in general. This was regarded by conventional Oxonians as "superior" and by others as "giving himself airs."[24]

Among the dons of the university Evans-Pritchard held a grudge against Radhakrishnan. H.H. Price and Collingwood were admirers of Radhakrishnan and were on very friendly terms with him. But the "high-ups" in Oxford generally "resented" Radhakrishnan's presence and did not hide their dislike for him.[25] They made no efforts to modify or alter the curricula to make Radhakrishnan's lectures the focus of a full course, with the result that his teaching was nothing but tangential to the main courses. According to A.J. Alston, "there he was an international figure housed at Oxford, but without any real roots there, all too like the Elgin Marbles removed from their natural setting and housed in the British Museum."[26] Radhakrishnan was aware of the despising attitude of those in the administrative wing of Oxford, and, in Katz's assessment, "was always anxious, perhaps too anxious, not to offend the establishment and that gave a muted tone to his activities at Oxford. It did not make the establishment love him more."[27] The attitude of the authorities was not at all affected by the low profile that he deliberately kept at Oxford. This became clear in their selection of his successor to the Spalding Chair. Though "Radhakrishnan, as well as both H.N. Spalding and K.J. Spalding hoped that D.M. Datta would succeed Radhakrishnan in the chair,"[28] the authorities showed utter disregard to their wishes, and elected R.C. Zaehner as the Spalding Professor when Radhakrishnan finally resigned on being elected as India's vice-president. In his inaugural lecture Zaehner is stated to have made "very offensive" remarks against Radhakrishnan.[29] On the day of his departure from Oxford, after tendering his resignation, Radhakrishnan was presented by his students with a silver pencil marked S.R.[30] and soon after All Souls College elected him as its honorary fellow.

Schilpp Volume

In 1950 Paul Arthur Schilpp, editor of the series "The Library of Living Philosophers," chose to edit a volume on the *Philosophy of Sarvepalli Radhakrishnan*. His inclusion in the series indicated that he was recognized as one of the great living philosophers of his time, as the series aimed at publishing volumes "on each of the greater among the world's living philosophers."[31] It put him on the same level as John Dewey, Santayana, A.N. Whitehead, G.E. Moore, Bertrand Russell, Ernst Cassirer and Albert Einstein, on whom this project had earlier brought out volumes. Justifying his choice, Schilpp wrote in the preface:

> [H]e also is one of the foremost living absolute idealists representing the great tradition in philosophy, which thus far, has had no representation in our *Library* . . . [he is an] excellent example of a living "bridge" between East and West . . . . Beyond this: more than any living philosopher of East or West Radhakrishnan has been devoting the major portion of his academic career as well as of his voluminous writings to what has almost become the passion of his life, namely that of bringing East and West together: by interpreting the great cultural tradition and spiritual insight of the East to the West, on the one hand, and by helping the East, on the other hand, to realize that—not merely in science and technology, but also—in philosophical thought and speculation the East can still learn some important lessons from the West.[32]

Acknowledging the cooperation received from Radhakrishnan in the preparation of the volume, he wrote, "Throughout the twelve years of the existence of this library, no other philosopher has given of his time more unstintedly to this project than has Professor Radhakrishnan. His advice and helpful cooperation have been available to the editor at all times."[33] When published in 1952, the volume contained his autobiography and twenty-five descriptive and critical essays by contemporary scholars on various aspects of Radhakrishnan's philosophy, followed by his "Reply to Critics." The autobiography was completed in the Indian embassy, Moscow, and the "Reply" in All Souls College, Oxford.

XIII.

The Vice-Presidency

As vice-presidential candidate Radhakrishnan arrived in Delhi quietly. As he was not a man involved in active party politics, the crowds that usually gather to welcome politicians nominated as the candidates by the ruling party for high offices were conspicuous by their absence. K. Iswara Dutt, a journalist and a family friend, and a representative of the External Affairs Ministry were the only two persons who had come to receive him at the airport.[1] In May 1952 Radhakrishnan was elected vice-president of India for five years by both Houses of Parliament—the Lok Sabha and the Rajya Sabha, and he assumed the office in the same month.

Chairmanship of Rajya Sabha

The vice-president of India is ex-officio chairman of the Rajya Sabha, the upper house of Parliament. Conducting the business of the Rajya Sabha, as per the rules and regulations laid down in the constitution, is one of the primary duties of the vice-president. Radhakrishnan took this duty very seriously. Every morning, when Parliament was in session, he would walk up to his chair in the house at 11 a.m. and call the house to order. Members watched with admiration as Radhakrishnan conducted the proceedings without relying too much on rules of procedure and matters of technicalities, but with skill, tact and good humor. Though, at times, members in the heat of the moment pressed their points of view, the impact of his personality was such that they never pressed it to the point of challenging the authority of the chair. But in the question hour (zero hour), or during some stormy debates when tempers rose, Radhakrishnan would take liberties with the concerned member and tell him in a stern schoolmasterly tone, though smilingly, "Mr. A. you have talked enough, sit down." The member would obey him as a kindergarten child would instinctively obey a much loved teacher, and be silenced. His reprimand was accepted with surprising meekness even by the most stubborn members of the House and the debate would proceed as if nothing unu-

129

sual had happened. The respect and affection that he commanded from every member of the House did not originate from his profound knowledge of the rules and regulations of the House, but from the confidence each member had in his impartiality, sense of justice, fair play, capacity for conciliation and compromise, and everyone's implicit faith that the rights of all would be protected by him even in the face of improper interference through the official whip.

His role in the House was appreciated by all, irrespective of their party affiliations. Gobind Ballabh Pant of the Congress party, lauding his role, told him, "The Rajya Sabha is a toy in your hands."[2] Bhupesh Gupta of the Communist party quipped, "Radhakrishnan is like a helicopter soaring with sudden vehemence in his speech."[3] K. Rama Rao, a senior journalist and member of Parliament (1952-1954), reminisced: "The life and soul of the House was its chairman, Dr. S. Radhakrishnan. As one looked on him one felt one was looking on a true son of Saraswati. He was a source of inspiration to me as few in my life have been. It was said of King Bhoja that merely a look at him inspired poetry. It was an honor to sit in a House over which the great Sarvepalli presided, a man of international reputation and a speaker of rare eminence. His sense of humor is remarkable and he would keep the House rollicking with laughter during question hour. In fact we seemed to be a lot of forward children before his gracious dignity and mellow wisdom. Even the obstreperous Communists stood in awe of him and respected and obeyed his rulings, always fair and never partisan or petulant."[4] Echoing a similar sentiment Hiren Mukerjee of the Communist party wrote, "He proved himself a great success in the chair of the Rajya Sabha . . . like Athens having been the school of Hellas, Radhakrishnan, a wag once said, proved to be able school master of a not easily tamed upper house! Of him it may be said, that he set the trend which has made the Indian vice-presidentship so much more than a decorative sinecure awaiting accidental glory in the event of the president's death or dislodgment."[5] He chaired the Rajya Sabha "with unmatched grace and authority, bending a sometimes turbulent house to his will in a manner that remains unique."[6] Recalling his role in imparting importance to the Rajya Sabha, N.G. Ranga, the doyen of Indian parliamentarians, wrote Radhakrishnan "presided over the first Rajya Sabha with dignity and distinction and endowed it with a special status, which does not usually accrue to such a second chamber. . . . He respected senior parliamentarians and encouraged juniors. Radhakrishnan used his great influence with Nehru and the cabinet and ensured that debates were held in the Rajya Sabha first whenever possible."[7] Reminiscing about Radhakrishnan's skill in managing the debates in the Rajya Sabha, Rajkumari Amrit Kaur of the Congress party wrote, "I was greatly impressed by his capacity to manage the House, in particular, some of the difficult members, with amazing tact and good nature. He was generous in giving us all time to put our points of view before him and whenever any difficult situation arose he was capable of handling it without offending anybody. His unfailing good humor and understanding sympathy made it easy for all of us to give him the loyalty and good behaviour he sought from us."[8] Jawaharlal Nehru, lauding Radhakrishnan's role in shaping the activities of Rajya Sabha, said: "You have made this House, with yourself as chairman, a rather unique place and converted it into a large family under your guidance."[9]

Based on his experience, Radhakrishnan expressed the view that the members of Parliament should undergo training to improve the quality of its functioning. During this training they, he advocated, should be imparted "thorough knowledge of the constitution, especially the directive principles, which form our 'national *dharma* or righteousness.' "[10]

Expositions Abroad of Indian Thought, Policies and Achievements

With Prime Minister Nehru's encouragement and also because he himself liked to do so, Radhakrishnan as vice-president undertook a number of foreign tours, each for a considerable duration of time. The purpose of these tours was (1) to disseminate knowledge of Indian life, culture, thought, religion, thereby increasing appreciation of them among the world's intellectuals and institutions of learning, and (2) to expound independent India's policies, especially of secularism and nonalignment and (3) to promote a sympathetic understanding of them among politicians in power abroad. In September 1952, he undertook a four-month tour of Europe and the Middle East. During his visit to the U.K. he was awarded the honorary degree of the doctor of civil laws by Oxford University. While in Egypt, he is said to have indicated clearly and unequivocally to General Neguib, the then president of the Revolutionary Council and head of the state, the dangers of military dictatorship and told him that power, if it was to endure, had to have a moral basis.[11]

In France, Radhakrishnan was unanimously elected president of the Seventh Session of UNESCO General Conference held in Paris in October, 1952. Thanking the delegates for electing for the first time a president from Asia, he said:

> It is essential . . . that we should will not merely peace, but the conditions that are essential for securing peace. . . . No man can attain happiness in this world if he feels hungry or cold, if he is slave to other men, if he is surrounded by filth and disease, and if he does not have some leisure for recreation, for reflection.[12]

Blaming human stupidity and "human cussedness" to be the chief obstacles to human happiness and well-being, and for making the world a better and happier place, he advised:

> If we wish to cure this element of vileness, wildness, cussedness, in the nature of man, it is essential for us to mobilise the great spiritual resources of mankind. The cure for that is to restore the truths of the spirit to the central place in the minds of men. Let those truths of the spirit sway the minds of men, transform the lives of men. The truths of the spirit are liberality, understanding, freedom. Those who deny freedom in the name of freedom are no less dangerous than those who deny freedom in the name of discipline and authority.[13]

A Secret Trip

There is a story that after his official visit to Bonn Radhakrishnan made a secret trip to East Berlin.[14] In the autumn of 1952 when the preparations for his visit to Brussels and Bonn were afoot, two emissaries of President Pieck of the German Democratic Republic secretly contacted N.B. Menon who was at that time looking after the Indian Military Mission in West Berlin. They conveyed to him their president's request to arrange for an unofficial visit by Radhakrishnan to GDR. They said, "President Pieck is interested in meeting Dr. Radhakrishnan for whom he has the highest esteem. Please convey this message to the vice-president and accept our assurances that the secrecy of the visit will be fully respected."[15] Menon sent a telegram to the vice-president conveying the invitation; and warning about the multifarious problems that, in his opinion, such a visit could create. Within two days he received instructions to go ahead with the arrangements for the visit. But he was asked to be doubly sure of the security of the vice-president and the secrecy of the visit.

On the appointed day Radhakrishnan arrived from Bonn. At the Berlin airport he brushed aside the inquisitive reporters by telling them that he had not come for sightseeing, but for spending a quiet day with a friend and his wife. He did not forget to send his greetings to the *Burgomeister* and requested his forgiveness for not being able to call on him since he had come just for one day on a private visit. In the privacy of Menon's residence he requested him (Menon) for briefing on the origin of the request and the arrangements for the evening. He told Menon that he had for a long time wanted to meet the leading personalities of East Germany, and was not unduly perturbed about the secrecy of the visit. He had already planned how he would react in the event of the visit becoming public. He firmly turned down Menon's suggestion that he substitute his prominent turban with a commonplace hat.

In the evening, Menon drove him through the Berlin Gate. They were escorted by the members of the Office of Protocol of GDR, whose car while in West Germany followed the car driven by Menon, and when in East Germany guided them to a big mansion. They were taken to a well-furnished room, where President Pieck, the GDR foreign minister and an interpreter were waiting for them. Noticing Radhakrishnan's admiring looks at the room and its furnishings, he informed them that the palace once housed one of the mistresses of Friedrich the Great. Radhakrishnan on hearing this quipped that "what was created for the pleasures of princes was now being used for the purposes of the people."

During the meeting President Pieck apprised Radhakrishnan of the origins of the GDR Government, its policies, ideology and the dangers to which it was exposed from the regime in West Germany; and in the end requested him to persuade the Government of India to recognize GDR. Throughout the meeting Radhakrishnan spoke very little. But to President Pieck's request for recognition, he replied:

> India itself was a victim of a surgical operation dividing it in two parts. The operation had brought nothing but death and destruction to both India and Pakistan. Reunification was not a realisable dream; the division appeared to be permanent. India was, therefore, firmly opposed to the division of a country as a solution to its political problems, whether it be in Korea, Vietnam or Germany. The division carried within it the seeds of future conflict in Europe. India, therefore, decided not to recognise both parts of a divided country unless, in its assessment, all hopes of reunification were irretrievably gone.[16]

After returning to Menon's house Radhakrishnan jokingly asked him, "Why on earth did you lure me here to play a role in a spy story?"[17]

Foreign Tours

In 1954 he undertook a six-week tour of Europe, USA, Canada, and Latin America. During this visit he was given the German Order Pour Le Merite and elected an honorary member of the Rumanian Academy of Sciences. In Montevideo, Uruguay, in his presidential address to the Eighth Session of UNESCO General Conference in October 1954, he said:

> Political freedom and economic justice are two sides of democracy, both are essential. We should lay stress on the improvements of the economic conditions of the people, as well as on liberty and freedom. No society can claim to be democratic if it does not permit political liberty, freedom of conscience, freedom of choice between parties, and opportunities of peaceful and orderly changes of government. No true democracy can remain satisfied merely with conditions which safeguard political liberty and freedom of the individual.[18]

Referring to the international situation he said, "There are many misunderstandings. We can build peace even on the basis of misunderstandings. When once peace is built, misunderstandings will diminish."[19]

Addressing the US Senate on November 17, 1954 he outlined India's policy thus:

> We, in our country, are now engaged in the enterprise of effecting a social and economic revolution. The word "revolution" need not scare us. It does not mean barricades and bloodshed. It means only speedy and drastic changes. We are interested not only in our objectives, but in our methods; not only in what we achieve, but in how we achieve. Through peaceful, constitutional processes we won our independence and integrated our country; and now we are striving to raise the material standards of our people. Even if we meet defeat in our attempt to replace force by persuasion, the politics of power by the politics of brotherhood, we are convinced that the defeat will be only temporary, for goodness is rooted in the nature of things; kindness and love are as contagious as unkindness and hate.[20]

He also lectured in many American universities and other institutions of higher learning, from the east coast to the west coast, on varied subjects ranging from global democracy to the future of modern civilization. Defining democracy as "the spiritual good manners," he said, "Democracy means the reconciliation of differences not the obliteration of differences."[21] He exhorted American youth to "produce the creative minority which will reveal to the American conscience the ideals which have animated this great people from the time they asserted their independence down to today."[22] He regretted that "there are times when America's voice is not heard in clear tones,"[23] and urged the universities to do their duty by standing as sentinels of democracy. In all his speeches he drew attention to the challenges posed by stark and ugly realities, such as hunger, poverty, and racial discrimination.

American intellectuals, like the president of Oberlin College, hailed him as a "renowned philosopher, educator, statesman, distinguished citizen of a great sister republic, champion of cultural interchange as the key to peace among nations . . . such a man as Plato dreamed of. A man who pre-eminently exemplified the Platonic ideal of a leader of men, one in whom genuine wisdom and political leadership have met."[24] The tremendous impression that he made on some Americans can be gauged by the inscription an American author made on his book which he presented to Radhakrishnan. The inscription read "To Sarvepalli Radhakrishnan, minister to and for humanity."[25]

He visited Canada next. There in a broadcast from Toronto, speaking on behalf of the Asian and African nations struggling to emancipate themselves from political, social, economic and racial bondage, he declared: "There is a world revolution in progress, and it is utterly independent of communism. The hungry, diseased, despised inhabitants who form the bulk of the non-communist world demand economic progress and development. If we hesitate to attack and answer these problems, others will exploit our inertia and inefficiency. What we want today is not the American way or the Russian way but the human way."[26]

Recognizing the services rendered by Radhakrishnan, specially as a roving cultural ambassador of India, in 1954 the president of India conferred its highest award *Bharat Ratna* on him.

In June 1956 he again undertook a tour of Europe, and East and Central Africa. The Free University of Brussels conferred on him an honorary doctoral degree on June 4. In his address to the university, Radhakrishnan appealed for the establishment of the "brotherhood of man" and "on earth one family," as science and technology had made it possible for us to attain these ideals. But he warned the world to be cautious about the method it adopts. "The future of mankind," he said, "depends on the future of man, on his spirit, on his approach to the problems which face him. If he relies on force and adopts a military approach the future is bleak indeed; if, on the other hand, he believes in the spirit, he will prosper."[27]

The Charles University, Prague, Czechoslovakia conferred on him its honorary doctorate degree on June 7. In his address to the university, he emphasized the importance of freedom to the being of man and said:

> It is an honour to be a man. The sanctity of the human soul, the dignity of the human personality is the ethical basis of democracy. Karl Marx denounced capitalist economy on the ground that it dehumanized man. By hardening man, by softening his head, by rousing his senses, by depleting his imagination, it mechanizes the human being. By debasing men's minds, by debilitating their wills, by destroying their vision, men are reduced to puppets, things of paint and sawdust, which have no life, but are moved by strings. Man is great when he is not a cog in the social machine, not an item in the series of objective happenings, not a unit in an anonymous crowd. He is great when he is able to think for himself. Pursuit of truth is the highest austerity, jnāna-mayaṁ tapaḥ."[28]

Referring to India's policy on nonalignment in his address to the University of Cracow in Poland on June 13, he said:

> If India and some other countries hesitate to align themselves with either of the two blocs, it does not mean that they are unwilling to decide between right and wrong. We are committed to peace, democracy and the U.N. charter. It is groups which compromise with these ideals. If we are convinced that war is a total disaster, then we should redouble our efforts in the peaceful settlement of our problems. The settlement of a dispute by agreement is more advantageous to the disputants than the continuation of it. Even if there were no such powers who have not aligned themselves, they will have to be invented. We are the states who can influence both sides to look at each other with discrimination. We are not attempting the impossible, to reconcile evil with good. We are asking all those who have control over nuclear weapons to discard them. We feel that the conflict between the two groups should be resolved through peaceful means and not catastrophic war. We believe that states which adopt different political systems can exist together. We believe that peaceful coexistence will help to educate totalitarian systems to a perception of individual dignity and the importance of civil liberties, and the democratic systems to care more for social justice, racial harmony and political freedom. India's adoption of the democratic outlook is sufficient proof that we are not neutral between peace and war. We are positively on the side of democracy and of peace.[29]

The honorary professorship of Moscow University was conferred on him on June 18, when he was on a state visit in the USSR. In his acceptance address to the university, he said:

Human development . . . is the development of the spirit of men. Independent reflection is developed by the quiet study of great books. We develop our souls by the study of great classics which reveal to us great minds. Though we belong physically to our country and our age, as students of universities we belong to all countries and all ages.[30]

Referring to the responsibilities of a university he said:

My appointment as professor of this university is a symbol of the oneness of the world of learning. We in the universities have to prepare the mind of the world for the establishment of a world community with a common consciousness and a common conscience. This is possible only if the nations which have the power to annihilate each other renounce that power. This requires an act of faith.[31]

Outlining the duties of a teacher he concluded:

It is the function of a teacher not to give the pupils what they want but make them want what he gives them. I will use my privilege as a professor to rebuke you, if I find that you go wrong. I hope you do not claim infallibility.[32]

To commemorate his visit, the Russian translation of his book *Indian Philosophy, Volume I,* was published.[33] The esteem in which the Russian leadership held Radhakrishnan was evident from the rare opportunity that he was given to address the Soviet people on television; and by the fact that both Khrushchev and Bulganin attended the reception held in the Indian embassy in his honor.[34] In Moscow, talking about religion, he said that like the Soviets, he as well as the Indian tradition were opposed to aggressive religious exclusivism. He proclaimed, "If there is hostility to organized religion in the Soviet Union, it is not entirely the fault of the Union. Those who sponsor religious propaganda in their zeal for the spiritual welfare of their fellow-men indulge in a vulgar competition about the know-how of salvation. Agencies for proselytization, which scramble for souls, are not in keeping with the true spirit of religion."[35]

In his broadcast on the Kiev Radio on June 25, discussing the essence of religion he said:

If religion is treated as an inward integration which each one has the freedom to achieve for himself, without interference from others, and a call to establish an equitable social order, there is not much in such a religion for the communists to complain about. In its essence religion is integration of human personality and redemption of human society.[36]

In a speech delivered at a reception held in his honor at the Kremlin and hosted by President Voroshilov, he warned, "Any system which suppresses the individual conscience is Un-Marxist. If we give people education and economic opportunity, they will demand freedom of inquiry and criticism," and suggested, "Now that the Soviet Union has consolidated its base and secured stability, what was necessary in earlier years may not be needed now."[37]

On his return, commenting on affairs in the USSR he declared that, "The present hatred of dictatorship, the emphasis on collective leadership, and the freedom of discussions within the party may well be regarded as the first step towards the liberalization of the Soviet state."[38]

In his address at the Inter-Racial Asian reception in Duthie Hall, Salisbury, on July 4, he said, "India is not a geographical expression—it is a living spirit. It stands for certain ideals. It tells us that this world of space and time is not all; it is something which is perpetually superseding itself."[39] Continuing the same theme in his address in Limbe, Nyasaland, he reiterated, "India is . . . an attitude of mind, an orientation, a particular outlook . . . when it is said that India is a secular state, it does not mean that India worships material comforts and luxuries or does not recognise that there are higher laws of the universe than those which govern the physical world of space and time. It only means it does not stand for any particular religion but deals impartially with all religions, that it adopts the philosophy of active co-existence among the religions of the world."[40] Advising the authorities of that country to work towards racial harmony through political methods he said, "Military solutions to political methods to political problems are good for nothing. Ultimately they will leave bitterness behind."[41]

Inaugurating the Gandhi Memorial Academy, in Nairobi on July 12, he said:

> If racial tolerance is to be implemented in the public life of the country, the work of re-education has to be started in our educational institutions. By living together, by working together we get to understand one another and bridge the gulf that separates us in feeling and imagination. When we do not know other people, we become frightened, angry, hysterical. When we know them, we understand them, appreciate them, make allowances for their weaknesses and accept them.[42]

Later, in September-October in 1956 he undertook a tour of Sing-
apore, Indonesia, Japan and China. In Tokyo on October 3, he inaugurated the International Congress of the World Fellowship of Faiths. In his
inaugural address, he castigated religious exclusivism and championed
the model of tolerance and brotherhood found in Indian religions. For
survival, he said, "it is essential for all those who have faith in the wisdom and love of God, whatever may be their religious denominations, to
get together, form a sacramental brotherhood and work for fellowship in
which alone lies the redemption of man."[43] In Shanghai, in the heart of
China, the champion of collectivism, he chose to speak on the value of
individualism. In his speech he emphasized how the discoveries of science, the great creations of art, and the masterpieces of literature and
music, were the outcome of the individual functioning often in his solitude. It needed exceptional courage to articulate such an idea in China at
that time. But then Radhakrishnan was not a man afraid of expressing his
views, whenever he felt like doing so.

In India, too, he delivered a large number of speeches. Of these,
mention may be made of those he gave in the convocations of Delhi
University, of which he was ex-officio the chancellor. Every year beginning with 1953, presiding over its annual convocations, he exhorted grad-
uating students, and delivered memorable speeches while presiding over
the special convocations held by the university to confer honorary degrees on the distinguished Indians and foreigners.

A Personal Loss

In 1956 he suffered a personal loss when his wife passed away, bringing to an end fifty-three years of their married life. During that long
period she had brought up five daughters and a son, and seen them grow
and flourish. She had also witnessed the rise of Radhakrishnan from his
student days to become one of the most eminent scholars and statesmen
of the world. It might have been his own attitude and behavior to her
and her fidelity, devotion and dedication to him, which made him write
as follows:

The Hindu ideal of a wife, exalted and exacting, still has a strong hold on
unsophisticated Hindu women. "If he is faithless, I must be faithful. If he is
shaken, I must abide. If he sees another, I must await his return." If there is a
taint in this blind devotion, then there is a taint in the eternal who loves us
with the same love, awaiting us patient and unwearied, when we return,

weary with false pleasures, to him. A pure unquestioning love that triumphs over the weaknesses of the loved one is perhaps the greatest gift of heaven.[44]

It could have been his married life which made him comment that among Indians "stable marriages are more numerous," and that this was due "largely to the character of Indian women, who are miracles of dignity, graciousness and peace."[45]

Towards a Second Term as Vice-President

On the eve of the end of his five-year vice-presidency in May 1957, Radhakrishnan made it clear to Nehru that he was not interested in continuing as vice-president for a second term. Nehru, who was impressed by what Radhakrishnan had achieved in those five years, particularly by his success in expounding in an illuminating way India's policies of secularism and nonalignment, and who also had a good rapport with him, was keen to see him elevated to the office of the president. Moreover, Nehru did not feel the same intellectual or spiritual affinity with Rajendra Prasad who was completing five years of his presidency. This was because, firstly, Prasad, Nehru thought, was too orthodox and conservative to continue to be the head of a secular and progressive state. Prasad washed the feet of learned Brahmins in public, consulted astrologers in drawing up his programmes, and was opposed to several "progressive" provisions in the proposed Hindu code. Consequently, Nehru considered that Prasad did not represent the modern secular India. Secondly, but more importantly, Prasad tended towards interpreting the constitution in such a way that it gave an active role to the president in the day-to-day functioning of the government. On the other hand, Nehru thought that according to the Indian Constitution the president was only the titular head of the state, who could only reign but not rule.

Without consulting Prasad, Nehru assumed that Prasad would like to retire, having been the president of the Constituent Assembly for two years and then of the country for five years. In fact, in the middle of 1955 Prasad had sent in his resignation as he felt that the spirit of the constitution required that no one should hold the office of president for more than five years.[46] But he did not press for its acceptance, because Nehru and others whom he had consulted did not like it. In his letter of July 2, 1956 addressed to Nehru he stated that while he would not be a presidential candidate again and would not seek election, he "may find it difficult to refuse an offer."[47] Moreover, the content, the tone and the manner of his speech in Madras in reply to a civic reception on Independence Day in 1956 appeared to be an indication of his wish to retire from the presidency. In the course of his speech he said that while he had established a second residence for the president at Hyderabad, he would not exclude the possibility of a third residence being fixed further South, and added, "I would leave it to my successor to take credit for that."[48] In view of all this, Nehru promised Radhakrishnan the Congress party's nomination for the presidency.

However, when Nehru approached Rajendra Prasad with a request to retire and not to seek a second term of presidency, Prasad told him that the matter was in the hand of the Congress party and that it was for the party's Parliamentary Board to decide. Prasad asserted he would accept only the Board's decision, no matter what it was.[49] So, when Maulana Abul Kalam Azad (1888-1958) met Prasad on behalf of the high command of the Congress party, the latter expressed his willingness for a second term.[50] Nehru tried his best and did everything he could to create a situation that would favor Radhakrishnan's nomination. He wrote letters to the members of the cabinet and chief ministers, and issued public statements advocating a change of president from a North Indian to a South Indian. He discussed the matter with the four chief ministers of South Indian states in particular, and tried to impress upon them the political advantage of having a South Indian president, as a North Indian had held the post for a full term. But they did not agree, as they claimed to be not influenced by regional considerations. They made it clear that Prasad should be reelected if he was available. To these chief ministers, who were 'Pukka' politicians, not overimpressed by the intellectual achievements of anyone, the idea of someone who was not a member of the Congress party and who had never participated in the freedom struggle becoming president was intolerable, especially when an intellectual who was also a past president of the Congress party and a distinguished fighter for Indian independence was willing to be reelected. Moreover, Prasad's gentleness, integrity and national service were well-known. According to some, it was not impossible that for the Southern chief ministers, Prasad's being a Kayastha (a non-Brahmin) and Radhakrishnan's being a Brahmin might also have been a factor which influenced them in favor of the former. It must also be said that for most long standing and devoted members of the Congress party, whether they be leaders like

Patel and Azad or ordinary party workers, Prasad was a tested insider who had suffered for decades to see India win its freedom, while the other person was an intruder who had prospered even in British days.

Though Nehru's efforts brought about some consensus in the press in favor of Radhakrishnan, most of the members of the Congress Parliamentary Board echoed the views of the chief ministers of the four Southern states and were in favor of Prasad. The Congress Parliamentary Board met in March 1957, considered both the candidates, and decided to renominate Prasad for a second term of presidency. Nehru had objected to the second term for Prasad on the grounds that Radhakrishnan was more popular in the South, that Prasad was old and in bad health, and that the principle of one term to one person should be applied to the occupant of the office of the president. But the members did not accept any of these grounds and accepted Azad's plea that in view of their past services to the nation and their relative images as national leaders, Prasad was far more eligible than Radhakrishnan for the office of the president, that Prasad was equally popular in the South and that his health was not inferior to that of some cabinet ministers. They accepted the argument that since the offices of prime minister and cabinet ministers had no limitation of tenure, it was unjust to put a limit on the tenure of the presidency. They also felt that the convention of one man-one term should apply to all, or to none.[51]

Nehru accepted the decision of the Congress Parliamentary Board, and personally conveyed it to Prasad, on April 1, 1957, and also reportedly suggested to him to retire after doing half the term of five years. But Prasad informed him curtly that he would go by his health.[52] When Radhakrishnan, who was hoping to be sponsored as president, with Rajkumari Amrit Kaur as his own successor in the vice-presidency, learnt about this, he was naturally disappointed. Outwardly, he kept up a show of unperturbed equanimity and an undisturbed composure, but to his close friends he poured out his deep disappointment and frustration.[53] His friends and probably he too felt, as has been observed by some, that his image as a liberal Hindu and not a conservative Hindu stood in the way of his nomination. They felt that Prasad's image as a conservative Hindu was responsible for his renomination, as most of the members of the Congress Parliamentary party were Hindu conservatives.[54] This, of course, could not have been a fact, because Patel, Azad and the Southern chief ministers were not conservative Hindus.

Radhakrishnan expressed his unwillingness to be renominated for a second term as vice-president, when he was first approached for his consent, on the ground that no useful purpose would be served by his continuing to be vice-president, as there was nothing to do as vice-president. The prime minister, Radhakrishnan complained, seldom came to him to talk about his problems; on the contrary he had to get hold of the prime minister at public functions to discuss with him the problems he was facing. Radhakrishnan was determined to leave Delhi.[55] But Nehru was not one to let him go so easily, because Nehru had known him as a sincere counselor who gave him wise and disinterested advice; as an eloquent emissary who interpreted his domestic and foreign policies abroad; and as an eminent philosopher-orator who expounded with conviction and rare felicity Indian tradition, culture, and aspiration in the post-war world. In addition to directly trying to persuade him, Nehru put pressure on him through Dhebar, Pant, Azad and Rajendra Prasad, to make him agree to continue for a second term.[56] But when all their efforts to retain him in Delhi failed, Nehru made certain written commitments to him, one of which was to make him the minister of education. But these too failed to yield any result. Finally, it was a letter from Indira Gandhi (1917-1984), saying that her father was very much upset, that in her opinion (which, of course, was shared by Nehru) Delhi without Radhakrishnan would be "unthinkable" and that "Delhi would not be the same without your presence," which moved Radhakrishnan and made him change his mind. He at once wrote to Nehru conveying his decision to place himself in his (Nehru's) hands.[57]

Vice-President Again

The news of Radhakrishnan finally agreeing to be nominated for the second term as vice-president pleased most people. He was formally elected vice-president for a second term of five years in May 1957. Nehru made Radhakrishnan happy by conceding a few prerogatives to the office of the vice resident. He changed the order in the warrant of precedence to make the vice-president, who until then ranked third after the prime minister, number two in the protocol. Rules were amended in such a manner that henceforth the vice-president was entitled to use Indian Air Force VIP aircraft to travel within India. He also arranged for Radhakrishnan to go on goodwill visits to foreign countries more often.[58]

Foreign Tours Again

In September, 1957 Radhakrishnan undertook a three-week tour to Southeast Asia, Mongolia, China and Hong Kong. In Peking, on September 27, explaining the traditional Indian concept of an ideal state he said, "The binding principle of democratic societies is spontaneous conformity, not enforced obedience. The people's will should prevail. We cannot crush their wishes, cannot trample on their dreams. Through mutual education the government and the people get near each other till the interests of rulers and the ruled coincide as in *Rāmārajya* or the ideal state of the Indian conception."[59] Talking about the importance of freedom for human development, he continued, "It is only in freedom that man can discover what he really is. It is the individual who feels pain and joy, who bears responsibility, does good or evil. If we overlook this side of human nature, we turn the subject into an object. The objectification is at once the necessary condition of freedom and a perpetual threat to it. Man must limit the objectification to what is essential for his freedom. As his fellowmen should be equally free, each individual has to submit to certain limitations. The submission is not servitude, as it is accepted in the freedom of the spirit."[60] In the course of this tour, Mongolia conferred on him the title "Master of Wisdom."

In July 1959 he toured America and Germany. In America he delivered a lecture at the East-West Philosophy Conference in Honolulu on "The Indian Approach to the Religious Problem." According to him, the Indian approach to the problem of religion could be indicated "by a reference to the first four aphorisms of the *Brahma Sūtra*, which are a part of the Vedas. The four *Sūtras* deal with (1) the need for the knowledge of Ultimate Reality, (2) a rational approach to it, (3) the experience of Reality, and (4) reconciliation of seemingly conflicting formulations of the nature of Ultimate Reality."[61] In his address "The Present Crisis of Faith" at the University of Hawaii he talked about the crisis faced by modern man and said, "The dilemma of the modern man is that though he despairs of life he does not wish to die. The instinct for survival gives us hope. The enemy we have to fight is not capitalism or communism. It is our folly, our spiritual blindness, our love of power, our lust for domination."[62] Outlining the importance of religion to life he said Religion "has some guidance and help to offer to a generation which is perplexed at its failure to find satisfaction and is now groping for light. Only a living faith in God will overcome the paralyzing sense of despair and create a less imperfect society."[63] But he emphasized that religions in order to be of help to the modern man "need to be rid of their irrationality, reactionary social character and of provincialism."[64]

In Frankfurt he addressed the International PEN Conference. Warning the delegates of the dangers of nationalistic egoism he said, "No nation is immoral. . . . If it is wrong for the individual to put his self-interest above national good, it is wrong for the nation to put its interests above those of humanity."[65] Later, in the same city, after receiving the Goethe Plaquette, in his thanksgiving speech he warned of the threats posed to the world by "rabid nationalism." He said, "Fanatic love of virtue has done more harm to humanity than anything else. Fanaticism is the greatest foe of friendship. . . . [Peace] is a hope that the invincible spirit of man will not suffer defeat. Even when all else fails, truth does not fail. Loved ones pass away, our friends fail, our cherished dogmas disappear but truth does not pass away, fail or disappear. . . . All those who think and suffer can cooperate in the creation of a new climate of thought, in the fostering of a new disposition of will which will make for brotherhood."[66]

Drawing the attention of the members of the National Assembly of the Federal Republic of Germany to the cause of erosion of values, he declared: "There is nothing wrong about technology. Signs of decadence do not originate from the machines. They are to be sought in the human soul. It is there that a change of direction is needed. We seem to have lost, at any rate when we work as members belonging to groups, national groups especially, a sense of values, a sense of the sacred. Decent human beings behave as a result in an immoral way."[67]

In January-February of 1960 he went on a goodwill tour of England and the Scandinavian countries, and later in November he went to Paris to attend the UNESCO Conference. Delivering the inaugural address at the UNESCO centenary celebration of Rabindranath Tagore, he pointed out that Tagore "worked for one supreme cause, the union of all sections of humanity." In 1961 he visited the USA to participate in the opening ceremony of the Centre for the Study of World Religions at Harvard University. On the occasion, in his speech "Fellowship of the Spirit" he expressed his firm belief that the spirit of religion can be the savior of the strife-torn, suffering world, and that it can provide us an ideal or a purpose to live for. Expressing hope that the Centre for the Study of World Religions would help improve the prevailing situation, and bring about brotherhood and friendship among different religions, he said:

A study of the different forms of religious life may give us some idea of the deep significance of religion for the life of man. The different religions are to be used as building stones for the development of human culture in which the adherents of the different religions may be fraternally united as the children of one Supreme. All religions convey to their followers a message of abiding hope. The world will give birth to a new faith which will be but the old faith in another form, the faith of all ages in the potential divinity of man which will work for the supreme purpose written in our hearts and souls, the unity of mankind.[68]

During this tour, when he visited Washington and met President Eisenhower, he had the frankness to tell the latter that as American diplomats did not know a "darned thing" about the Kashmir problem, all that Eisenhower knew about it was wrong. Eisenhower reportedly got a jolt by such an act of outspokenness.[69]

UNESCO

In addition to the goodwill visits, Radhakrishnan went to various countries to attend the annual sessions of UNESCO held there. He had been representing India in these sessions since the inception of UNESCO. He was head of the Indian delegations to UNESCO Annual General Conferences from 1946 to 1954 and again in 1958. While he attended ten conferences of the UNESCO, he presided over only the Seventh General Conference held at Paris in 1962 and was a member of its Executive Board for two terms of three years each from 1946 to 1951. He was the chairman of the board during 1948-1949. In the board's meetings, as in other forums, he put forward the Indian viewpoint fearlessly, clearly and earnestly.

In the early years of UNESCO, most Western countries, especially the USA, were advocating conquest of ignorance as a principal aim of that organization. They presupposed that ignorance of the Western democratic way of life was the cause of Nazism and fascism, which in turn led to the World War. Radhakrishnan forcibly countered this self-righteous Western approach and argued that "the way of life we are growing accustomed to requires to be altered radically," that the correction of the Nazi and fascist mind was not the primary objective of the UNESCO education program, and that the whole world needed reeducation. He pleaded for inculcation in men's minds of respect for all cultures; and asserted that any effort to impose a particular way of life on Germany was unjustifiable, as that would be cultural fascism. He criticized any exaggerated or exclusive emphasis on scientific and technological education, pointing to the equal importance of humanistic education: "The way in which sciences, national and social, have to be employed is studied by ethics and philosophy. The concepts of right and wrong do not belong to the sphere of science, and on the study of ideas centering around them human happiness ultimately depends. A balanced culture should bring the two great halves of science and wisdom into harmony."[70]

Accepting the importance of adult education he declared that "it should aim not just at attainment of literacy, but at a total development of human personality. It should be able to increase the work efficiency of adults and improve their standard of living."[71]

Radhakrishnan did not hesitate to pinpoint the drawbacks of the organization of UNESCO and suggested remedial measures. Drawing delegates' attention to the fact that in the UNESCO secretariat out of 557 positions, 514 posts were occupied by the citizens of Western Europe, England and the USA; and only forty-three of those belonged to the Middle East, China, India and the rest of the world, with Africa conspicuously absent, he observed, "If we are to avoid the suspicion that the UNESCO is an Anglo-American or West European organization, we must make serious efforts to correct this disproportion."[72] He suggested that "though the salaries of the secretarial staff must be based on need, the policy of recruitment should be such that it does not encourage careerists."[73]

On another occasion, he addressed the delegates thus in a forthright way: "Cannot we from here in the name of UNESCO call upon the leaders of the world to listen to the voice of humanity in anguish, and give up the ways of the jungle and inaugurate a new chapter in the history of man? Can we not stop getting angry with each other?" Continuing in the same candid tone, marked by prophetic insight he added, "We cannot continue to live as an armed camp in a state of perpetual alarm."[74] The present state of perpetual alarm he said could be avoided if we turned to the ancient Indian view regarding the causes of war, and try as far as possible to remove them. The Indian seers, he said, have maintained that there are two main causes of war. The first cause is the fear, suspicion, hatred and jealousy among peoples. All these are offsprings of frustration. The source of frustration lies in the loss of human and spiritual values, and the economically backward condition of the people. The second cause of war is the wide disparity in the standards of living. Consequently, he suggested that the UNESCO in order to establish a peaceful world order, must not only concentrate on the economic development of nations ravaged by wars, but also on other parts of the world. It should aim at the economic reconstruction of Asia and Africa along with other continents to ensure freedom from hunger of the people living in these subcontinents, for fulfillment of material needs and the eradication of poverty which is a stronger guarantee than any other ideal for the establishment of a peace-oriented mind.[75]

UNESCO, he suggested, must aim at the "rehabilitation of men not of schools, libraries, shops and factories. We must recreate men if we are to recreate a new world community."[76] This, he said, can be done by the propagation of spiritual values. In a world rich in spiritual values there is no place for suspicion and fear. It necessarily produces "men of dignity and integrity, free in spirit, men who will obey the moral law."[77] If we fail in our enterprise, he warned, civilization will descend into the abyss for "concentration of power, no matter whether it is political or economic, is a threat to democracy. It is certain to be abused whether it is by politicians on account of their position or by rich men on account of their wealth. Aggregation of wealth in a few hands and growth of corporate monopolies do not make for democratic process. Big business and high finance will control politics, will control intellectual life, will control machines of propaganda like the press and radio, will establish economic fascism."[78]

Peace, he said could not be "achieved by imposition of disciplinary measures or use of sanctions but by fostering goodwill and understanding among people of the world." The main task of UNESCO, according to him, was "to effect ideological harmony and diminish tensions" by promoting "a new life, a new outlook, a new philosophy which will inspire humanity."

Every religion, he asserted, teaches truth and love. The pursuit of truth makes us respect the individual—the bearer and carrier of values. Love asks us to respect humanity. Calling upon the representatives to UNESCO to stand above narrow national loyalties and to maintain their integrity he said, "We are a priesthood of the spirit. We cannot compromise, though politicians may. No false word should escape our lips, no wrong thought should enter the mind. I am concerned that we in this body should stand above politics and for universal values."[79] He believed in the parity of all cultures and treated a belief in the superiority of one's own culture as "cultural fascism."

It was primarily due to Radhakrishnan's presence and his persistent efforts that the UNESCO conference held in New Delhi in December 1951, after discussing the need for reconciliation between the conflict of ideologies of East and West resolved, "The conventional distinction between the active West and the contemplative East was fallacious. Therefore, the distinction between the East and the West should not be emphasized.

Instead a spirit of cooperation under which man can deal with man on the basis of equality must be promoted. This is new humanism."[80]

Due to his penetrating observations and deep insight Radhakrishnan was looked upon by the delegates to the conferences as the embodiment of the ancient wisdom of the East, and as one who contributed, more than anyone else, towards building up a bridge between the cultures of East and West. His speeches in these conferences were crisp, to the point, and packed with thought-provoking ideas. Because of his reputation as "the bridge builder," "the liaison officer," and a lucid and clear speaker, he was the greatest "crowd puller" at the conferences. The delegates sought personal interviews with him. But this popularity in no way affected the humanity and jocosity of Radhakrishnan.

An interesting episode may be mentioned here. In a conference in Buenos Aires, Ms. Myrna Loy, a famous Hollywood film actress, was a member of the US delegation. Like other delegates she too had heard of Radhakrishnan and was keen to meet him and discuss with him some problems of philosophy. When she came to meet him in his hotel room, he was, as usual, lying in his bed in his thin muslin dhoti and vest, with books strewn around him. In his characteristic way, he pushed away a pile of books and asked her to sit beside him on the same bed. She was taken aback for a moment, but such was his personality and his friendly gesture that she lowered herself gingerly on his bed. He took her hand in his hand without any display of emotion and in a matter of fact manner, asked her, "And, my dear, how many husbands have you had so far?" She poured out her heart to him. They discussed everything else under the sun, but not philosophy.[81]

According to Prem Kirpal,[82] among the many programs launched by UNESCO, resulting from the initiatives taken by Radhakrishnan, three stand out: (1) It was primarily due to Radhakrishnan's initiative that UNESCO prepared material in humanities both for the specialists and for the general public, which for the first time incorporated besides the Western thought, the wisdom of the East. These publications by highlighting the "contributions of seers, sages and scholars of India and China," shifted the balance of knowledge and information in favor of Eastern and African countries, and alleviated the neglect of these countries due to the "egocentricity of the Western nations." (2) The UNESCO adopted, because of Radhakrishnan's emphasis on knowledge and synthesis of cultures and his persuasion, a major project "for the mutual appreciation of the cultural values of East and West." This "helped in constructing new bridges of knowledge and understanding in the minds of men, so essential to a *world order* struggling to be born." (3) It was due to Radhakrishnan's influence that UNESCO undertook a project for "An objective study of world religions" with an aim to project and practice "human values and for the meeting of historic cultures and civilizations."

Relations with President and Prime Minister

At home, Radhakrishnan himself took the initiative to restore between President Prasad and himself the friendly relationship and rapport that they had before the presidential election in 1957, and to a large extent succeeded in doing so. Radhakrishnan went to see Prasad regularly every Saturday. In privacy they both reportedly ridiculed the idea of suggesting a change in the presidency in 1957 on the ground of placating South India. Radhakrishnan appears to have told him that a change on that ground would have been unfair to Prasad as well as to the South, and commented that "the prime minister was too much of an innocent who lent his ear to others too readily."[83] In their private meetings Radhakrishnan brought to the attention of Prasad matters which in his opinion deserved serious consideration by the government, such as the anti-Hindu propaganda, the scandal relating to Insurance Corporation funds,[84] release of Sheikh Abdullah,[85] etc. Prasad confided in Radhakrishnan whenever he felt miserable on account of his inability to reconcile with the policies and actions of the prime minister, and this was not infrequent. Though Radhakrishnan on such occasions suggested to Prasad that a "straight and uninhibited talk with Nehru was the best way out," he agreed with Prasad that Nehru would not accept his views on the constitutional relationship between the president and the prime minister, and therefore it was useless to talk to him.[86]

The president and vice-president, according to some accounts, agreed on most of the major issues. On the super-session of the Communist government in Kerala by the central government in 1959, Prasad and Radhakrishnan shared the view that "the Kerala government could hardly be called a sinner in the face of the doings of some Congress governments in the states,"[87] and both agreed that "by its action against the Communist government in Kerala, the Congress government in India has lost some of its moral prestige."[88] Prasad also shared with Radhakrishnan his critical views regarding the National Integration Council which was constituted by the government and consisted of union ministers, chief ministers and government officers as its members, with the prime minister as its chairman. Radhakrishnan was highly critical of the constitution of the council for he thought that it gave an impression of being a government body rather than a public organization. He felt "it was going to end up a joke." For he believed that an organization which was supposed "to guide, if not educate, the government, should not have been dominated by ministers and government officers themselves."[89] The two also agreed in their assessment of Nehru as a person who though himself guileless and incapable of intrigue, was not able to see through the guile and intrigue of people around him, despite his experience of men and matters.[90]

Radhakrishnan practically attended on Prasad whenever he suffered from illness. Acknowledging his gratitude to Radhakrishnan, Prasad wrote, "My most intimate experience of his kindness and large-heartedness, sympathy and genuine love came during my serious illness; for weeks he not only showed the keenest interest but practically and literally attended on me. I can never forget the words of encouragement and solace which even in those difficult days I never missed, coming as they did from the depth of his heart."[91]

Radhakrishnan acted as president in June-July 1960 when Prasad was away on a tour. He was again the acting president when Prasad fell ill in August-September 1961.

If the above account of the rapport between Prasad and Radhakrishnan and their unanimity on a number of issues after the former's 1957 election is authentic, it would be another illustration of Radhakrishnan's capacity to be able to relate and interact with two persons or groups adverse to each other, because, from all accounts, he was at the same time more friendly and closer to Nehru. In the preindependence period he was able to be so with both the British authorities in India and the Indian nationalists, and in the later period he had no difficulty in being equally friendly with congressmen as well as communists. One may also wonder why Prasad and Radhakrishnan, together or singly, did not choose to have a serious discussion with Nehru about the important matters on which they both agreed, but differed from the prime minister, and have it out with him, *if* they felt so strongly about them. It would have been surprising if Nehru, considered to be flexible and amenable to rational persuasion, had not accepted their views at least on matters like the composition of the National Integration Council, if they had chosen to make them known to him directly. A plausible explanation is: as Nehru perhaps did not consult the president or the vice-president on these issues in advance, the president might have felt it *infra dignitatem*, and the vice-president imprudent, to give unsolicited advice. It may be remembered that Aristotle rated prudence very highly among virtues.

As Vice-President, An Assessment

The fact that Radhakrishnan was becoming a sort of legend as vice-president was evident when Lyndon Johnson, the then vice-president and later president of the USA, on a visit to India said to him, " 'Ambassador Bunker tells me that I should model myself on you.' "[92] Radhakrishnan discharged his duties as the vice-president of India—whether it was to receive Eisenhower, Khrushchev or Yuri Gagarin or the routine chairing of the Rajya Sabha—with great skill and dignity. He claimed to be also detached from everything around him. During that time, on a visit to Patna to deliver a convocation address, he told the governor of Bihar, R.R. Diwakar, that for him only Bala Ravi, the early morning rising sun, was important—as meditation on him fed the roots of his being, and all else, including the office he held, was but a *tamāshā* (fun) for him.[93]

Though Radhakrishnan might have considered his occupancy of the office of vice-president a *tamāshā*, he took the two functions attached to this office, namely, presiding over the Rajya Sabha and traveling in India and abroad to give lectures and speeches regarding the government's policies, very seriously.

In the Rajya Sabha through his constant alertness, unfailing courtesy, scrupulous fairness, complete impartiality, wit and humor, he was able to create an atmosphere in which the members of the treasury benches and the members of the opposition had matching opportunities in which "everybody won a point and there was no sense of vanquishment."[94] As a result there was hardly any occasion of protest or walkout by the members resenting his ruling. Though as a rule he never attended the afternoon sessions of the House, he kept a close watch on its proceedings by listening to them at his residence. He kept a strict discipline in Rajya Sabha and did not hesitate to admonish those who violated it irrespective of who it was, as is clear from the following episode, narrated by Lakshmi N. Menon: "Once it happened that the prime minister wanted to tell me something. He sauntered to my seat as though we were at some informal social function. With unusual firmness the chairman said, 'Mr. Prime Minister, what are you doing?' Panditji . . . apologised and walked back to his seat."[95]

In his lectures and speeches abroad Radhakrishnan was successful in projecting government policies and plans and secured a sympathetic and friendly response for them. Of his foreign trips and his attempts to create concord through his formal lectures as well as extempore speeches, Nehru remarked: "Wherever he went, his words brought comfort to the people and his wisdom brought people nearer to each other."[96]

Throughout his vice-presidency "he had only two persons in his personal staff: a personal assistant (stenographer) from the Rajya Sabha Secretariat and an assistant private secretary in the vice-president's office. He used his own private car and never used the official staff car. Even on his trips abroad he never took any member of his family or staff with him. On these tours, he traveled alone as an ordinary first class passenger in a commercial aircraft."[97]

In the farewell function organized by the members of Rajya Sabha on Radhakrishnan's election as the president of India, the members of the ruling as well as the opposition parties paid rich tributes to the contribution he made and the conventions he set in conducting the proceedings of the Rajya Sabha. Bhupesh Gupta, a fiery and eloquent member of the Communist party, lauding the role of Radhakrishnan as chairman of the House, said, "In this role of yours what has attracted us and the people most is your broad vision and your fundamentally nonpartisan outlook. In the present context of our political life it is not easy for anyone to be a dignitary of the state and yet maintain such an attitude. You have been, Sir, a guide and teacher in our House."[98] A.D. Mani, recalling the influence of Radhakrishnan's personality on the members, observed, "This House has witnessed many memorable spectacles and one of them has been very recent when at your request the leaders of the Opposition withdrew their amendments that they had submitted to the motion of thanks on the president's address. I think it is without any parallel in the history of the world that because of the personal influence of the chair, the members of the opposition have withdrawn [their amendments] which have been tabled on behalf of their parties."[99]

Replying to these tributes, Radhakrishnan explained the secret of his success as the chairman of the Rajya Sabha thus: "I should like to say that if my chairmanship of this House has been successful it is due to the goodwill and affection which all these members have shown to me. My ignorance of parliamentary processes and procedures is condoned; my faults are forgiven and my errors are overlooked. I do not pretend that I conformed to the strict rules and procedures of parliamentary business. I have not done that and if you still are tolerant with me, it shows your generosity of mind and tolerance of spirit."[100]

XIV.

The Presidency Part I

As President

In 1962 Radhakrishnan completed his second term as vice-president, and Prasad his second term as president. The Congress party unanimously nominated Radhakrishnan as a candidate for the presidency. In the election he secured 97.98 percent of the total votes, and became the second president of India for a term of five years. He assumed office on May 13, 1962. In his place Dr. Zakir Husain was elected the vice-president. Initially, Nehru's sister, Mrs. Vijayalakshmi Pandit, had also staked her claim for the vice-presidency but she later kept herself out. Radhakrishnan persuaded her to do so on behalf of Nehru, on the latter's request. Like Prasad, accepting only Rs. 2,500 per month out of a total presidential salary of Rs. 10,000 per month, Radhakrishnan donated the remaining to the prime minister's National Relief Fund. In fact, after the deduction of income tax, his salary was reduced to just Rs. 1,900 per month.

On Radhakrishnan's election as president, Bertrand Russell declared: "It is an honor to philosophy that Dr. Radhakrishnan should be the president of India and I, as a philosopher, take special pleasure in this. Plato aspired for philosophers to become kings and it is a tribute to India that she should make a philosopher her president."[1] Pearl S. Buck commented, "I congratulate India." *The Times* of London wrote, "It might have been thought a reflection on India, had a man of Dr. Radhakrishnan's attainments not ended his years in public life, with a period of service as India's President."

On the Platonic concept of 'philosopher king', Radhakrishnan was to say later:

Generally, whenever addresses are presented to me, Plato is brought out as one who said that philosophers should rule the State. This is not a Platonic axiom. It is something common to all great cultures. In our own country we said that thinkers must be actors:

154

Ātma rati ātma krida kriyāvān
eṣa brahamavidām variṣṭhaḥ

He must be *kriyāvān*, a performer of works. Similarly, it is said:

Vivekī sarvadā muktaḥ kurvato nāsti kartṛtā
alepavādam āśritya śrikṛṣṇa Janakau yathā

Even Śrikṛṣṇa and Janaka were men not only of philosophical wisdom but also of practical efficiency. We should also behave in the same way. So the Platonic axiom is something which is common to all great cultures. It again shows the universality of culture. We must have vision, we must have practical work. Vision is illumination of solitude. Once you have the vision, you must try to transform that vision into reality, by efforts, dedicated work. That is what all great people are expected to do. All students of philosophy are called upon not merely to interpret but to change the world, not only to exert their vision but also to exert honest service, honest dedication.[2]

This, one may assume, was Radhakrishnan's manifesto to which he tried to be true.

In his inaugural address Radhakrishnan pledged "to do my best to deserve in some modest measure, the great faith of my people, and devote the few years left to me to their service."[3] Referring to the ideals on which democracy is founded he said: "These ideals of freedom, equality and justice are not possessions to be defended but goals to be reached. We have often lapsed from them and suffered in consequence. In a mood of humility and repentance, we should strive to correct our past mistakes, remove the indignities which we have imposed on our fellowmen and march forward. We cannot move into the future by walking backwards."[4] Expressing his commitment to the pursuit of truth, he said, "The Supreme is truth according to all religions. Men of all creeds and no creed are devotees of truth, the great comforter, the great awakener. When other things fail, truth does not. *Tat Satyam, sa ātma, tat tvaṁ asi*, as the Chāndogya Upanishad has it."[5] The themes of truth, democracy, equality and social justice were to be repeatedly reflected upon in most of his speeches in the following five years.

Soon after assuming office, Radhakrishnan conferred India's highest civilian award, *Bharat Ratna*, on his predecessor, Rajendra Prasad. Speaking on the occasion he said, "Rajen babu, as he is affectionately called, is essentially a religious man, . . . who symbolizes . . . the age-old spirit of the country."[6]

Though one expected that a philosopher of Radhakrishnan's standing would consider the hurly burly of politics an anathema and would like to spend most of his time reflecting on abstruse and abstract philosophical questions about the meaning of life, Radhakrishnan "knew everything that was happening in Delhi." With "his feet firmly planted upon the earth and his ears close to the ground," he without any delay came to know of the maneuvers and manipulations in the Congress party, what was going on in the government, what the cabinet discussions were about, the attitude of the prime minister and other ministers to various questions, who was on the way out of the cabinet and who was going to be in. "He knew all the scandals and how far they were true and to what extent manufactured with ulterior motives."[7]

Rashtrapati Bhawan, the dwelling of the president of India, is the old Viceregal Lodge which the British built in a most lavish and impressive way. Even after Radhakrishnan became its occupant, his way of life did not change. He continued to be accessible to as many people as he could. Politicians came to acquaint him with their views, make suggestions to him as to how he should guide or advise the government on different issues, or to complain to him against some of the policies or actions of the government. Foreign and Indian scholars and students came just to have the honor of meeting him, or to present their books, or seek his advice and comments on educational, philosophical or cultural issues. Sometimes ordinary men came to seek redress of their grievances. He received those whom he knew and with whom he could chat, lying on his bed, wearing a dhoti and full sleeved shirt, with heaps of books on small tables around his bed as well as on a bed by its side. He received others in the reception room wearing a long coat and turban.

He used to get up early in the morning, and after getting ready lie on the bed, sipping coffee and listening to devotional music and news on the radio, or reading newspapers and magazines. Throughout the day, whenever time permitted, he would glance through the latest literature especially on philosophy and other humanistic and social sciences.

Later in the day he attended to official papers, and personally replied to every letter he received. Often he wrote just a line or a few lines in reply, and in some rare cases his reply ran into a number of pages; but no one failed to get a reply from him.

After lunch he used to have his siesta and in the afternoon he fulfilled official engagements, attended social functions or addressed public meetings. In the evenings he strolled in the Mughal Gardens in Rashtrapati Bhawan, often accompanied by a couple of his relatives, friends or visitors whom he knew well.

His dinners were simple and consisted of vegetarian dishes of the South Indian type. Sometimes he ate only two or three varieties of fruits. At receptions and other functions, he avoided eating anything except two or three cashewnuts.[8]

In order to acquaint himself with the views and grievances of the public and develop contact with the masses, Radhakrishnan started holding open *durbārs*[9] everyday at 5 p.m. Anyone could attend these and have a word with him and also give him a note or petition. These were held in the beautiful Mughal Gardens of Rashtrapati Bhawan. The people who came to attend them were made to sit in rows, and the president, followed by his staff and a couple or so of his relatives and friends, slowly walked among them, stopping near each person, listening to what he might have to say, receiving any papers he might give, responding in a polite and gentle way, and moving on to the next person. Those who came included some who merely came to see him; others sought jobs, money or scholarships; and yet others requested redressal of wrongs or injustices. Some came to lodge their complaints about inordinate bureaucratic delays, and some came to beg for clemency for their imprisoned or condemned friends or relatives. In the beginning the attendance at each *durbār* was around 2,000. A Petitions Committee was established in Rashtrapati Bhawan to sort out the petitions received by the president at these *durbārs* and send them to the concerned ministries, offices or institutions for necessary action. The latter took more or less the usual time to deal with the papers transmitted by the president's office. The concerned authorities also resented people directly petitioning the president for any and everything. Thus the president's office in effect became a post office. Soon the public realized the ineffectiveness of the president's *durbārs*, and, consequently, the number of people attending each of them dropped to just sixty or seventy, even though the frequency at which they were held was reduced from once a day to twice a week in view of declining numbers. While this experiment failed in so far as it could not provide any satisfactory solution to public grievances, it succeeded in exposing the shortcomings in administration and the highhandedness of certain ministers, ministries and departments. Some like Chief Minister Pratap Singh Kairon and others were reported to have called these *durbārs* "nonsense," did what they could to discourage holding them. It may be said that most politicians in the ruling party and a majority of officials viewed with skepticism Radhakrishnan's attempt to have a direct contact with people in this way. On a number of occasions even Nehru asked the president sarcastically how his *durbārs* were going on.[10] Eventually they were stopped.

Relations with Nehru

The relationship between Radhakrishnan and Vice-president Zakir Husain remained excellent throughout their terms in office. The president's relations with Nehru, who had a great regard for his scholarship, eloquence and international reputation, were warm and cordial to begin with, but changed slowly with the passage of time and turn of events. Radhakrishnan once confided to Chagla that at the beginning of his term, Nehru would come into his room unannounced, sit down, stretch his legs and tell him, "I want some relaxation, and I can only find it in telling freely to you, and gathering your reactions to what has happened today."[11] That Nehru valued and acted on Radhakrishnan's advice in the beginning can be illustrated by the following episode.

It so happened that when Rajendra Prasad died at Patna, Nehru was about to leave on a tour of Rajasthan. He wrote to Radhakrishnan that he himself would be unable to attend Prasad's funeral and that there was no reason for President Radhakrishnan also to attend it. But Radhakrishnan replied that Nehru must attend it, as such respect was due to Rajendra Babu and it must be paid, and that he should abandon his tour and come with him to the funeral. Nehru did as advised.[12] With his informal ways, Radhakrishnan was able to influence Nehru to a considerable extent in the beginning, but soon Nehru began to be suspicious of his advice and became indifferent. This may be because Radhakrishnan gradually began to offer advice, express opinions, or make comments on political issues or about appointments to the cabinet and embassies, etc., which Nehru did not like. But, with regard to educational and cultural policies and matters of propriety, Nehru almost always deferred to him.

Soon after Radhakrishnan took over as president, the government of India decided to celebrate his birthday as "Teacher's Day" each year. Besides collection of funds for the betterment of the lot of teachers, on this day, national awards were to be presented to honor the outstanding primary and secondary school teachers, and teachers of Sanskrit Pathashalas by the president of India.

Radhakrishnan kept himself abreast with the latest happenings in India and abroad, and used to keep track of the debates in Parliament through microphones by his bedside and on his desk. He encouraged members of Parliament and others who met him to express their views on public issues, sometimes also expressed his personal views on such occasions and, in a way, sought to propagate them. According to some accounts, a desire to have an independent and decisive role in Indian politics began to be manifested by Radhakrishnan after he became president; for otherwise, he would not have told Chester Bowles on several occasions that "the whole country could operate under 'President's rule' for a few months." This, he said, would enable him in his role as president to ease some of the accumulating political conflicts and make some of the difficult but necessary decisions before turning the government over to a new prime minister and cabinet."[13]

Some time after he became president, he began to criticize in private Nehru's government policies and actions unsparingly. He particularly disapproved of the way the government dealt with Sheikh Abdullah, and blamed Nehru for agreeing to a ceasefire in Kashmir in 1948, for, he opined that Nehru's decision in this matter was taken while keeping in view international opinion rather than national interest. Likewise, when Nehru issued a statement on Cuba, Radhakrishnan said, "Let us not bother about the rest of the world. Let us be national for a while, and cease being international."[14] Such a statement was surprising as it was made by a president who in his inaugural speech had declared "We should not put national security above world security. The absolute sovereign national state is outmoded."[15] This was a reflection of Radhakrishnan's subjectivity prevailing over his objectivity which started clouding his idealism. He considered Nehru to be a "poor judge of men," as he protected and placed his confidence in (according to him) unworthy persons like V. K. Krishna Menon, Pratap Singh Kairon and Dharma Teja.[16] He used his influence as president to persuade and press Nehru to drop Krishna Menon from the cabinet after the military debacle of India in the armed conflict with China; and to institute an enquiry into the charges of corruption and maladministration against Kairon, as a result of which Kairon had to quit as chief minister of Punjab. Dharma Teja was granted a loan of rupees two hundred million by the government to finance a company floated by him. But when the company, due to speculation, adventurism, mismanagement and bungling, landed in a financial crisis, Teja fled the country.

Nehru, in turn among other things, became suspicious of Radhakrishnan's growing intimacy with Chakravarti Rajagopalachari (Rajaji), a leading figure of the Indian independence movement and the first gover-

nor general of independent India. In earlier years Nehru was an admirer
of Rajaji. He had proposed his name for presidentship against Rajendra
Prasad, had him in his cabinet, appointed him as governor of West Bengal
and later helped him to become chief minister of Madras (1952-1954).
Then they began to differ, and finally fell apart after 1959 when Rajaji
formed a rightist party called Swatantra party, which Nehru thought was
a reactionary one. Rajaji, on the other hand, called Nehru's government
"pure autocracy or dictatorship." He scathingly criticized Nehru's domestic
and foreign policies. Nehru and others appear to have believed that Radhakrishnan was being counseled by Rajaji, because he made it a point to call
on Rajaji, whenever he was in Madras and used to spend hours with him. In
Delhi he gave easy access to members of Swatantra and other parties which
bitterly opposed the Congress party and were carrying on a devastating criticism of Nehru's policies and actions, and frequently had long discussions
with them. It was said that Radhakrishnan's increasing criticism of government policies and his alleged inclination to the West as opposed to
Nehru's pro-Soviet attitude, was largely due to Rajaji's influence.[17]

However, whatever concord Nehru and Radhakrishnan might have
had on political issues and matters of State, vanished after the Sino-Indian
conflict. Radhakrishnan like the whole nation, was disappointed, dejected
and depressed by the ignominy India suffered in this conflict. The happenings preceding this event may briefly be narrated to give the context
of this souring of relations between Nehru and Radhakrishnan.

The Sino-Indian Conflict

China had been carrying on a boundary dispute with India since
1960. On September 8, 1962, in a way most unexpected by the Indian
government, Chinese forces advanced into Indian territory, which they
claimed to be theirs. In his address to the United Chambers of Trade
Associations in Delhi on October 14, without getting prior clearance from
the cabinet or Nehru, Radhakrishnan announced that India would be
prepared to consider negotiations with China provided the Chinese troops
withdrew to their September 8 positions. But on October 20 the Chinese
forces advanced further. On October 22, Nehru publicly supported Radhakrishnan's proposal. On November 21 the Chinese unilaterally declared
a ceasefire and withdrew their troops.

During the conflict Radhakrishnan visited the frontline areas in NEFA
and Ladakh, as well as military and civil hospitals where injured officers

and jawans were being treated. Wherever he went he addressed the soldiers whose morale was very low and told them that all those who were responsible for their plight would be punished. Criticizing the government for the debacle he said, "The country had been brought to this sorry pass—a matter for sorrow, shame and humiliation—because of two blunders in policy—credulity and negligence on the part of government."[18] He urged all MPs to stand united and to strengthen the armed forces and patriotic phalanxes.

Calling the Chinese "aggressors" publicly, Radhakrishnan boosted the morale of his countrymen and the army in his speech on October 25:

> The country is faced by perhaps the greatest crisis we have had since we achieved independence. Our officers and soldiers are fighting—fighting so gallantly, fighting so well as to be a challenge to our selfishness and to our pettiness and narrowness. They are facing superior numbers, superior equipment, giving up their lives. There is no question that so far as this struggle is concerned, there is only one end to it and that is victory for our forces and for ourselves. It is the trespassers into our country, those who violated our boundary, it is they who are to be thrown out. We are defending, we are not on the offensive. We are trying to defend our land, trying to throw out people who have entered into it. We told them times without number that for centuries these borders had been within the territorial limits of India and that we are prepared to enter into negotiations. Spurning all these efforts, rejecting, so to say, every effort we made for negotiations for a settlement, they came determined to decide the issue by might. That is the position in which we are. And in this world, whatever upsets we may have, whatever reverses we may pass through, ultimately victory is for the just cause.[19]

In private, Radhakrishnan expressed doubts about the capability of Lt. General B.M. Kaul (1912-1972), the area commander of NEFA, a favorite of Nehru and Defense Minister Menon, and believed by many to have been catapulted into his then key position due to nepotism. After a meeting with Kaul Radhakrishnan is reported to have remarked "he sounds hollow."[20] When, after serious setbacks, Kaul got admitted to the Military Hospital in New Delhi, and began directing military operations from there, Radhakrishnan like many others, suspected that he was shamming sickness, and remarked that he must be thoroughly examined by a full medical board and exposed to the public, if necessary[21] but, due to confusion prevailing in New Delhi at that time, Kaul escaped a thorough medical examination. While the conflict was on, whenever he visited Poona, Radhakrishnan discussed with Lt. General J.N. Chaudhuri (1908-1983) of the Southern command the operations against the Chinese. Most of the time he found that Chaudhuri's observations were correct, and that his predictions came true. When General Thapar submitted his resignation, Nehru, despite the poor performance of Kaul wanted the latter to be promoted to the post of General. But Radhakrishnan put his foot down. Pointing out to Nehru the injustice and foolishness of such a proposal, he suggested that Chaudhuri, a soldier of proven merit and competence, be appointed to replace General Thapar. Nehru yielded and Lt. General Chaudhuri was promoted as general.[22] Radhakrishnan is reported to have been amused when under heavy fire from the opposition in the Parliament, the treasury benches resolved to drive out the Chinese from Indian soil and muttered to himself, "They won't be able to do so in centuries the way they are going on."[23] And on Chinese unilateral ceasefire and withdrawal he is reported to have remarked, "They came into our house, slapped us, and have gone back."[24]

After the ceasefire, while there was a demand for Nehru's resignation from some quarters, there was almost a universal demand for Defense Minister Menon's resignation. Menon was a trusted lieutenant of Nehru, against whom Radhakrishnan had been complaining since 1960 when he had requested Nehru to stop sending Menon as India's representative to the United Nations, in view of some (in Radhakrishnan's view) irresponsible statements he had made before the General Assembly. These statements, Radhakrishnan felt, not only did not project Indian policies correctly, but also tarnished the country's image. Moreover, when he was the vice-president, he had suggested to Nehru not to include Menon in the cabinet on the ground he was a bad administrator and was careless about financial matters. But, Nehru, to the disappointment of Radhakrishnan had first included Menon in the cabinet as a minister without portfolio and later appointed him as the defense minister. Even after the outcome of the conflict with China, Nehru was quite unwilling to remove Menon from the cabinet. So, to appease all quarters, Nehru on October 31, 1962, took over as minister of defense, and created a new ministry called the Ministry of Defense Production and put Menon in charge of it. Menon was at that time in Tejpur, far away from Delhi. When this change in his portfolio was brought to Menon's notice, he issued a public statement that nothing had changed and that he continued to be the defense minister. On hearing this, senior cabinet ministers asked Nehru for an immediate ouster of Menon from the cabinet. Radhakrishnan, when apprised of this demand by ministers and Congress M.Ps, advised Nehru to drop him from the cabinet. But the prime minister was too attached to Menon and he requested the president to write to him advising that Menon be dismissed from the cabinet. Radhakrishnan sarcastically told Nehru that to do so would be a reversal of the roles of the prime minister and the president, for, under the constitution the prime minister was supposed to advise the president, and it would be a bad precedent for the president to suggest the dismissal of a minister. Nehru saw reason, obtained Menon's resignation, and on November 7 wrote to the president requesting him to accept it.[25]

A view has been expressed that Radhakrishnan's criticism of the defense minister for military unpreparedness was not fair, because the president, too, was equally responsible for it. As the supreme commander of the armed forces President Radhakrishnan had never tried to persuade the government before the conflict, "that the defense set-up should be modernized to meet any threat of foreign aggression. Even as supreme commander he acted only on the advice of his Council of Ministers. In his messages to the nation through Parliament he made little mention of the armed forces." It has been further pointed out that "Radhakrishnan as supreme commander did not effectively function as such. He did nothing more except dittoing what the government put forward to him for signatures, besides making exasperated remarks. Radhakrishnan never emphasized the need for modernizing the services into a firstclass fighting machine."[26] According to such criticism from 1950 to 1962 "Radhakrishnan talked about armed forces only on three occasions during his addresses to Parliament, i.e. 1950, 1951 and 1952. These talks never enlightened the nation on the progress being made to defend the country."[27]

Soon after the debacle Radhakrishnan assumed the role of friend, philosopher and guide to the nation. In his public speeches he tried to assuage his countrymen's feeling of humiliation by telling them that the government in its negotiations with China would not compromise with the nation's self-respect and honor. In a speech in Madras in November 1962 he said, "We do not want to appease China. . . . We have to tell them that what they are doing is wrong. The way in which many nations, whether democratic or communist, have responded to our call shows that they have recognised that there is a fundamental distinction between right and wrong, that we are the victims of aggressions and so we should be supported and that the aggressors must be condemned."[28] In his 1963 Republic Day speech he admitted that, "The large-scale attack on our frontiers took us by surprise. On account of our traditional adherence to the methods of peace and the habit engendered by it we were psychologically unprepared for meeting this sudden aggression."[29] But he advised his countrymen not to be gloomy in the face of defeat and drew their attention to the silver lining under the cloud of gloom. The silver lining referred to was the hope that "we as a nation will grow better, grow chastened and will become more unified, with the one common purpose of preserving human dignity and helping the onward march of humanity."[30] The Chinese aggression, he said, "has warned and steeled us and made us resolve to protect ourselves from the menace and to strengthen our defense and economic structure to the utmost."[31] It had brought to the fore, he told his countrymen, what he called India's essential unity. Before the aggression, the divisive forces and separatist tendencies were manifesting themselves at an alarming rate, but soon after the invasion, he observed, "all of a sudden overnight as it were, when this attack came, we woke up and found ourselves one united nation with a common purpose and object."[32] Assuring all Indian citizens to take advantage of this manifest unity, he said, "If we are able to utilize this opportunity, this attack by the Chinese will be a blessing in disguise. We should try to bring together all our people whatever their caste or community, into one single whole; coordinate their activities and make them feel that they are participating in this work (of strengthening national purpose)."[33]

If some reports could be relied upon, Radhakrishnan would have liked Nehru to resign. N.G. Ranga (b. 1900) and others were criticizing Nehru for clinging onto power even after the Chinese debacle, despite having remained prime minister for seventeen years. They were, indeed, demanding his dismissal, because of his failure to provide effective leadership to the nation during the crisis. Radhakrishnan, it is said, encouraged and advised such persons.[34] He is reported to have exclaimed, "We all wish to cling to power unto the last."[35]

The Kamaraj Plan

At this juncture what came to be known as the Kamaraj Plan came to the fore. Kamaraj (1903-1975) was at the time the undisputed leader of Tamilnadu, who had risen from among the masses and was known for his closeness to and rapport with them, as well as for his patriotism, administrative ability, simplicity and integrity. He was then chief minister of his state. It is not known for certain who conceived the plan and for what purpose. It was ostensibly aimed at rejuvenating the Congress party whose image had suffered a major setback in early 1963, when J.B. Kriplani, an independent, R. M. Lohia, a socialist, and Minoo Masani, a Swatantra candidate, had won the Parliamentary elections, defeating the Congress candidates. They were all, at that time ruthless critics of the Nehru government. The Kamaraj Plan was advertised as a method by which the Congress party would regain the confidence of the people, and tackle internal problems like food shortage, almost nil foreign reserves, communal tensions, and, above all, the tensions created in the aftermath of the defeat suffered at the hands of Chinese. Biju Patnaik, a Congress leader of Orissa, claimed that he was the author of this plan, and that he had discussed it with Nehru when the latter was on a holiday in Kashmir.[36] On the other hand, it has been alleged that it emerged from Kamaraj's discussion with Radhakrishnan during the latter's stay in the Rashtrapati Nilayam in Hyderabad, and that its real purpose was to remove Nehru as prime minister.[37] According to Kamaraj himself, although the plan came to be named after him, it was the Congress leadership and Nehru who were largely responsible for its formulation.[38] Nehru talking about the plan said, "it was an idea taking hold of the mind and growing by itself."[39]

The plan, on the face of it, required the resignations of the prime minister and all cabinet ministers, and thereafter undertaking full-time organizational work among the people to refurbish their party's dwindling image. According to one account, Kamaraj and others who formulated it with Radhakrishnan's connivance, expected that Kamaraj would be able to persuade Nehru to accept the plan by informing him that President Radhakrishnan would accept all the resignations except Nehru's and then ask the latter to form another government and carry on. But the actual plot, it is alleged, was to accept Nehru's resignation with alacrity as soon as it was tendered and eject him from the prime minister's office. However, this did not work. Whoever might have conceived it, Nehru himself asked Kamaraj to place the plan before the Congress Working Committee, which in its meeting held at Nehru's residence on August 8 and 9 accepted the plan with the modification that the services of Nehru as head of the government were indispensable, and, consequently, he would not have to resign till the country had resolved all difficulties.[40] The implication of this was that Nehru could accept any resignation that he liked and reject others.

According to one source, that Radhakrishnan had some interest in the Kamaraj Plan and eagerly awaited the outcome of the Congress Working Committee meeting held to discuss it, was supposed to have been demonstrated by his not going to sleep early that night as was his habit, and by his pacing up and down in his study and bedroom till late that night. When the news of the acceptance of the modified plan reached Radhakrishnan, he was apparently disappointed.[41] Some political observers have suggested that the plot to secure Nehru's resignation failed because Kamaraj revealed it to Nehru.[42] Others like H.N. Pandit and Marry C. Carras consider the story that Radhakrishnan and Kamaraj plotted to get rid of Nehru as prime minister to be "a fantastic tale," which "strains credulity, given the reputations for integrity of both Radhakrishnan and Kamaraj."[43] It would appear reasonable to agree with this and dismiss with contempt the allegation of the involvement of Radhakrishnan in any plot against Nehru. It would appear equally reasonable to reject the contention that Nehru used, if not also formulated, the Kamaraj Plan to regain his eroded supremacy by getting rid of his inconvenient rivals and critics along with some nonentities from the cabinet. It seems difficult to identify with certainty the idealists who first conceived this plan and the altruistic ends they intended to achieve through it.

After these happenings, while Radhakrishnan became more or less *persona non grata* with Nehru and their relations became cold and strained ever after, Kamaraj's relations with Nehru became very cordial and he became since that time a close confidant of Nehru.[44] Nehru used the Kamaraj Plan to restore his political power fully, by purging all his potential successors and critics from his cabinet. Among those so sacked were two of Radhakrishnan's favorites, K.L. Shrimali and B. Gopala Reddy, and also one of Nehru, Lal Bahadur Shastri, the man who actually succeeded him in 1964.[45]

Criticism of Government

Thereafter Radhakrishnan began to assert himself by criticizing the government openly. Addressing the first convocation of the Uttar Pradesh Agricultural University in November, 1963, he blamed the government for the stagnation of India's agriculture; and in his Republic Day broadcast in 1964 warning the country against complacency about corruption he said, "it would be well to recognize that tolerance of our society for a weak, inefficient and unclean administration is not unlimited." In private too, Radhakrishnan expressed a very poor opinion of the government and its foreign policy. He did not hesitate to make his views explicit.

Regarding India's policy of extending friendship to all nations he said that it resulted in friendship with none. As a result of this policy, he felt, India's relations with major powers like the USA depended on their mercy, with the USSR they could not rise above being just cordial; with China they were at their worst; with Britain, Germany, Japan and France they were at the level of mutual bargaining. The policy had resulted in a onesided friendship with the Asian and African countries, with the latter barely reciprocating India's gesture of friendship. Consequently, he felt that the policy of friendship with all had resulted in friendship with none. This, according to him was amply demonstrated during the Sino-Indian conflict, when none but Malaysia came to India's help in its hour of crisis.

With respect to the failure of the government to comprehend and punish the people responsible for India's debacle in the Sino-Indian conflict, he thought that the real culprits had escaped as the government, "searched for scapegoats." He felt that "The real culprits were the vast majority of the *Jee Huzurs*. They drew the wool over the eyes of those in power to harsh actualities. When the realities became too vivid, the courage of conviction and the character to own up to a mistake were lacking, barring a few. We built up tremendous propaganda clouds around and against people who failed to discharge their duties."[46]

Nehru, whose image and position became rather dim and weak respectively after the Sino-Indian conflict, could not do anything to prevent Radhakrishnan from making derogatory and critical statements against his government. Unlike the mild, gentle and accommodating Rajendra Prasad, Radhakrishnan became a devastating critic of the Nehru government.[47] One wonders whether it was proper for a constitutional president, whose position was analogous to that of the British monarch, to have launched upon what amounted to a campaign of public criticism of his own elected democratic government, headed by a prime minister almost solely responsible for his own elevation to the highest office.

Posthumous Tribute to Nehru

Nehru, who took pride in his good health, suffered a serious paralytic stroke affecting his left side on January 8, 1964. After he recovered from it, he once again started coming to Radhakrishnan whenever he had time. On such occasions they not only discussed the political problems, but also talked about philosophy and other things. On May 27, 1964, Nehru passed away at 1:44 p.m. In his public speeches Radhakrishnan described Nehru "as a man of many moods,"[48] who led "a life of great service and dedication."[49] Nehru, he said, was "a person of immense intellectual gifts and of genuine social passion. He was one of the greatest figures of our country, an outstanding statesman whose services in the cause of human freedom were unparalleled."[50] Nehru, he further said, "identified himself with the life of the people and tried to make their lives somewhat richer and fuller. He was great in spirit, and true greatness consists in the realization that one is born not for oneself, but for one's kind, one's neighbour and one's people."[51] He proclaimed Nehru as "One of the greatest figures of our generation, an outstanding statesman whose services to the cause of human freedom are unforgettable," who had during "the long years of his premiership tried to put the country on a progressive, scientific, dynamic and noncommunal basis."[52] Describing Nehru as "a great believer in world peace and the concept of one world community" he wrote, "[Nehru] had a love of liberty not merely for his own people, but for all people of the world. . . . He believed in the liberty of all without distinction of class, creed or country."[53] Appreciating Nehru's role in national integration he continued, "his [Nehru's] courage, wisdom and personality have held this country together."[54]

This seems to be Radhakrishnan's lifelong assessment of Nehru because even from his Moscow days he considered Nehru to be "a great and good man, but . . . surrounded by fools."[55]

XV.

The Presidency Part II

Radhakrishnan-Shastri Relations

Nehru's passing away gave Radhakrishnan an opportunity to rule the country directly by declaring "President's Rule," through exercise of his emergency powers, which would have been, according to one interpretation, in accordance with the Constitution of India.[1] Some political observers also believed that if he "had in fact proposed that the political leaders of all parties should be given a chance to catch their breath and refocus their plans and policies . . . [it] would have been almost unanimously accepted by Indian people and their political leaders."[2] But he did not do so, for he realized that he was in the historic situation of being the first president of India to interpret the constitution on the occasion of the first change of government and hence in a position to establish a precedent to be followed by future presidents. So instead of suspending the Parliament even for a brief period as provided by the constitution, he invited the most senior member of the cabinet and the then Home Minister Gulzari Lal Nanda to be the interim prime minister on the condition that he would have his party elect a leader who would then be installed as prime minister.[3] Nanda agreed to this and was sworn in as prime minister. In asking Nanda to be the acting prime minister, Radhakrishnan was practicing what he had preached to the governor of West Bengal, when B.C. Roy, the chief minister of the state, died. He had then suggested to the West Bengal governor, who had sought his advice, to appoint the most senior member of the cabinet as chief minister till the Congress Legislature party* elected a new leader.[4]

Though Nanda wanted to continue as prime minister for a few months before a new leader was elected and appointed prime minister, Radhakrishnan insisted that the election be held as soon as possible to avoid any intrigue and asked Kamaraj, the party president, to hold the meeting of the Congress Parliamentary party** immediately and let him

---

* The state wing of Congress Party
** The central wing of Coingress Party

have the name of the leader so elected within a week. The Congress Parliamentary party met on June 2, 1964, and elected Lal Bahadur Shastri (1904-1966) as its new leader. Radhakrishnan invited him to form a government the same afternoon, and he was sworn in as prime minister a week later. It is reported that Radhakrishnan treated Shastri, who was unsure of himself in the beginning of his term, with "unconstitutional sternness—indeed almost bullied him," but later on "a more confident Shastri virtually ignored Radhakrishnan."[5] That Shastri did not bother about Radhakrishnan was amply demonstrated when he accepted the resignation of T.T. Krishnamachari, the minister of finance in his cabinet, on the eve of his departure for Tashkent, despite Radhakrishnan's suggestion to take a final decision in this matter after his return from Tashkent.

The year 1965 was marked in the directive principles of the constitution as the year for the switch-over from English to Hindi, which had been accepted as the official language. So, in the beginning of 1965 some states in North India announced that they would send and receive all communications in Hindi. Irked by this, the South reacted violently for over a month, and the army had to be called out to control the situation. Property worth lakhs of rupees and many lives were lost in the agitations in the whole of South India. In this situation Radhakrishnan assumed the role of an ideological adviser and helped Shastri to overcome the crisis. Though Radhakrishnan himself had never learnt Hindi, he supported it as a national language. At the same time he understood the importance of English. Arguing that multiplicity of languages was neither an obstruction nor a threat to national unity or integration, he referring to India's past history said: "Even though different languages have been spoken in this country for centuries, its fundamental unity has not been impaired. The ideals of spiritual endeavour, righteous living and devotion are to be found in the literatures of various languages. The culture has been a progressive one, a dynamic one, one that has been renewing itself perpetually from the period of Ṛg Veda down to our times. Our culture has been assimilating the ideas in all the languages with which it has been brought into contact. Every creative writer picked up the past heritage and made it into the living present."[6] In his address to the Parliament on February 17, 1965, he "deplored" the acts of violence which had occurred and extended the government's deep sympathy to those who suffered. Announcing government policy on official language, which he had persuaded Shastri to accept, he said, "We wish to state categorically that the assurances given by the late Shri Jawaharlal Nehru and reaffirmed by our prime minister will be carried out without qualification and reservation. This is essentially for the unity of the country. While Hindi is the official language of the union, English will continue to be an associate official language. This will continue as long as the non-Hindi speaking people require it. We earnestly hope this will allay the apprehensions of the people and lead them to return to their normal work."[7] Thus Radhakrishnan, though himself a Southerner, not knowing Hindi, rose above regional politics on the official language issue. There was general agreement on the decisive role Radhakrishnan played in reaffirming the language policy as laid down by Nehru.

An incident revealing an aspect of Radhakrishnan's character may be mentioned. During the Indo-Pakistan conflict of 1965, for protection of the citizens of Delhi from air raids many trenches were dug throughout the city, so that people could take shelter in them whenever air raid sirens blared. In Rashtrapati Bhawan in the basement there were some cellars made during World War II. When advised to use them during Pakistani air raids, Radhakrishnan refused to do so saying he "preferred to die with his fellowmen breathing fresh air."[8]

Declaring that the conflict was thrust on India by Pakistan and asserting, "We have friendly feelings for the people of Pakistan," Radhakrishnan advised his countrymen that in the moments of anger "we have also to avoid any form of hatred of the people of Pakistan, who are our kith and kin. Friendship with them has always been our primary objective. It is not our desire to hurt Pakistan to save India. Our commitment to peace is well-known. We do not believe in any unbridgeable chasms. There are more things which bind us together than keep us apart. In this dreadful situation, let us have a few moments of introspection and make our spirit capable of compassion and sacrifice prevail."[9] Reporting the signing of the ceasefire pact and its implementation, and jubilant at the success of the military operation, he said, "We have today retrieved our prestige and it is my hope that our army, air force and navy will continue to function with daring, heroism and skill, and be treated as a force to be reckoned with."[10] But even on that occasion, the philosopher-statesman in Radhakrishnan expressed himself thus: "China and Pakistan are our neighbors and they should be persuaded to become our good and friendly neighbors. This is not impossible, difficult though it may seem today. We should work for that goal. *Dīrgham paśyata mā hraṣvam*. Look far ahead; do not be short-sighted."[11] But in private he appears to have expressed the view that India should have taken Lahore and not rested content with what it had achieved.[12] It is difficult even for a philosopher to consistently and completely overcome patriotic and nationalistic sentiments in a situation of war.

Prime Minister Shastri passed away in Tashkent at 2:02 a.m. on January 11, 1966, a few hours after signing an agreement with the president of Pakistan. Before his departure for Tashkent, Shastri was advised by Radhakrishnan that in his meeting with the president of Pakistan, "his attitude must be one of bringing people together, not breaking them; emphasizing the things which unite us, not emphasizing the things which separate us."[13] On January 3, 1966, on the eve of Shastri's departure for Tashkent, in a speech at Chandigarh, Radhakrishnan outlined his expectation of Shastri thus: "He goes [to Tashkent] with an open mind, with no prejudices. Any prejudice or any fanaticism is the opposite of the scientific spirit. If we want to adopt the spirit of science, we must rid our minds of prepossessions, of all fixed habits. Never have any rigid hypothesis. Fanaticism is the opposite of fellowship, falsehood is the opposite of truth. We must, therefore, adopt an attitude of mere scientific pursuit, not bother about our views and previews; we must go, seek each other, adopt a scientific habit of mind, know the realities and what are the facts of the whole, help in the betterment of humanity. That must be our endeavour. It is with that idea that our prime minister has left . . . . And I have no doubt he will do his best."[14] On the day Shastri passed away, conferring on him the Bharat Ratna award posthumously, Radhakrishnan said, "Lal Bahadur Shastri's case is an illustration of the strength of democracy in this country. From humble beginnings, without any advantage of birth, position or wealth, he rose to the highest position in the government of the country. It is due entirely to his force of character and integrity of life. These things enabled him to rise to the top. If democracy were not well-grounded in our conscience, in our minds and hearts, such a thing would have been difficult to achieve. . . . If we are to get any lesson from Lal Bahadur's life, it is to work in a detached way and an unattached way also, and work for unity, harmony and friendship among all peoples of the world."[15]

Advent of Indira Gandhi

In accordance with the convention that he himself had set after Nehru's demise, viz., of not keeping the office of the prime minister vacant even for a short duration, and filling it with the most senior member of the cabinet, Radhakrishnan immediately asked G.L. Nanda to be interim prime minister and swore him in. On January 19, when Mrs. Indira Gandhi was elected the new leader by the Congress Parliamentary party, he invited her to form the government. On January 24, she submitted a list of her council of ministers, when all of them were sworn in the same afternoon. In both cases a smooth transition of power was effected and Radhakrishnan played a historic role as the "guardian of constitutional continuity."

Abroad as President

President Radhakrishnan traveled extensively in India and in some foreign countries, not merely giving an account of the achievements of his government and explaining its policies, as heads of states do; but expounding Indian thought and culture, clarifying the concepts of democracy and justice and pleading for peace and harmony in India and in the world. But his foreign tours were far less in number than when he was vice-president. In May 1963 he went on a state visit to Afghanistan and Iran. In June of the same year he visited the United States of America and Britain. In September 1964 he went to the Soviet Union, and in September-October 1965 he undertook the last of his foreign tours when he visited Yugoslavia, Czechoslovakia and Ethiopia. On all these tours with his characteristic informal manners, simplicity and humanitarian approach, he won the hearts of all those he met. By his demeanor, eloquent speeches, philosophical wisdom and excellent understanding of contemporary problems, he enhanced India's prestige wherever he went. The impact that he made on his foreign audiences is best summed up in the following remark that Queen Farah of Iran made after listening to him in a banquet given in his honor during his visit to Iran: "I could have listened to him for hours. He explains complex ideas so clearly. His personality is so gentle and compelling, for once I could understand so much I never understood about Indian philosophy."[16]

Radhakrishnan's visit to the UK was the first ever visit of a head of a republican state within the Commonwealth. So, the queen took a personal interest in the details of his visit. She had already decided to award him the "Order of Merit." At Victoria Station where he was received by the queen, besides others, about 200 Indians living in the UK had gathered to welcome their president. According to protocol, after the reception and introduction of the dignitaries present, Radhakrishnan should have accompanied the queen to the gate, and then left for Buckingham Palace. But, Radhakrishnan, to everyone's surprise, completely unperturbed, and perhaps quite oblivious of the flutter he was causing by leaving the queen alone, walked up to the Indians gathered there and after responding with a *namaste* to their resounding cheers, came back to her. Though this was a breach of protocol, all those present including the conventional Englishmen were moved by the simplicity and naturalness with which he took note of his fellow countrymen.[17]

During Radhakrishnan's stay in England another interesting incident occurred. While he was returning from the Commonwealth Exhibition in London, he expressed a wish to go to his publishers. When the protocol officers remonstrated that such a visit was not scheduled, and that if he wanted to see the publishers, proper arrangements would have to be made and the publishers informed in advance of his arrival, he retorted, "Nonsense, tell the driver to drive to Allen and Unwin, and I should like to see Allen whom I know well." The car was diverted and the outriders informed. On arrival at the office of George Allen and Unwin, Radhakrishnan went up to Allen's room and knocked at the door. Allen almost fainted with surprise on seeing the president of India. Allen asked, "Why did you not inform me? I would have made proper arrangements." Radhakrishnan replied, "Never mind the arrangements. I have come to find out how my books are selling."[18]

During this visit, Queen Elizabeth invited him to stay with her and her family at Windsor Palace. When Radhakrishnan reached the palace, the queen was in a summer dress and ready to go to the races at Ascot. Radhakrishnan after greeting her said, "Hello, I see you are dressed for the races," and patted the children on the head. This was something which had never happened in the past, as the queen was not accustomed to being treated and addressed thus as one human being to another. Another surprise was in store for the queen when Radhakrishnan noticing the absence of Princess Anne at dinner told her, "I know you punished her." She was pleasantly taken aback by this behavior. But this made the relationship between the two cordial and the two were chatting pleasantly for long hours at private dinners as well as at public places.

Politically his visits to the UK and the USA were great successes, as he made a very favorable impression on both Prime Minister Macmillan and President Kennedy in particular, and on the people of the two nations in general. On that occasion, *The Daily Telegraph* paid the following tribute to Radhakrishnan:

No living head of the state in the world approaches his intellectual distinction. In his writing he has been the outstanding interpreter to the West of the thoughts of the East concerning the ultimate mystery of man. That such a man should have been elevated by a great people to the first place of its polity rather than one immersed in the controversies of politics is remarkable evidence that India sees society, of which the president is the supreme representative, as something greater than, and including the state.[19]

In Washington too, he left the indelible imprint of his personality. One of the noted political commentators wrote:

Time and again Radhakrishnan would turn to the same theme, that India is a model of democracy for Asia, and stands in stark contrast to mainland China's commitment to political dictatorship. The theme was stressed during two days of intensive discussions here with President Kennedy and Secretary of State Rusk.[20]

On his return, Radhakrishnan summed up the results of his visit in the following words:

We tried to do our best to tell them about our general policies of individual freedom, social justice and welfare, non-involvement in military blocs and also about our prime minister's leadership in consolidating the country and modernizing it. On the international situation, our policy is to work for peace, bring about a ban on nuclear test and work for disarmament without losing patience or hope. The essential conditions of peace are that colonialism must be ended as soon as possible, racial discrimination stopped, and emerging nations which are sunk in economic miseries should be assisted to grow and make themselves self-sufficient. Let other people deal with economic aid and military aid. That is not my concern. Mine was merely to create a climate of goodwill and friendliness and I tried to do what I could in that direction.[21]

In Ethiopia the Haile Selassie I University conferred on him, on October 12, 1965, the honorary degree of doctor of letters. On that occasion he said that inward awareness and outward compassion are the two fundamental principles of true religion. Consequently, to be really religious, "We must deepen our awareness and must extend the objects of our compassion till they embrace the whole university."[22] Speaking on the real function of a university he said:

A university is intended to promote not merely knowledge but wisdom . . . [Wisdom] is something which you acquire by the spending of a few moments in your life, when you recollect your thought, when you sink within yourself, get beneath to the layer of your mind, body, etc., and get into the very quick and nerve of your consciousness where the "Supreme" dwells. It is there that you get into contact with your own fundamental reality that dwells there. You will realise that all men are akin to each other and they form one family. Our duty today is to look upon others as members of one family for the pursuit of wisdom. Our own great prophet Gandhi said, "People say God is truth, I say, Truth is God." Even the atheist cannot deny it. He may deny God, he cannot deny the pursuit of truth. That is what a university stands for.[23]

Back home in India on February 5, 1964, Radhakrishnan who had already completed seventy-five years of his life underwent an operation for cataract. He was confined to bed for more than a fortnight. During this period Zakir Husain officiated as president. His eye operation was not totally successful. Consequently, his eyesight deteriorated.

Sahitya Akademi and Shimla Institute

In 1964, he was elected president of the Sahitya Akademi. He had been its vice-president since its inception in 1954. Nehru was its president and continued to be so till his death. Radhakrishnan took such keen interest in the affairs of the Akademi that he did not miss even a single meeting of its Executive Board.[24] He believed that creative writers alone can bring about a change in the society, and make the change acceptable to the people at large.[25] The function of literateurs is "to endow people with faith, to give them some cause to live for and to die for, . . . to give them that kind of impulse, that kind of urge, make them feel that life is worth living and not merely to be thrown away. Its purpose is not merely to produce stability, but to produce a ferment, to produce a kind of confusion of mind from which they will be able to rise to the achievement of some proper goal and purpose."[26]

It was due to his insight and initiative that the Indian Institute of Advanced Study was established in Shimla. Soon after taking over as president, he started looking for a place where an Institute of Advanced Study, on the pattern of the Institute at Princeton could be established. On investigation, he found that Rashtrapati Niwas at Shimla, which was the summer capital of the British and was meant for the use of the president was actually visited by presidents during the fifteen years after independence for just one hundred and twenty days, i.e., for about eight days a year.[27] He was also informed that a huge expenditure was incurred by the government in maintaining the establishment. He discussed the matter with Jawaharlal Nehru and persuaded him to put it "to a more useful purpose than merely the pastime of the president." Justifying the stress on humanities as "necessary and very essential," in his inaugural address on October 20, 1965 he said, "humanities . . . enable us to expand our consciousness, to transcend, to make us understand clearly what it is we are attempting to do."[28] Talking about the importance of men in building the Institute he warned, "Let me tell you, whether this Institute prospers, grows, succeeds or not depends on the men who participate in it."[29] He expressed his idea of the future and the purpose of the Institute thus, " . . . we should not merely rest on our laurels, think we have got a beautiful building, a climate which is suitable for high intellectual endeavours, but we should try to collect men of merit from all parts of the world and try to see to it that our education itself improves."[30]

Honor from Pope

In December 1964 Pope Paul VI, on the first ever visit of any Pope to India, conferred on Radhakrishnan the Vatican's highest honor for a head of a state, the 'De Equestrine Ordine Militae Auratae' (Knight of the Golden Army of Angels).

Hosting Foreign Statesmen

During his tenure as president, Radhakrishnan received a large number of heads of states and other visiting dignitaries to India. Among them were President Brezhnev of USSR, the king of Laos, the pertuan of Malaysia, the king of Greece, President Luebke of the Federal German Republic, the president of Bulgaria, Lebanon, Mexico, Poland and Rumania, President Tito of Yugoslavia, Archbishop Makarios of Cyprus, Prime Minister Tunku Abdul Rehman of Malaysia, Prime Minister Ikeda of Japan, Mrs. Srimavo Bandarnaika of Ceylon, Wing Commander Ali Sabry of the United Arab Republic, Prime Minister Michel Debre of France and Prime Minister Diefenbaker of Canada, Earl Attlee, British Commonwealth Secretary, Duncan Sandys, Pakistan's Foreign Minister Zulfikar Ali Bhutto and King Mahendra of Nepal.[31] An example of how fearlessly and frankly he talked with visiting dignitaries was indicated in his reply to Brezhnev, who referring to Carl Chessman's case mused, "Justice in America does not take a correct course" and Radhakrishnan responded, "I do not know where justice takes a correct course."[32]

Radhakrishnan-Mrs. Gandhi Relations

Commenting on the election of Mrs. Indira Gandhi, whom he regarded as his niece and who attended his lectures in Oxford in the 1930s, he is reported to have said, "With all the problems that India faces, she now has the most beautiful prime minister in the world. At least everyday papers will carry to us in the mornings a beautiful picture."[33] In the early period of her prime ministership, Mrs. Gandhi heeded Radhakrishnan's advice. For instance, he could persuade her to let Nanda continue as home minister. He in turn helped Mrs. Gandhi in bringing Ashok Mehta to the cabinet, despite Congress party President Kamaraj's opposition to it, on the ground that he was a new entrant to the party. But, soon the relationship between the two cooled off. Most probably this started from the time he sensed that she was not inclined to have him as president for a second term, and she, on her part, felt he was treating her as a student and often giving her gratuitous advice.

It would appear that in private conversations Radhakrishnan conveyed that he valued the pursuit of truth more than the highest office in the country and that he preferred an academic environment and living in college rooms to working with politicians and living in Rashtrapati Bhawan. It is reported that he used to say to his friends and acquaintances "What is a president after all? Anyone nearing seventy-five and who has lost his will power is fit enough to be the president of India!"[34] During his state visit to the UK in 1965 he visited Oxford. Naturally he traveled from London to Oxford in a luxurious saloon. In Oxford he preferred to spend the night in the room he had occupied during his tenure there, and not in the more comfortable saloon. To Indian High Commissioner Chagla, who was accompanying him, he explained: "I am happier in this room, moving about in an academic atmosphere than as president in Rashtrapati Bhawan with its glamour and prestige."[35] Nevertheless, there is evidence that he would have liked to continue as president for a second term.

As the year 1966 was coming to a close it became clear that Kamaraj and a number of important members of the Congress party and some opposition parties would support Radhakrishnan's candidature for a second term, while Mrs. Gandhi was not in favor of it. In the general elections for Parliament in February 1967, the Congress party under Mrs. Gandhi's leadership came back to power with a considerably reduced majority in the Parliament and loss of a number of states to the opposition. In this situation some opposition parties were considering putting up their own candidate for the presidency. In the Congress party there was no unanimity with regard to its candidate. Some congressmen favored having Radhakrishnan again on the ground that he was a fair and impartial person, a scholar-statesman known all over the world, and one whose democratic and secular credentials were not doubted by any section of the Indian people. Other congressmen thought it was better to have a change as (in their opinion) he was old and ailing, as he had been vice-president and president altogether for fifteen years, and as Vice-President Zakir Husain, being an eminent educator, a consistent nationalist from a minority community and a person of the highest integrity, was an excellent candidate for the highest office. The supporters of "Radhakrishnan Again" line also reportedly argued that the nation was not yet ready to have a Muslim as president and that, consequently, Husain's nomination might divide the Congress party while uniting the opposition against him.

The supporters of Husain's candidature within the Congress party, led by Prime Minister Mrs. Gandhi herself, thought it was high time to have a person from the minorities as president, as that would satisfy "an important religious stratum" of the country, as earlier having Radhakrishnan was satisfactory to "an important geographical part" of the country.[36] Moreover, this (the latter group also thought) would demonstrate to the world that India was not only democratic, but also secular. Some have also surmised that Mrs. Gandhi "felt uncomfortable with Radhakrishnan who, she feared, might one day exercise the inherent and undefined powers of the president to dismiss the ministry and assume control of the nation's affairs."[37] It may be conjectured that as Mrs. Gandhi knew the relationship between Radhakrishnan and her father in the post-Sino-Indian conflict period, and her father's account of the reasons for it, and as she must have also heard some accurate and some fabricated reports of Radhakrishnan's assessment of her father's rule, as well as hers, she concluded that it was safer to have someone else as president, especially as one who was not only the vice-president, but also a distinguished and reliable person, and, above all, a Muslim, was readily available.

It is reported that in view of the prime minister's stand, the supporters of "Radhakrishnan Again" line put forward as a compromise that

Radhakrishnan might be reelected with a private understanding that midway during the second term he would retire of his own accord enabling Husain to succeed him without the risk of an election. This was not acceptable to Mrs. Gandhi.[38]

Critical Speeches

As already said, by the end of 1966 it became known that Mrs. Gandhi was not in favor of Radhakrishnan's reelection, and no one could be sure of becoming the president without the prime minister's support. On January 25, 1967, on the eve of the Republic Day, and on the eve of the fourth general elections in February 1967, Radhakrishnan's address to the nation had portions like the following which were highly critical of the government and which, many understood, favored a change in it:

> Charges of corruption are frequently made against people at all levels of government, central and state. Immediate disposal of these charges is essential. If the charges are false, their falsehood should be exposed. If there is any basis for them, this should be admitted and rectified. Such admission will enhance the prestige of the government. . . . We cannot forgive widespread incompetence and the gross mismanagement of our resources.[39]

To political leaders, whom he in an earlier speech had described as persons tormented by "greed and personal ambitions," he gave this advice: "Our political leaders should have a clear vision of the future of the country and not be content with their own individual comfort and survival."[40] Stating that "We treated some of us as more equal than others, and denied to the majority the right for self-development," and that "internal differences are crippling our democracy as sectional interests and regional pressures are increasing," he admonished: "all public questions require to be decided on principles of justice and equality and not as a result of pressure politics and such other methods as blackmail."[41] He concluded his address thus:

> The pursuit of wisdom has attracted me for many years. Whatever my other preoccupations may have been, this search has been my main inspiration. Even in public activities, I have tried my best to apply ethical considerations to the solution of our problems. I have had understanding from those with whom I worked, the President Rajendra Prasad and the three Prime Ministers, Jawaharlal Nehru, Lal Bahadur Shastri and Shrimati Indira Gandhi, as well as from representatives of all parties. The goodwill

and affection that I enjoyed from the people has been much more than I ever earned or deserved. It is my earnest hope that the country will be vigilant and ever-renewing and vibrant with idealism and relevance to modern life.[42]

Many political interpreters felt that this sounded as if it were a farewell address.

On April 10, 1967, as expected, the Congress party's nomination of Zakir Husain as its candidate for the presidency was announced. On the same day newspapers published Radhakrishnan's statement issued on the previous day:

> Some months ago I indicated clearly my desire to retire from office. Since then, after the results of the general elections and the formation of governments of different complexions in the states, many leaders of various parties have been urging me to reconsider my position in view of the difficult times through which we are passing. Recent developments in connection with the two highest offices in the country have made me most unhappy and strengthened my resolve to retire. I hope all those who have sought to persuade me to continue in office will understand, and I wish the next president success.[43]

Zakir Husain won the election and was sworn in as president on May 13. In his inaugural address on assuming office as president of India, Zakir Husain described Radhakrishnan as one of "the most distinguished sons of India" who "brought to the presidency a mental equipment, a degree of erudition and a wealth of experience rarely to be found anywhere. During a lifetime devoted to the pursuit of knowledge and truth, he has done more than probably any other man to bring out and explain Indian philosophical thought and the oneness of all true spiritual values. He has never lost his faith in the essential humanity of man and himself has never ceased to champion the right of all men to live in dignity and with justice."[44]

In his farewell speech to the members of parliament on May 7, 1967, Radhakrishnan exhorted politicians to identify themselves with the lowest of the lowly, and urged them to do their utmost to alleviate the suffering of humanity and to raise their material conditions. He edified them further:

> Politics should not absorb all our life; it is indispensable but not the whole life. Our spiritual strength, our intellectual achievement and artistic experi-

ence, these have contributed to the greatness of our country. All those who are patriotic must know not only the politics of the country but also of the greatness of our endeavour in all these different fields. It is my hope that we shall try to understand the true spirit of our country and be able to transform the spiritual vision into practical reality.[45]

Farewell

In his farewell address to the nation on May 12, Radhakrishnan reaffirmed his faith in the spirit of India:

The culture which we have inherited is an ancient one and it has faced many waves of invasion of Yavanas, Sakas, Hunas, Pathans and Mongolas, among others and is still enduring. It is not only the quality of antiquity—*prācinatā*—but also of enduring vitality—*mṛtyunjayata*—which has enabled it to last all these centuries. The secret of this staying power is the quality of tolerance and understanding. The saints and sages have been the great integrators of our society. They humanize the universe by humanizing man. . . . We are going through a period of doubt and uncertainty but such periods often occurred in our past history. We require a good deal of patience and wisdom to make effective contribution to our age. We have to chart our course by the distant stars and not by the dim street lights.[46]

Last Years

On May 13, 1967, after laying down office in the forenoon, he left for Madras in the afternoon by a special train. In Madras he lived in "Girija," 30, Edward Elliots Road, the house he had built in 1936. After his retirement he did not involve himself in politics and was completely involved in pursuing his favorite pastime, reading. The two public speeches he made after his retirement were in 1968. One of them was on the occasion of his receiving the fellowship of the Sahitya Akademi, the other was when Bharatiya Vidya Bhawan conferred on him the title *Brahmavidyā Bhāskara*.[47]

His health deteriorated faster than was expected. He suffered a stroke in September 1968, and after that he could express himself only in monosyllables. But, he continued to read voraciously. Whenever he read anything distressing about the political or economic situation in India, he would only utter, "Oh! my poor Indira."[48]

A year later in 1969 cataract problems again started troubling him. He underwent an eye operation, but it was not very successful. As a result he could not read and write. In 1973 a fall resulted in a hip fracture. He had to be in a nursing home for a fortnight. Then, he suffered a major cerebral stroke on June 22, 1974, and was admitted to a nursing home from where he was discharged on July 30. He had to be readmitted to a nursing home on August 19 for gastrointestinal bleeding where he remained till he passed away. In February 1975 he became the first non-Christian to be awarded the Templeton Foundation Prize for Religion valued at £ 40,000. He suffered repeated cardiac arrests from April 6, 1975 onwards. On the morning of April 16, 1975 his condition suddenly deteriorated further. He was pronounced critically ill, was put on oxygen and drugs and fluids were administered to him intravenously. Thereafter his condition was constantly monitored, but in spite of it, it gradually worsened. Finally, the end came at 12:45 a.m. on April 17, 1975. He was cremated the same day at the Mylapore cremation ground after a state funeral. The nation went into a period of seven-day mourning.

Posthumous Tributes

The prime minister of India, Indira Gandhi, in her tribute said, "Radhakrishnan's scholarship was phenomenal in its range and it was not of the ivory tower variety." In a message to his son S. Gopal and the other family members, she described Radhakrishnan as, "one of the most brilliant exponents of our philosophy, striving untiringly to explain that India's message was a positive one—not flight from life but action, action unattached to its fruits. His inspiring eloquence made people aware of the human heritage and enabled us to reaffirm our faith in future." Describing his role as a statesman, she continued, "As a statesman he had a deep understanding of the practical problems of nation-building. He contributed significantly to the consolidation of our political and parliamentary tradition." Queen Elizabeth in her condolence message recalled the love Radhakrishnan had for Oxford University and said, "I am sure that his many friends and admirers in the University will feel a great sense of loss today." Sheikh Mujibur Rahman described him "as a profound scholar, statesman and humanist who made an enduring contribution to the rich spiritual heritage of India." V.V. Giri described him as "an *Ajātaśatru*, loved and respected by everyone without distinction of caste, colour, creed or race." Jayaparkash Narayan said Radhakrishnan has "bestowed upon humanity a fund of wisdom to guide future generations."

The *Daily Telegraph* in a tribute to Radhakrishnan in its obituary column wrote, "No living head of the state could approach the intellectual distinction of Dr. Radhakrishnan. Aside from political services, he was a world famous philosopher and a pioneer interpreting Eastern thoughts to the West." The *Indian Express* in its editorial wrote, "Dr. Sarvepalli Radhakrishnan showed that a commoner could combine the 'Spirit and Power of philosophy' with political judgement and acumen. With his death one of the nation's rare moulds has been broken." In its editorial *The Statesman* wrote, "Radhakrishnan was not a political leader in the usual sense of the term. . . . It was not only in private that he gave forthright advice. When he thought that a situation required plain speaking in public, he never hesitated to provide it." *The Hindustan Times* in its obituary, matter of factly, wrote, "Very few leaders of modern India combined the scholarship and statesmanship, the philosophy and patriotism displayed by Dr. Sarvepalli Radhakrishnan."

XVI.

Reflections on His Thought

During his lifetime and even today there are some philosophers who hold the view that Radhakrishnan cannot be considered to be a philosopher in the real sense of the term. Their chief argument is that he did not propound any 'ism' distinct from the prevalent systems of thought. They at the most are willing to call him a historian of philosophy; or a chronicler of "Indian Thought." In this, too, some of them think that he has misinterpreted or misunderstood the texts of Indian philosophy. They allege that his expositions are not faithful to the texts; and that he has read into them Western ideas. Regarding his comprehension of religions other than Hinduism some of his critics feel that he had "almost total lack of understanding of, and feeling for, Christian theological categories."[1] They allege that when he writes about Christianity he writes about "what seems to him to be Christianity . . . and not with Christianity as Christians understand it."[2] The consequence of this kind of interpretation of Christianity is that it "gives a slightly hollow ring to his statement that the meeting of East and West may pave the way for unity 'if mutual appreciation takes the place of cold criticism and patronizing judgement.' "[3] So, some among Eastern and Western scholars have charged him with being faithful neither to Hinduism nor to Christianity. They also feel that he almost totally ignored Islamic and Chinese philosophies and religions. Even in his writings on Hinduism, they allege, he has paid scant attention to the causes of historical conflicts within it and highlighted its universal character alone.

One of the earliest scholars who has done so was Leonard Woolf[4] who in 1935 stated that while Radhakrishnan was a writer of "considerable intellectual power," he used his capability "to decorate this [the kind of mysticism indigenous and endemic in the Asiatic mind during the last two thousand years] sterile oriental mysticism with the flowers and purity of western rationalism."[5] He thought that Radhakrishnan added nothing to Indian or Western mysticism. He further argued that Radhakrishnan just started his exposition with "a categorical statement about intuition

185

and direct perception and their infallibility for providing us with absolute metaphysical truth."[6] Radhakrishnan's philosophy, he said, is "an extreme form of intellectual quackery," "a revolt against reason." He holds 'intellectual quackery' at par with 'metaphysical quackery' by which he means "abandonment of and contempt for reason as a means to truth in nonpolitical speculation and the substitution for it of so called intuition, magic and mysticism."[7] To prove his point, namely, that Radhakrishnan's philosophy falls in the region of metaphysical quackery he challenged the infallibility of the intuitive method adopted by the latter.

Woolf argues that the leap made by Radhakrishnan from saying that "I have a direct and immediate experience of the fact that the universe is good, spiritual and in some sense personal" to have a direct and immediate experience of the fact that the universe is good, spiritual and in some sense personal" is unjustified. He says:

"But who is this 'we'? I personally have no such experience and, what is more I do not even understand what is meant by the extraordinarily vague statement that "the universe is in some sense personal." There are thousands of persons in the same mental condition as myself; yet the statement implies that everyone has a direct perception of these metaphysical truths. . . . But when Sir S. Radhakrishnan says: "I have a direct perception that the universe is good, spiritual, and in some sense personal," he is making a statement which may or may not be of psychological interest, which is capable of neither test nor proof, and which has no scientific, intellectual, spiritual, or metaphysical interest or importance. All that one can say of it is that it may or may not be true. But when instead of saying "I," Sir S. Radhakrishnan says "We," and implies that "We,' means "everyone," and further that the direct perception of everyone that the universe is good is a guarantee that the universe is good, then we are in the region of pure metaphysical quackery.[8]

Woolf's conclusion was that the contents of Radhakrishnan's statements are unknowable and incommunicable. Therefore, according to him, Radhakrishnan was a "force destroying civilisation."[9]

In reply to the above sort of criticism there are other scholars who maintain that the position of Radhakrishnan was based upon experience and logic. One of the earliest philosophers who accepted and lauded Radhakrishnan's way of philosophizing was C.E.M. Joad.[10] In 1933, analysing An Idealist View of Life, Joad showed that Radhakrishnan ably reformulated the ontological argument and showed that human religious aspirations are grounded in reality, because they are the outcome of action between human beings and the environment in which they are interplaced. Human beings, according to him, are "part and parcel of the process of nature." So their religious aspirations as they "point to some feature in the universe which provokes and corresponds to them," guarantees their fulfillment.[11] In other words, religious aspirations are at least in part objectively valid because they are the result of interaction between the self and the objective world, external to it. As such they give human beings the assurance that something other than them exists.[12] Joad accepts Radhakrishnan's contention that like science and sense experience the deepest religious convictions give human beings trustworthy knowledge of ultimate reality. This in Joad's words is "a simple statement of psychological fact."[13] Joad concludes that "by means of a positive system of metaphysics and a consequential doctrine of ethics," Radhakrishnan has sought to answer questions concerning religious experience.[14]

In the light of his own philosophy and experience, as well as by invoking the religious insight of the East, Joad declares, Radhakrishnan has confirmed "by the light of the spirit the practical ethics which we in the West have hammered out by the experimental methods of science."[15] So Radhakrishnan has been hailed by him as "a bridge builder" and "a liaison officer" between East and West. Joad characterized Radhakrishnan's contribution in the world of philosophy as "counter attack from the East."

Others like E.S. Brightman and George P. Conger have evaluated Radhakrishnan as one of the "greatest philosophers of mysticism in modern times,"[16] and as "one who has surpassed the personalists in his philosophy of spirit and rivalled the pragmatists in promulgating a philosophy of life."[17] The Times Literary Supplement of May 3, 1934 hailed Radhakrishnan "not merely as the distinguished exponent of a lofty spiritual philosophy (as he assuredly is), but as the initiator of a new synthesis." It is interesting that while for J.H. Muirhead, Bergson and Radhakrishnan were "leaders of thought in Europe and India,"[18] for Leonard Woolf they were to be ranked among "intellectual quacks."[19] In our opinion, Radhakrishnan is undoubtedly an eminent philosopher of our time and the foremost among those produced by Indian universities.

In reply to those who criticize him for relying on intuition Radhakrishnan's answer was that philosophy is "the pursuit of wisdom" and "not an intellectual pastime." Philosophy, according to him, "is intensely practical, being a way of life, an enterprise of the spirit. It is a human effort to comprehend the problem of universe, or determine the nature of reality and so subject to the influence of race and culture."[20] He did not undermine the importance of 'conceptual knowing' for two reasons. *One*, 'conceptual knowing' is a preparation and necessity for intuitive insight.[21] *Second*, one's integral experience or vision has to be expressed, explained and communicated to others, because philosophy, according to him, does not merely aim at an integral experience but also at "an exhibition of insights." For such an exhibition or exposition, logical proof has to be employed so that others may be convinced of the truths seen in visions.[22]

It is true that Radhakrishnan did not profess any new 'ism'. He did not even try to build any entirely new system of philosophy. He more or less devoted himself to the clarification or reinterpretation of what has already been said. According to him, "All great teachers restate the teachings of their former masters. They do not lay claim to be original but affirm that they are but expounding the ancient Truth. It is the final norm by which all teachings are judged."[23] Radhakrishnan did so more or less in all his works in general, and particularly so in his translations of and commentaries on the four basic works, *Dhammapada, Principal Upaniṣads, Gītā* and *Brahmasūtra*. He thought that significant works like these have "to be understood by each generation in relation to its own problems."[24]

Though he believed that we must study our ancestors, for him "traditional continuity is not mechanical reproduction; it is creative transformation, an increasing approximation to the idea of truth. Life goes on not by repudiating the past but by accepting it and weaving it into the future in which the past undergoes a rebirth."[25]

Describing the main aim of his writings, which he kept throughout in his mind while reinterpreting the works of the *Ācāryas*, he wrote:

> In my writings my main contention has been to make out that there is one perennial and universal philosophy which is found in all lands and cultures, in the seers of the *Upaniṣads* and the Buddha, Plato and Plotinus, in Hillel and Philo, Jesus and Paul and the medieval mystics of Islam. It is this spirit which binds continents and unites the ages that can save us from the meaninglessness of the present situation, and not any local variant of it which we find in the Indian tradition. It is absurd to speak of any Indian monopolies of philosophic wisdom.[26]

Though Radhakrishnan essentially emerges as an exponent of the Indian philosophical tradition, he cannot be described as a "mere interpreter," as he tried to interpret Indian wisdom in a way and in an idiom that was relevant to the time he was writing in. While he tried to avoid all "conjectural interpretations," he strove not to confuse objectivity with unimaginativeness. He believed that the thinkers of the past had "profundity of mind and motive which we ourselves possess," and claimed that in his writings he had creatively interpreted their thought. In his writings he sometimes questioned, criticized and doubted the teachings of the ancient seers. Though he admitted that in his writings he commended the general spirit of Śankara's philosophy, yet on many essential issues he developed his thought on independent lines. His endeavor was "to expound a philosophy not to state a dogmatic theology, a philosophy which offers an interpretation of the universe, which is at once rational and spiritual, which depends on logical reflection and not on acts of faith."[27] One may say his method was not merely historical and critical, but hermeneutical.

Radhakrishnan declared himself to be a "modernist" who gave a modern interpretation of ancient Indian values and texts in a manner that preserved "whatever is valuable in our ancient heritage and discarding whatever is not of value."[28] He admitted there were many things in tradition which had to be discarded and a number of others which are vital and sustaining.

Some critics alleged that Radhakrishnan was not faithful to the texts, while others held that he had misunderstood and misinterpreted them. While it is quite possible that when a man had written so much he might have erred in a number of cases, it is difficult to believe that there are any major mistakes or deliberate misinterpretations in his writings. His *Indian Philosophy*, Volume I, was read in manuscript and proofs by J.S. Mackenzie, V. Subrahmanya Aiyar and A.B. Keith. The first edition of Volume II of that book was read in manuscript and proofs by V. Subrahmanya Aiyar, J.S. Mackenzie and A.B. Keith; and for its second edition he got "valuable suggestions" from M. Hiriyanna, and "valuable advice" from Mahamahopadhyayas S. Kuppuswami Sastri and N.S. Anantkrishna Sastri. It is in this volume that developed systematic philosophy is dealt with, and some of the best available authorities then read its manuscript, proofs and first edition and made suggestions and comments, which he utilized. The proofs of his translations and commentaries of the scriptures were read by Suniti Kumar Chatterjee and Siddheswar Bhattacharya. It is unlikely that these great scholars did not locate and point out to him the mistakes and misinterpretations in them, if there had been any; and improbable that he did not care to remove them when they were brought to his notice.

While Radhakrishnan admitted that he admired great masters, "ancient and modern, Eastern and Western," had learnt a great deal from

them, and was influenced by their teachings, he asserted that he was neither "a follower of any, accepting his teaching in its entirety" nor his
thought complied with "any fixed traditional pattern." He claimed that
his thought "proceeded from my own experience, which is not quite the
same as what is acquired by mere study and reading. It is born of spiritual experience rather than deduced from logically ascertained premises."[29]
About his works he said: "I have tried to communicate my insight into
the meaning of life."[30]

According to Radhakrishnan himself, and others as well, *An Idealist View of Life* is his major philosophical work. In this book understanding philosophy as "conceptual knowing" which leads to, and is preparatory
for an "intuitive insight," he classified idealism into three types: (1) epistemological or subjective; (2) ontological or objective, which may appear
in pluralistic forms e.g. personalism; or monistic forms; and (3) axiologi-
cal or valuational. For the first type of idealism whatever is real in the
universe is such stuff as ideas are made of. The term "idea" is taken as a
particular mental image peculiar to each individual. In the second type
also whatever is real in the universe is such stuff as ideas are made of, as
in the first type, the difference being that here the term 'idea' is taken as
quality of the existent shareable by other existents, and knowable by
other minds. The third type emphasizes the worth of things rather than
their knowability or nature. A thing is a 'meaning' or a 'purpose'. An idea
is an 'operative creative force'; 'the principle involved in a thing' and the
'purpose' of the being of a thing. According to the third type of idealism,
"the world is intelligible only as a system of ends." An idealist of this type
holds that the world is purposive. In his work Radhakrishnan rejected the
first two types of idealism which regard as their core either the mind-
dependent nature of reality or the internality of relations, and have been
accepted by the idealist philosophers of the West. He upheld the third
type of idealism which interprets ideas as ideals or values.

Radhakrishnan considered himself to be an idealist of the type who
asks the question "what is the idea?" In the sense "what is the purpose of
its being, for its acting?" or "Does reality depend on minds?" The core of
his argument was the claim that the universe is not a blind process but a
teleological one and that the course of evolution is not accidental and
haphazard but in some way expresses a purpose. He tried to show that
though this view of idealism underlay the teachings of the greatest philosophers, prophets and saints in the East as well as in the West, and was
the undercurrent in Indian and European philosophical systems, which

on the surface appeared to be so widely different, there was a need for a fresh statement of idealism as it had, due to changed circumstances in the world, to reckon with the new challenges generated by natural, social and human sciences. He also analyzed naturalism, atheism, agnosticism, skepticism, humanism, pragmatism and modernism which offer a substitute for religion to the dissatisfied spirit of modern man, and showed that they also failed to satisfy the intellect of modern man even as much as many religions did.

Radhakrishnan contended that man can only be satisfied when he recognizes the spirit in him as the highest reality and value. This knowledge, according to him, could be attained by intuition alone. Intuition is not opposed to the intellect, but is its completion, perfection or consummation. It gives an integral view of life and reality, and is a true and abiding source of the true and enduring religions of the world. He presented his thesis not as a "prophet" who "sets forth some new fangled paradox," but merely as a point of view which "constitutes the very essence of the great philosophic tradition of idealism." To support his claim he gave apt quotations from great philosophers, poets, scientists, prophets, saints, preachers, politicians, atheists and skeptics of the world which made his work attractive to many, scarcely boring to any, and offensive to none.

An Idealist View of Life strikes a sympathetic chord in most readers irrespective of whether they are Christians, Hindus, Buddhists, Taoists, Sufis, or even if they do not follow any religion. It presents Radhakrishnan's thinking on religion and philosophy at its best, and also shows the extent of his own contribution to philosophy.

Whereas Radhakrishnan's *An Idealist View of Life* is mostly metaphysical, his *Religion and Society* is predominantly ethical. In it, unlike in his previous work in which he had depicted an idealized Hindu society, he presents a realistic picture of it. He is quite frank and outspoken in showing up the defects in Hindu social institutions. He advocates in unequivocal terms the need for the reformation of Hindu society.

The caste system, *Religion and Society* admits, had led to the "humiliation of the lower classes," had prevented the development of "homogeneity" and "the organic wholeness and the sense of common obligation" among the Hindus.[31] Strongly pleading for the abolition of the caste system, he declared that the issue of the removal of any discrimination against the lower castes "is a question not of justice or charity, but of atonement. Even when we have done all that is in our power, we shall not have atoned even for a small fraction of our guilt in this matter."[32]

In this book, while favoring monogamy, Radhakrishnan says that while it is "assumed" to be "natural," "It is not quite so simple. We have passions. Fidelity, though essential, is not easy." "If love without marriage is illegal," he concludes, "marriage without love is immoral."[33] Advocating a change in the Hindu law to permit divorce "where married life is absolutely impossible," he argues: "For two people to remain together in unhappiness, because they have entered into a bond which only death can break, is a sin against the best in us. It sometimes blasts the soul. It is better for the children that unhappy parents should not live together. Our laws make havoc of our domestic intimacies, in deference to dogmas we no longer respect."[34]

Disagreeing with Mahatma Gandhi that self-restraint is the most moral way for birth control, Radhakrishnan wrote, ". . . control of births by abstinence is the ideal, and yet the use of contraceptives cannot be altogether forbidden. . . . It is wrong to think that sexual desire in itself is evil, and that virtue consists in dominating and suppressing it on principle. . . . Men and women want each other as much as they want children. To remove from the lives of masses of men and women their one pleasure would be to produce an enormous amount of physical, mental and moral suffering."[35]

In this work Radhakrishnan criticizes communism as a way of life to be intellectually inadequate and its assumptions unsatisfactory. He admits that the communist emphasis on economic conditions is correct, but feels that "the suggestion that they are exclusively determinant of history is incorrect."[36] Marx, according to him, identifies "objective dialectic"—the way in which matter behaves, with the "subjective dialectic," its reflection in consciousness, without offering any proof for it. Dialectics cannot be regarded as an explanation for the development in nature and social reality. It can at the most be regarded "as a method of interpretation." Communism also fails, according to him, to appreciate the value of individuality. In it there is no place for individual action or initiative. It reduces the individual to just a moment in the universal historical process. But if we look at the history of the world we find that "all progress is due to the initiation of new ideas by exceptionally endowed individuals. Without intellectual freedom, there would have been no Shakespeare or Goethe, no Newton or Faraday, no Pasteur or Lister."[37] Asserting his faith in the supremacy of the individual as compared to the nation or society he wrote, "there is nothing final or eternal about states or nations which wax and wane. But the humblest individual has the spark of spirit in him which the mightiest empire cannot crush. Rooted in one life, we are all fragments of the divine, sons of immortality, *amṛtasya putrāḥ*."[38]

During the period of his vice-presidency and presidency Radhakrishnan in his numerous speeches had spoken on a number of contemporary issues. The concepts of secularism, democracy, equality (both political and economic) etc. received from him a good deal of attention, bringing forth a number of inspired utterances.

He rejected the concept of secularism which upheld that it meant neglect of religion or indifference to religion. He gave a positive definition of secularism as an attitude of "respect for all religions; respect for all faiths . . . respect for everything which a human being holds sacred."[39] Secularism, according to him, is based on the understanding that "the aim of religion is the realization of the Supreme and every pathway to it has to be recognised, validated and appreciated."[40] It, therefore, implies that, "we care for religion so intensely that we believe that everyone who is seeking the Divine, whatever pathways he adopts, is to be extended some kind of appreciation and encouraged to go forward."[41] A truly secular person or society, according to him, is one which respects "whatever is held sacred by any other individual." His definition of secularism is in tune with what some Indian sages and saints taught. Often he referred to this saying of a Sikh guru: *mandira masjid tere dhām īśvara allāh tere nām*, which means that the same God dwells in temple and mosque, and is addressed by the different names of *Īśvara* and *Allāh*.[42] His definition has been generally accepted in India.

The concept of democracy, he believed, had its basis in "the sanctity of the individual, the divine possibilities which he has," and its essence in "consideration for others."[43] The prerequisite of a democratic society is an attitude "of respect to each individual as sacred, as an embodiment of the Supreme, and never to regard ourselves as the only repositories of the ultimate truth."[44] Democracy, he said, "is toleration of differences, it is accepting the variety of the world as something to be encouraged and not as something to be destroyed or obliterated."[45] Democracy for him was "not merely a political arrangement," but a moral commitment—"a commitment to hope, to the advancement of the human race, to the future development of human beings."[46]

Radhakrishnan considered all talk of democracy, and all discussion of freedom meaningless and phony unless it led to the establishment of an equitable and just social order. He insisted that "we must purge our society of man-made inequalities and injustices, and provide all men and women opportunities for personal well-being and development."[47] Without bothering about what system a society or nation may adopt, he advocated a system in which wealth is not concentrated in the hands of a few. He considered increase in wealth and its equitable distribution to be important, and between the two the latter more important than the former.[48] He called for a "socialist reconstruction of society," by which he meant a reconstruction of society in such a way that it would "bridge the differences between the rich and the poor and try to bring them both together."[49] This reconstruction of society would necessarily lead to a fellow feeling, equality of opportunity and pursuit of happiness. For achieving such a state he advocated varying degrees of social control. These social controls, he realized, can only be applied through a social revolution for he felt that "social revolution is the only way to achieve national unity,"[50] as "social equality is the primary basis of national cohesion."[51] But in his scheme of things a social revolution has to be brought about "through democratic processes, persuasion, argument and peaceful change of opinion,"[52] and not through violent means. He also believed that such a state of affairs would not get established automatically. He advocated a conscious effort on the part of all individuals, societies and nations to work for the establishment of a new social order. He was aware of the fact that "our trouble has been that we have professed these ideals for centuries but we have not implemented them."[53] In the best tradition of Indian dynamism and activism, he said, "things do not improve of their own accord. We have to exert our utmost to build up our future: *Kuru pauruṣam ātmaśaktya.*"[54]

In reply to those who criticized Radhakrishnan for not making any original contribution to philosophy, Muirhead wrote, "It is Radhakrishnan's modesty that disclaims any originality for the views his books expound. But if originality in philosophy, as in poetry, consists not in the novelty of the tale, not even in the distribution of light and shade in the telling of it, but in the depth with which its significance is grasped and made to dominate over the details, his books never fail in this quality."[55] Many of the readers of his works would agree with this.

XVII.

Attempt at a Vignette

R adhakrishnan wrote an autobiographical essay for a collection of similar essays, edited by Vergilius Ferm, published in 1937. In 1936 he had given up the vice-chancellorship of Andhra University and had become the Professor of Eastern Religions and Ethics at Oxford, while retaining the King George V Professorship of Philosophy at Calcutta. He was forty-nine years old then. He entitled that essay *My Search for Truth* (forty-nine pages). Mahatma Gandhi's autobiography entitled *Story of My Experiments with Truth*, in its English version had appeared in 1927. The two, however, differ vastly: While the latter is the revealing and edifying story of one of the greatest figures of the modern world who wanted to "achieve . . . self-realization, to see God face to face, to attain Moksha;"[1] the former is the *tour de force* of a brilliant academic who had achieved international fame and cherished as his ideal: "to imitate in some small measure" the examples of "truly religious souls from Buddha and Christ down to lesser mortals, [who] . . . have striven to lighten the load of humanity, to strengthen the hopes without which it would have fainted and fallen in its difficult journey."[2] Schilpp was not wrong in referring to this essay of Radhakrishnan as "a veritable gem."[3]

Radhakrishnan wrote an "ostensible 'autobiography',"[4] while he was India's ambassador to Moscow, for the volume on his philosophy, edited by Schilpp, and published in 1952. He gave it the subtitle *Fragments of a Confession*. He was sixty-four years old then. St. Augustine's *Confessions* is a great classic of religion and philosophy, as well as a soul-baring account of a deeply moving cathartic spiritual odyssey. On the other hand, Radhakrishnan's *Fragments* (actually seventy-eight pages) consists of ten chapters: How I Came to the Study of Philosophy; The Philosophical Situation; Indian Philosophy; Scientific Outlook; Technological Civilization; Religion and Social Conscience; Samsara or the World of Change; The Human Condition and the Quest for Being; The Religion of the Spirit; and Religion and Religions. Of these only the first has an autobiographical touch inasmuch as it mentions that he chose philosophy as the special subject of his study in college as one of his cousins who graduated that year passed on his (the cousin's) textbooks to him, and that because (1) he spent the first years of his life in "a great centre of religious pilgrimage," (2) his "parents were religious in the traditional sense of the term" and (3) he studied in Christian Missionary institutions for twelve years, "he grew up in an atmosphere where the unseen was a living reality" and his "early training" "determined" his "approach to the problems of philosophy from the angle of religion."[5] The remaining chapters in the *Fragments*, not logically connected with each other, reiterate his views on the topics just mentioned.

It is intriguing that in both the *Search* and the *Fragments* Radhakrishnan did not say anything about his parents, except this: They were "Hindu parents, who were conventional in their religious outlook" (*Search*); they "were religious in the traditional sense of the term" (*Fragments*). He was strangely silent about his ancestry, his father's education and occupation and his siblings. In the *Fragments* he stated it was not his intention to speak of these things, and of his "likes and dislikes," "struggles and disappointments," and his "own share of the burdens and anxieties of life." While these were of "immense importance" to him, "discretion" forbade him to speak of them![6] It is difficult to conjecture the reason for this "discretion" of his, when he admitted "No man's story of his own life can fail to be of interest to others, if it is written in sincerity." He dismissed the whole matter thus: "I have not had any advantages of birth or of wealth."[7]

Radhakrishnan began the second section of *My Search for Truth* with the heading "Home Life," referring to Hegel's saying to the effect that a man makes up his account with life "when he has work that suits him and a wife whom he loves."[8] This allows one to draw the implication that when he wrote this at forty-nine, he thought philosophy and education suited him and he loved his wife, whom he had married when he was fifteen and she ten. It could be inferred that he had his wife in mind when he further wrote in the same section that Hindu women "cling to the deeper and more ultimate reality," and are "found conspicuously fighting on the side of eternal values," and that they have "perhaps the greatest gift of heaven," viz., "a pure unquestioning love that triumphs over the weakness of the loved one." Is it possible that to some degree their conjugal life reflected his following quotation in the same context? "If he is faithless, I must be faithful. If he is shaken, I must abide. If he sees another, I must await his return."[9]

This question appears to be legitimate, because in the last and fourth section of *My Search for Truth*, under the heading "Life's Problems," there are the following passages: "Whose life is so clean, whose character is so spotless that he can sit in judgement on others? . . . Most of us find ourselves in absurd positions when some overmastering passion reduces us to unreason. . . . Most of us are slaves of our passions. . . . Society has queer notions about right and wrong. Unorthodox personal relationships are wrong, while acts involving whole nations in war are right. Cruelty, treachery, and exploitation are condoned, while loving the wrong person not wisely but too well is condemned, though the latter is only a misfortune, not a crime."[10]

Is it wrong to construe all this as an apologia for any actual cases of "unorthodox personal relationships" and "loving the wrong persons?" Here an allusion to a passage in Vyasa's *Yoga Sūtra Bhāshya* (II.4.) may be relevant: "If love is experienced for someone, it does not mean that it is not experienced for another. When Chaitra is found to be in love with a woman, it does not follow he is out of love for another."

While about his parents, siblings, wife and other teachers in school and college he was unduly reticent, of one teacher he wrote: "My distinguished teacher Professor A.G. Hogg,. . . a thinker of great penetration in theological matters."[11] A.G. Hogg, was "one of the greatest Christian thinkers we had in India, with whom I studied philosophy for four years 1905-1909."[12] It has, however, been stated by one whom nobody can know better, that while Radhakrishnan's "parents created a religious background," not only Hogg but two other teachers too (Meston and Skinner) "influenced" him.[13] Their criticism of Indian tradition and Hinduism disturbed his dogmatic faith in these.

Another great formative influence on Radhakrishnan was that of Swami Vivekananda. In *My Search for Truth* he wrote that his "pride as a Hindu [was] roused by the enterprise and eloquence of Swami Vivekananda." In 1963 he spoke of the courage Vivekananda's "humanistic, man-making religion" gave him and his contemporaries when they were young. Vivekananda's letters, he recalled used to be circulated in manuscript among students when he was perhaps in the last year at school. They all felt "thrilled" to read the letters which gave them a "mesmeric touch," and they, according to Radhakrishnan, effected a kind of transformation in the young men.[14]

The dialectical interaction between the Christian Missionary criticism of Indian culture and Hinduism and Vivekananda's definition and defense of Hinduism as "eternal religion" (*sanātana dharma*) applicable to actual social problems and his criticism of the West, helped to shape Radhakrishnan's understanding and definition of Indian heritage and his own religion.

ॐ

If his own self-analysis in 1937 was correct, Radhakrishnan seems to have given a sincere account of his personality traits then. This may be summarized as follows: His was a meditative frame of mind; he loved loneliness. Though involved in external activity, he loved to "linger in his inner life of increasing solitude." While he did not feel at home in conventional social functions, or in the company of those whom he did not know well, he had "an uncanny knack" of developing rapport with anyone, if he needed it. On the one hand, as he was shy and lonely, so withdrawn and socially timid, some considered, that it was difficult to know him; on the other hand, some found him social and sociable. Though he was not so, some believed he was cold and strong-willed. Nervously organized, sensitive and highstrung, he was capable of strong and profound emotions, which he generally tended to conceal. Such was the result of Radhakrishnan's self-analysis.[15]

A sketch of Radhakrishnan by not an entirely uncritical admirer, published in 1936, somewhat confirms his own self-assessment. It may be summarized as follows: He was not a messiah, but "Nature's great gentleman," with fascinating human qualities. He was a man of the world, steeped in its wisdom and ways. He had alert, attentive and affable manners. He had no pomposity or snobbishness; he could talk to anyone as if he had known him all his life. He could read others' thoughts and anticipate what they were going to say. This enabled him to be the leader of any institution, hurry up and rush through organizational matters. In councils and debates he could hustle people to agree with him, and see through a hundred-topic agenda in one hundred minutes. If he wanted, in a party he could talk with anyone most entertainingly.

The summary of the same sketch may be continued thus: He was inscrutable, vigilant and circumspect. While others might confide in him, he confided in none and kept his own counsel. For days on end at a stretch he confined himself to his house, reading, writing, and relaxing only in the companionship of his own family. He led a simple and austere life, with few wants and partaking of a frugal fare. Describing his house

as a caravan-*Sarai*, he never furnished it properly. Though a man of delicate sensibility and not indifferent to beauty, who would enjoy pictures,
plays, music, and in later days cricket, he never visited places of natural
beauty or historical interest. Though he visited Europe and passed through
Cairo a number of times, he felt no desire to go to see the Acropolis, Venice
or the Pyramids. He never went for a walk. A voracious reader, he read
almost anything, except books of a technical nature. A poet and a dreamer
at core, with a romantic vein, when he deeply felt the injustice or suffering
around him, his revolutionary fervor was roused and he expressed himself accordingly, combining clarity of mind with compassionate forgiveness, he tolerated all without adopting a moral line, and had no hostility
even towards those who meant harm to him. He was helpful to all without rancor and malice. According to what his wife told the writer of the
1936 sketch, while in his younger days he tended to be Bohemian, in later
life through discipline he attained self control, serenity and equipoise.[16]

From available records of reminiscences and comments of various
persons who worked with him or had interaction with him at different
times and places, including such august persons as the British and the
Iranian Queens, the American President's wife (Mrs. Kennedy, then preg-
nant, requested him to pray for her child!), Communist M.P.s like P. Sundarayya and Bhupesh Gupta,[17] and great national leaders such as Rajendra
Prasad and Nehru, the accuracy of Radhakrishnan's personality as delin-
eated in his own *My Search for Truth* and in the 1936 sketch summarized
above, appears to be borne out to a considerable extent.

In a recent critical sketch, a well-known writer and a leading journalist, after pointing out that Radhakrishnan liked flattery, was parsimoni-
ous with money, prone to hearing and spreading gossip and to favoritism
towards those who worked for him, effusively concluded as follows: "Dr.
Radhakrishnan remains for me the greatest interpreter of Hinduism that
India has produced since Ādi Śankara. Also, one of the greatest orators I
have heard. He had some human weaknesses, but was nevertheless a great
and a good man."[18] While no deep student of Hinduism could agree with
the estimate in the first sentence of this quotation, no fairminded person
would disagree with the contents of the rest of it. Here one may be reminded
of a line from Kalidasa:

> A single blemish gets submerged in a multitude of virtues,
> even as the stain in the moon in the latter's rays.
> (*Kumāra Saṁbhava*, I.3.)

One of the personality traits of Radhakrishnan was his great aptitude for politics, which was noticeable by the time he was in his late forties. The author of the 1936 sketch summarized above observed that if Radhakrishnan cared to enter politics, he would become one of the biggest men of that epoch, because he was the only man of his generation capable of providing Indian nationalism with a creed, a theory, reconciling India's immemorial intellectual tradition with the demands of a changing social order.[19] In that sketch it is also mentioned that though several of his friends urged him to enter politics, he put them off, saying that he was very much content with his work and the fellowship of his friends. In an earlier chapter it has been mentioned that in a public speech in a felicitation function in 1936, the British head of the education system of the Madras presidency prophesied that if and when India became a republic, Radhakrishnan would become its president.

Likewise, a reference has been made in a previous chapter to the perceptive article in the late forties of Khasa Subba Rao forecasting the possible imminent entry of Radhakrishnan into politics as well as his very probable success in it, because he was so well-equipped for it. This was indeed so, because by then Radhakrishnan had enough independent income of his own; he had ingratiated himself with the most important national leaders;[20] and, above all, through his writings and speeches he had by the late 1940s established himself as a forceful and fearless advocate of independence for India.[21] Indeed, C.Y. Chintamani, editor of the *Leader*, and one of the foremost journalists and public figures of his time, remarked that he "would unhesitatingly describe Radhakrishnan as an academic extremist."[22] Besides, the arts of manipulation and intrigue were not unknown to him.

Radhakrishnan, his critics point out, never participated in the struggle for independence in any way whatsoever, and never went to prison. On the other hand, he maintained cordial relations with the British rulers in India, and was friendly with British academics, and was admired by them. Consequently, he was knighted by the King-emperor in 1931; and invited to be a professor at Oxford in 1936 and a fellow of the British Academy in 1939. At home, the Mysore government under the distinguished Diwan Visvesvarayya appointed him a professor in their newly established university in 1916, but Asutosh Mookerjee snatched him away to Calcutta in 1921. He got himself elected vice-chancellor of Andhra University in 1931, while Madan Mohan Malaviya got him elected as vice-chancellor of Banaras Hindu University in 1939. When India became free, he became member of the Constituent Assembly, ambassador to the USSR, the vice-president for two terms, and finally, the president. Thus according to his detractors, without subjecting himself to the least inconvenience (he relinquished his knighthood only in 1947, after India became free), and without doing anything concrete for India's independence, he got the maximum benefit in free India.

When compared to Gandhi, Bose, Nehru, Prasad or Patel, he may be said to have done nothing substantial for the independence of India. But, adopting (what he called) a lateral approach to and without making a frontal attack on political problems,[23] he attempted to convince the English-knowing world that India with its great culture and high intellectual tradition, extending back to centuries, cannot and should not remain a subject nation and that it was not moral for Britain to continue its domination.[24] No Indian academic with a world-wide reputation advocated complete independence for India so eloquently, forcibly and frequently in as open a manner and for so long a time as Radhakrishnan did at home and abroad. From the 1920s till he had a stroke in 1968, in every available forum he asserted the equality of East and West, urged that imperialism and colonialism be ended, and pleaded for the replacement of the existing world politico-economic order by a new one based on social and economic justice. It was to Nehru's credit that he perceived the advantage to the nation of having a man like Radhakrishnan as its ambassador, vice-president and, finally, president. His becoming president, it may be recalled, won the applause of some of the best minds like Bertrand Russell and of almost the entire informed Indian public, and was editorially hailed by the world media.

ॐ

One of the admirable things about Radhakrishnan is that though he spoke and wrote about religion and spirituality (*ad nauseam* according to some; or to a tiresome extent according to many), it was not an escapist, traditional or irrational religion and an unsocial and unscientific spirituality that he expounded. For him "nothing can be true by faith if it is not true by reason."[25] What he expounded, he claimed, depended on logical reflection.[26] It did not "comply with any fixed traditional pattern." His thinking "proceeded from," was "born of," his own "spiritual experience." In his writings, he asserted, he tried to "communicate" his "insight into the meaning of life."[27] This is not the right place either to analyze these statements and examine their self-consistency, or to determine with precision the nature and value of what he expounded, and to what extent he had developed it on "independent lines." Radhakrishnan expressed himself against taking any philosopher as a *guru*.[28] Though some considered him a follower of Śaṅkara, he himself denied this, and affirmed that only "the general spirit of Śaṅkara's philosophy" was "commended" in his writings[29] (whatever that may mean!). Someone has testified that Radhakrishnan himself told him that he regularly meditated on the early morning rising sun, and that it was the most important thing for him. As against this, perhaps the person closest to him and who could speak about him with utmost authority has answered three specific questions as follows: (1) To him Radhakrishnan never claimed he had *Brahmanubhava* (experience of Brahman), mystic vision, or integral experience. (2) To his knowledge Radhakrishnan did not practise any spiritual discipline (*sādhanā*), yoga, or worship (*upāsanā*). (3) He did not perform any daily or occasional rituals (*nitya* and *naimittika Karmas*, like *sandhyā vandanā* [morning and evening prayers] or *śrāddha* a funeral or obsequial rite). He occasionally visited temples, but believed in no rituals.[30]

This shows Radhakrishnan was really an exceptional man, for it is almost impossible to mention readily any South Indian Brahmin of his generation, background and class who did not quite regularly perform *sāndhyāvandanā* and *śrāddha* and some sort of daily *pūja*. Even today a good number of South Indian Brahmins (e.g. university men, civil servants), at least in their fifties and above, seem to be performing these almost regularly. One does not hear that he ever went on a pilgrimage (*tīrthayātrā*) with his wife, or had any *pūjas* performed when he visited temples. He did not acknowledge anyone *as his guru*. This author of *The Hindu View of Life* neither habitually smeared sacred ash nor wore *tilak* on his forehead.

He had the courage to declare in 1927: "The Sastris and the pandits, the Maulvis and Maulanas, the missionaries and clergymen of the conventional type are not likely to be of much help to us in our present condition."[31] In 1934 at Haridwar he addressed an assembly of sannyasins on the theme "Beware of Sadhus!" In 1942, in the course of lectures at Calcutta and Banaras he observed: "The *muṭṭs* have outlived their function. They have ceased to learn and to teach, to inspire and to illumine."[32] This great exponent of Vedānta and famous commentator of its triple canon, on whom the Bharatiya Vidya Bhavan bestowed the title of "the

Sun of Brahman-knowledge," (*Brahmavidyā Bhāskara*) was never initiated by any guru and never performed any ritual; and did not engage himself in meditation or worship. But, in later years he was often seen humming some *ślokās*, sometimes gently tapping with fingers on a desk or table in front, or using cymbals.[33] He might have been trying to remember always the Supreme Being by constantly chanting His names and hymning Him. The *Gītā* teaches: I am easily accessible to him who always remembers Me (*smaratī nityaśah*), without any mental diversion. (VIII.14.) Those who are determined to make a strenuous effort are constantly hymning Me (*kīrtayanto mām*). (IX.14.) This easiest and best type of spiritual practice might have been what Radhakrishnan chose.

What were Radhakrishnan's objectives in different spheres of activity and what did he actually achieve?

As a teacher, his ambition was to educate his pupils to "a belief in a spiritual and ethical universe."[34] His attempt as a philosopher was "to expound a philosophy ... which offers an interpretation of the universe, which is at once rational and spiritual." His "main contention" in his writings was to make out "that there is one perennial and universal philosophy."[35] His "supreme interest has been to try to restore a sense of spiritual values to the millions of religiously displaced persons."[36]

The results of his academic work may be briefly described now. He presented for the first time Indian philosophy in an attractive and elegant way. Wherever he could, he compared Indian with Western ideas and tried to show that in a considerable number of cases the former were more cogent, and more advanced than the latter, as well as anticipatory of the latter. While admitting that India did not have any monopoly of wisdom, and believing that Hinduism has some aspects which are eternal, he identified them and incessantly urged that they should constitute the spiritual foundation for a new world inspired by ethical principles. Hundreds heard his formal class lectures wherever he taught, several thousands all over the world heard his speeches directly and on the radio, a million or more may have read his works. It is possible many were convinced by his arguments and accepted his views. For the sophisticated among the English-educated middle class in India (e.g. Nehru, J.P. Narayan) his works were the main source books of Indian thought.

As a philosopher he gave rise to no new school, invented no methodology, and discovered no new truth. His writings, however, developed and popularized "a comparative method," and for decades this and idealism were dominant in Indian educational institutions. Ideas such as equality of all religions, all religions having the same essence and the same goal, the possibility of a world philosophy emerging from a synthesis of Eastern and Western philosophies, the establishment of universal peace and harmony through an awareness of the presence of the same Divine Spirit in all human beings: these were commonly accepted by many Indian intellectuals. Meticulous study of texts taking into account their historical setting, chronology and philology, rigorous analysis and tracing the growth and gradual development of ideas, paying attention to interrelationships among ideas and drawing out their implications and consequences: these were generally neglected in most Indian university philosophy departments. All these, though not exclusively, were to a significant extent, due to his influence. He was, the ideal and the fashion, more than any other Indian philosopher, for quite a large number of teachers and students of philosophy in India.

There have been some academics who did not consider him to be a profound and systematic thinker, and were certain he was not at all original. Yet, no Indian academic philosopher was ever, nor is anyone even now, better known than him in India and abroad, and no other Indian academic philosopher's works have had more sales than his. This last fact is explained away by some due to his works being more popular than profound, and more attractive than original, and also due to the glamor of their author's Oxford professorship, foreign honors and high public offices.

In addition to being a professional philosopher and a university man, Radhakrishnan throughout his life concerned himself with issues related to contemporary civilization, world peace, effects of technology, cultural and politico-economic imperialism and colonialism, social and religious reforms, education, and, more particularly, India's freedom, unity and development. No other Indian academic has had such wide interests, pursued them so seriously and none has done reading, thinking, lecturing and writing about them in a sustained manner for such a long time. Russell, Dewey and Sartre are comparable persons in this matter. Very few Indian university men have even tried to emulate his example in this respect. If examination and criticism of contemporary civilization, society and life, and putting forward suggestions for their improvement, is philosophical activity, Radhakrishnan would have to be considered the foremost modern Indian academic philosopher.

In the foregoing relevant chapters Radhakrishnan's achievements as (1) university administrator, (2) diplomat, (3) vice-president and (4) president and (5) his role in the deliberations of the League of Nations Committee and UNESCO have been described. But, what is most noteworthy in each of these will be briefly highlighted in the following.

(1) As educator and university head, he tried to make universities, and also pleaded for universities to be made, centers where knowledge which is useful as well as spiritually enriching would be *freely* pursued, taught, learnt and developed. Universities have a responsibility for preserving and advancing culture and civilization in addition to providing education and training which will lead to gainful employment.

(2) Radhakrishnan succeeded in Moscow because, not being either a career diplomat or a politician with an office in his own country, he conducted himself in the Soviet Union in an authentic way, i.e. in a way conforming to his own nature, profession, reputation, and scholarship. He behaved simply and naturally and treated all alike, speaking to everyone frankly. He did not feel inferior or superior when meeting or talking to anyone. He acted on the principle that trust begets trust, and that if one spoke no lies to another the other too will not do so. His learning and humanism made him respected and loved. His personal prestige and behavior contributed to the steady friendship between the two countries.[37]

(3) His most notable contributions as vice-president are two. (a) He presided over the Rajya Sabha in almost an ideal way, by being thoroughly impartial, by caring more for the parliamentary spirit than for rules of procedure and by the ability to intervene in a charming, yet firm, manner through persuasive power and the right way of speaking. (b) Visiting several countries, he expounded free India's objectives, policies and achievements in an impressive, scholarly and authoritative manner. He enjoyed the prime minister's confidence throughout his vice-presidency, he had the necessary gifts (knowledge and eloquence) and the aura of international reputation. His success was unprecedented and unsurpassed by any American or Indian vice-president.

(4) Due to the steady aging and ailments of both Radhakrishnan and Nehru, as well as their growing mutual nagging suspicions, the former's five-year presidency does not appear to be so great a success as his ten-year vice-presidency. Neither often was his counsel on major matters sought by the prime minister. Things like his making Nehru attend Prasad's funeral are not important. Only after the debacle following the Sino-Indian conflict did Radhakrishnan assert himself and prevail to some extent. In Krishna Menon's exit and General Chaudhuri's promotion his advice seems to have mattered. According to a most

credible authority, "he had no knowledge of the Kamaraj Plan before it was announced."[38]

He had a historic role in deciding and selecting the successor to Nehru and Shastri when they both passed away while in office; and he acquitted himself admirably on both the occasions. He and Shastri could not remain close and friendly to each other. It is said, he advised Shastri to be reconciliatory in his talks at Tashkent, and that the latter was so. Indira Gandhi was quite close to Radhakrishnan when he was vice-president, and is believed to have been also responsible for persuading Radhakrishnan to remain in Delhi and be vice-president for a second term. Yet, they moved away from each other and ceased to give each other mutual support some time after she became prime minister. Neither of them could have been solely responsible for this.

The fact that Radhakrishnan could not continue to be Nehru's confidant after becoming president, that Shastri distanced himself away from him and Indira Gandhi grew distrustful of him, raises the question: Had something gone wrong with him? What happened to his wonderful capacity to win and retain friends? It is also reported that some time after he became president, Radhakrishnan got into the habit of criticizing in private the prime minister and his government's policies and actions, and this became known to Nehru. He began to do so rather openly during the Sino-Indian conflict and more so later. He did not entirely stop doing this in the Shastri interregnum; and though he was quiet for a while after Indira Gandhi's ascent to power he indulged in public criticism rather freely on a couple of occasions. Naturally, this produced a reaction, and it is widely believed that his desire to continue for a second term was not heeded. President Radhakrishnan would have remained more exalted if he remembered that like the British monarch he had only to reign, not rule, and give advice if and when sought, especially, as the attorney general, in Rajendra Prasad's time, expressed the opinion that the president should not embarrass the government through his public criticism of it. According to Radhakrishnan himself, "the president symbolizes national purpose and national unity and can be a great influence for stability and progress."[39] If he had adhered to this superb ideal more completely and sincerely, he would have been a far greater president than he had been.

(5) In the League of Nations Committee and UNESCO, Radhakrishnan brought home to the West that the cultures and civilizations of the East are as great and valuable as those of the former, that they have their unique contributions to make to the advancement of a common human

civilization, and that the preservation, study and mutual appreciation of all of them had to be promoted by these international bodies. Everyone in the world should have access to and opportunities to enjoy the literatures, arts, music and thoughts of both East and West. UNESCO should try to be the intellectual reservoir and the ethical conscience keeper for the whole world, rising above all differences among nations. In a similar manner, Radhakrishnan attempted to obtain for Africa and Latin America equal attention, and get parity for them and for Asia in getting employment within UNESCO.

ॐ

In the beginning of this chapter it has been said that Radhakrishnan's supreme ideal was the imitation of Buddha and Christ. How far an individual has progressed in realizing such an ideal only he can know inwardly. One can have only certitude of one's perfection; others can have no certainty about it. Radhakrishnan never claimed he was anywhere near his ideal.

Radhakrishnan asserted that he highly valued kindness to others and sincerity with oneself and in one's intimate relations with others, because (he wrote) for him "a human and intimately personal life" was "more important than that of a pedantic scholar or a dull dispenser of thought."[40] He claimed he was granted the 'invaluable and magic gift', namely, to have the "confidence of a few of the unhappy men, the lonely ones, the misfits," who are persecuted by society. From such men, he wrote, he received letters asking for "advice and help in every conceivable perplexity," and he was able to show them sympathy or understanding.[41] Suniti Kumar Chatterjee has testified that Radhakrishnan used to receive many such letters. Ms. Vina Majumdar, in whose parental home Radhakrishnan used to stay in early years of the Second World War and even after that whenever he visited Calcutta, has given this information: "An incredible number of people came to visit him in our house—university teachers, students, political personalities, and many other persons from the field of journalism to hard scholarship. A lot of people came to tell him of their personal problems, as he had a soft corner for people who had to face individual crises."[42] Radhakrishnan wrote glowingly about his "wonderful experiences" which "forged links of human affection and regard," giving him "high joys as well as deep sorrow," in a sense "fulfilling destiny" (whatever that may mean!).[43]

The above account is from his 1937 autobiographical essay. It ends with a beautiful *śloka* from the *Bhāgavata* (IX.21.12.), without giving its translation. It may be translated thus: "I do not wish for a kingdom, heaven or rebirth; but I wish for the destruction of the anguish of living beings subjected to suffering." The ideal of imitation of Buddha and Christ, the ethics of compassion towards others and sincerity with oneself and in interpersonal relations, portrayed here, might have been theoretically adhered to by him throughout his life. It is not known whether he was able to cultivate or practice them in later life, as he might have at a certain period in his life. If anyone held such an ideal and unwaveringly practised compassion and sincerity all through life, he must have been indeed a blessed person.

૨ટ

John James Tigert, former commissioner for education in USA, and president emeritus of the University of Florida, who served as a member of the Indian University Education Commission, of which Radhakrishnan was the chairman recorded his impression of him thus: "He is a very great man—not only a remarkable scholar but also a good man with some saintly qualities while retaining his simplicity. He is about as nearly a perfect speaker as you will hear."[44]

Notes

CHAPTER I

1. This information was conveyed by Mr. T. Ramalingeswra Rao in his letter dated March 27, 1982, to K. Satchidananda Murty.

2. "The Religion of the Spirit and the World's Need: Fragments of a Confession," *The Philosophy of Sarvepalli Radhakrishnan*, edited by P.A. Schilpp (New York: Tudor Publishing Company, 1952), pp. 6-7, hereafter "Fragments of a Confession."

3. *My Search for Truth* (Agra: Shiva Lal Agarwal and Co. (Private) Ltd., Second Indian Reprint 1956), p. 3.

4. "The Aim of Education," *President Radhakrishnan's Speeches and Writings, May 1962-May 1964*, (New Delhi: Publications Division, 1965), p. 115.

5. "Fragments of a Confession," p. 6.

6. "The Aim of Education," p. 114.

7. Ibid., p. 114.

8. *My Search for Truth*, p. 9.

9. "The Fulfillment of Man," *President Radhakrishnan's Speeches and Writings, May 1962-May 1964*, p. 65.

10. "Reply to Critics," *The Philosophy of Sarvepalli Radhakrishnan*, p. 806n; *My Search for Truth*, p. 9.

11. S. Radhakrishnan, "Foreword", Eric Sharpe, *The Theology of A.G. Hogg*, (Madras, 1971), p. ix.

12. *The Theology of A.G. Hogg*, p. 24.

13. Quoted in *The Theology of A.G. Hogg*, p. 94.

14. His other publications are: *Christ's Message of the Kingdom* (1911) which is a compilation of morning devotions; *Redemption from the World or the Supernatural in Christianity* (1922) which is highly theological rather than philosophical in its content; and *The Christian Message to the Hindu* (1947).

15. *The Theology of A.G. Hogg*, p. 41.

16. *Karma and Redemption* (1909); reprinted 1970, (Madras), p. xix.

17. Ibid., p. 33.

18. Ibid., Preface, p. xix.

19. Ibid., Preface, p. xx.

20. *Christ's Message of the Kingdom,* quoted in *The Theology of A.G. Hogg,* p. 58.

21. *My Search for Truth,* p. 5.

22. Ibid., p. 8.

23. Ibid., p. 9.

24. "Fragments of a Confession," p. 9.

25. Ibid., p. 9.

26. *My Search for Truth,* p. 9.

27. Ibid., p. 12.

28. Ibid., p. 12.

29. *The Ethics of the Vedanta and its Metaphysical Presuppositions* (Madras: The Guardian Press, 1908). Quoted in Robert N. Minor, *Radhakrishnan: A Religious Biography,* (State University of New York Press, 1987), p. 18.

30. Ibid., p. 82 [Quoted in Minor.]

31. Ibid., p. 66 [Quoted in Minor.]

32. Ibid., p. 83 [Quoted in Minor.]

33. Ibid., p. 86 [Quoted in Minor. We owe this analysis to Minor.]

34. Quoted in *My Search for Truth,* p. 10.

35. Ibid., p. 9.

36. Ibid., p. 9.

37. "Reply to Critics," *Philosophy of Sarvepalli Radhakrishnan,* p. 802.

38. Bhimsen Sachar, "India's Noble Son," *The Radhakrishnan Number,* ed. Vuppuluri Kalidas, (Madras, Hyderabad: Vyasa Publication, 1962), p. 31.

CHAPTER II

1. Joseph Pothan, "Student Prince," *The Radhakrishnan Number*, p. 53.

2. K. Chandrasekhran, "A Realist," *The Radhakrishnan Number*, p. 111.

3. Khasa Subba Rau, "Ageless Radhakrishnan," *The Radhakrishnan Number*, p. 41.

4. P. Sankaranarayanan, "Recovery of India," *The Radhakrishnan Number*, p. 141.

5. Reported to be said by his wife, quoted in S.P., "Sir Sarvepalli Radharishnan (A Sketch)," *Triveni, New Series*, (September, 1936), pp. 6-16.

6. *My Search for Truth*, p. 12.

7. Pyarelal, "Gandhiji's 'Krishna'," *The Radhakrishnan Number*, p. 55.

8. "The Man and His Evolution," *Sarvepalli Radhakrishnan*, edited by K. Iswara Dutt, (New Delhi: Popular Book Services, 1966), pp. 109-110.

9. Quoted in V.S. Narvane, "Radhakrishnan's Thought," *The Radhakrishnan Number*, p. 108.

10. Ibid., p. 108. [Quoted in V.S. Narvane]

11. Quoted in *My Search for Truth*, p. 13.

12. Ibid., pp. 13-14.

CHAPTER III

1. *President Radhakrishnan's Speeches and Writings, May 1962-May 1964*, p. 246.

2. *My Search for Truth*, pp. 14-15.

3. Translated from V. Sitaramaiah, *My College Days* (Kannada), by K.B. Ramakrishna Rao and sent to K. Satchidananda Murty.

4. A.R. Wadia, "A Forgiving Heart," *The Radhakrishnan Number*, p. 92.

5. "In Accord with Spinoza," *The Radhakrishnan Number*, p. 149.

6. Ibid., p. 149. [Quoted in M. Yamunacharya.]

7. A.R. Wadia, "A Forgiving Heart," p. 92.

8. "Students' Idol," *The Radhakrishnan Number*, p. 23.

9. A.R. Wadia, "A Forgiving Heart," p. 92.

CHAPTER IV

1. Mookerjee said this in 1924. Quoted in Narendra Krishna Sinha, *Asutosh Mookerjee, A Biographical Study*, (Calcutta, 1964), p. 123.

2. Quoted in K. Iswara Dutt, "The Man and his Evolution," p. 89.

3. Ibid., p. 89.

4. "In Accord with Spinoza," *The Radhakrishnan Number*, p. 149.

CHAPTER V

1. From a letter to K. Satchidananda Murty, dated July 8, 1981 from an old student, now a well-known scholar who wishes to remain anonymous.

2. "A Philosopher Looks at Life," *The Madras Mail*, April 1, 1936.

3. *My Search for Truth*, p. 16.

4. "Radhakrishnan's World," *The Philosophy of Sarvepalli Radhakrishnan*, p. 87.

5. His letter published in *The Modern Review*, February, 1929.

6. Ibid.

7. *The Statesman*, May 4, 1933.

CHAPTER VI

1. *The Radhakrishnan Number*, p. 115.

2. Quoted in A.C. Underwood, *Contemporary Thought of India*, (London, 1930).

3. Quoted in K. Iswara Dutt, "The Man and His Evolution," p. 110.

4. *My Search for Truth*, p. 18.

5. K. Chandrasekharan, "A Realist," *The Radhakrishnan Number*, p. 111.

6. *My Search for Truth*, p. 17.

CHAPTER VII

1. Quoted in K. Iswara Dutt, "The Man and His Evolution," p. 107.

2. *My Search for Truth*, p. 20.

3. Ibid., p. 21.

4. Ibid., p. 26.

5. Ibid., p. 24. [Quoted in]

6. Ibid., pp. 24-25.

7. Ibid., p. 33.

8. "A Rare Man," *The Radhakrishnan Number*, p. 64.

9. "Symbol of India," *The Radhakrishnan Number*, p. 14.

10. "As Diplomat," *Sarvepalli Radhakrishnan*, ed. K. Iswara Dutt, pp. 63-64.

11. For his brilliant and nonparochial speech, see *Sadhana Patrika*, (November 24, 1928).

CHAPTER VIII

1. He was vice-chancellor, Madras University, from 1925 to 1928.

2. Quoted in Prema Nandakumar, "Dr. Sir S. Radhakrishnan, a Master Mind and Speaker," *Triveni* (July-September, 1988), p. 16.

3. M. Venkatarangaiya, "A Real Kulapati," *The Radhakrishnan Number*, p. 104.

4. 'W, P, E and B' stand for initials of their names.

5. Lakkaraju Subba Rau, "A Synthesizer," *The Radhakrishnan Number*, p. 105.

6. Under the acronym "Gora" he later became famous as a propagator of atheism and humanism and a Gandhian constructive worker. His conversations with Gandhiji have been published in a brochure by Navjivan Trust, Ahmedabad.

7. Gora, *We Became Atheists*, (Vijayawada, 1975), pp. 27-28, 33-34. V. Kasi Visvanatham, *Gora, Nastikuni Jivitam*, 2nd revised edition, (1980), pp. 61-62. Sri Lavanam's letter of Dec. 12, 1988 to Sri Y. Anjaneyulu, Telugu University, Hyderabad. Lavanam is Ramchandra Rao's son and Director, Atheist Centre, Vijayawada.

8. Sri A. Radhakrishna Murti's letter of July 31, 1981 to K. Satchidananda Murty. Sri A. Radhakrishna Murti was a student of Philosophy at Andhra University when Radhakrishnan was its vice-chancellor.

9. *Andhra University Golden Jubilee Celebrations Souvenir 1926-76*, p. 87.

10. M. Venkatarangaiya, "A Real 'Kulapati'," p. 104.

11. Sri T. Bullaiah, a philosophy student (1932-35) of B. A. (Hons) gave this information in a talk with K. Satchidananda Murty on June 6, 1981.

12. Sri A. Radhakrishna Murti's letter.

13. Ibid.

14. Ibid.

15. Ibid.

16. Ibid.

17. Ibid.

18. Ibid.

19. Ibid.

20. Quoted in K. Chandrasekharan, "A Realist," *The Radhakrishnan Number*, p. 112.

21. Quoted in K. Iswara Dutt, "The Man and His Evolution," *Sarvepalli Radhakrishnan*, p. 91.

22. Quoted in K. Chandrasekharan, p. 112.

23. Quoted in J.C. Coyajee, *India and the League of Nations*, Waltair, 1932, p. 189.

24. Ibid., p. 189.

25. B.K. Malik, "Radhakrishnan and Philosophy of the State and Community," *The Philosophy of Sarvepalli Radhakrishnan*, p. 719.

26. *Minutes of the Senate Meeting*, 1932-33, p. 7.

27. M. Chalapathi Rau, "A Profile," *The Radhakrishnan Number*, p.56f.

28. Sri A. Radhakrishna Murti's letter.

29. *Pariah*, literally means man of the fifth caste, untouchable.

30. This account of the Mālapalli incident is based on Bangorey, *Mālapalli navala pai Prabhutva Nishedhālu*, (Madras, 1979).

31. *Minutes of the Academic Council*, 1935-36, pp. 76-77.

32. *Minutes of the Senate Meeting*, 1934-35, p. 109.

33. *My Search for Truth*, p. 33.

34. Sri A. Radhakrishna Murti's letter.

CHAPTER IX

1. "A Nation Seeking Its Soul," *The Hindu*, (April 1, 1936).

2. Ibid.

3. Ibid.

4. Ibid.

5. Ibid.

6. Ibid.

7. "A Philosopher Looks at Life," *The Madras Mail*, (April 1, 1936).

8. Ibid.

9. "A Nation Seeking Its Soul."

10. This information was provided by the late Mr. Kenneth Henderson, Secretary, Spalding Trust, Oxford, to K. Satchidananda Murty (*Vide* his letter dated January 22, 1981).

11. *Vide* W.H. Dawes' letter dated June 15, 1981 to K. Satchidananda Murty.

12. Quoted in Partap Singh Kairon, "Sage Statesman," *The Radhakrishnan Number*, p. 46.

13. D. Padmanabhan, "Reservoir of Compassion," *The Radhakrishnan Number*, p. 174.

14. Ibid., p. 175.

15. S. Natrajan, "A Non-Party President," *The Radhakrishnan Number*, p. 80c.

16. Hiren Mukerjee, "Reminiscences," *Facets of Radhakrishnan*, ed. B.K. Ahluwalia, (Delhi: Newman Group of Publishers, 1978, p. 14.

17. S. Natrajan, "A Non-Party President," p. 80c.

18. Quoted in "A 'Seer'," *The Radhakrishnan Number*, p. 85.

19. G. Rama Rao, *Sarvepalli Radhakrishnan*, (Hyderabad: Telugu University, 1988), p. 34.

CHAPTER X

1. S.L. Dar and S. Somaskandan, *History of the Banaras Hindu University*, (Banaras Hindu University Press, 1966), p. 651.

2. Ibid., p. 652.

3. Ibid., p. 653.

4. Ibid., pp. 657-658.

5. Ibid., p. 658.

6. Ibid., p. 664.

7. Ibid., p. 670.

8. Ibid., p. 677.

9. Ibid., p. 679.

10. Ibid., pp. 682-683.

11. Ibid., p. 683.

12. Ibid., p. 685.

13. Only three persons who had this privilege are known, T.R.V. Murti, P.T. Raju and P. Nagaraja Rao.

14. *History of the Banaras Hindu University*, p. 700.

15. Ibid., p. 703.

16. Ibid., p. 708.

17. Ibid., p. 719.

18. "A Wartime Episode Recalled," *The Radhakrishnan Number*, p. 56c.

19. *History of the Banaras Hindu University*, p. 725.

20. Ibid., p. 732.

21. Ibid., p. 733.

22. Ibid., p. 722.

23. Ibid., p. 737.

24. Ibid., p. 688.

25. Ibid., p. 749.

26. Ibid., p. 753.

27. Ibid., p. 755.

28. Professor T.R.V. Murti said so in a conversation with K. Satchidananda Murty on June 17, 1980.

29. Quoted in K. Iswara Dutt, "The Man and His Evolution," p. 92.

30. Ibid., p. 92.

31. "As Diplomat," p. 64.

32. Pyarelal, "Gandhiji's 'Krishna,' " *The Radhakrishnan Number*, p. 55.

33. See Pyarelal, *Mahatma Gandhi—The Last Phase*, (Ahmedabad: Navjivan, 1956), pp. 569-607.

34. See K.L. Shrimali, "Dr. Radhakrishnan: A Philosopher King," *Dr. Sarvepalli Radhakrishnan, A Commemorative Volume*, ed. Sudarshan Agarwal, (New Delhi: Prentice Hall of India, 1988), p. 28.

35. Pyarelal, "Gandhiji's 'Krishna,' " p. 55.

CHAPTER XI

1. *My Search for Truth*, p. 5.

2. Ibid., p. 9.

3. Ibid., p. 10.

4. "Fragments of a Confession," p. 19.

5. *Radhakrishnan Reader, An Anthology*, (Bombay: Bharatiya Vidya Bhavan, 1988), p. 64.

6. Ibid., p. 495ff.

7. Ibid., pp. 512-513.

8. In *The Nehru Birthday Book*, (Delhi, 1949).

9. K. Subba Rao, "Sir S. Radhakrishnan," article reprinted in *Triveni*, (July-September, 1988), p. 11.

10. S. Natrajan "A Non-Party President," p. 80d.

11. Tej Bahadur Sapru, et. al., *Constitutional Proposals of the Sapru Committee*, (Bombay: Padma Publications, 1945), p. 216.

12. Ibid., I:18.

13. D.P. Singhal, *History of Indian People*, (Metheun, 1983), p. 389.

14. "Our President," *The Radhakrishnan Number*, p. 9.

15. Quoted in Karunakar Gupta *India in World Politics*, (Calcutta: Scientific Book Agency, 1969).

16. "A Wartime Episode Recalled," *The Radhakrishnan Number*, p. 56d.

17. Quoted in Humayun Kabir, "As a Writer and Speaker," *Sarvepalli Radhakrishnan*, pp. 30-31.

18. The Report of the University Education Commission (December 1948-August, 1949), vol. 1, (Publication Division Government of India, 1949), p. 49.

19. Ibid., p. 39.

20. Ibid., p. 40.

21. Ibid., p. 36.

22. Ibid., p. 44.

23. Ibid., p. 36.

24. Ibid., p. 49.

25. Ibid., pp. 36-37.

26. Ibid., pp. 48-49.

27. Ibid., p. 52.

CHAPTER XII

1. Quoted in K.P.S. Menon, "As Diplomat," p. 62.

2. Ibid., p. 63.

3. Quoted in B.N. Pandey, *Nehru*, (London: MacMillan, 1976), p. 328.

4. This account of Radhakrishnan's meeting with Stalin is based on C.L. Datta, *With Two Presidents: The Inside Story*, (Delhi: Vikas Publications), pp. 74-75; K. Iswara Dutt, "The Man and His Evolution," p. 94; Pyarelal, "Gandhiji's 'Krishna,'" p. 56.

5. Pavlov told this to Rajeshwar Dayal when the latter asked him "How did your boss like the meeting with our Ambassador?" in a reception on January 26, 1950. Quoted in Pyarelal, p. 56.

6. K. P.S. Menon, "As Diplomat," pp. 66-67.

7. Ibid., p. 67.

8. Mrs. Lakshmi N. Menon in her letter of Nov. 30, 1981 to K. Satchidananda Murty.

9. Y.D. Gundevia, *Outside the Archives*, (Sangam Books, 1984), p. 83.

10. For this acount we depend upon Gundevia, pp. 95-97.

11. Mrs. Lakshmi N. Menon's "Letter."

12. S. Gopal, *Jawaharlal Nehru, A Biography, Vol. II*, (Bombay: Oxford University Press, 1976), p. 101.

13. S. Radhakrishnan *Occasional Speeches and Writings October 1952-February 1956*, (New Delhi: Publications Division), p. 35.

14. Gundevia, *Outside the Archives*, pp. 108-109.

15. Ibid., [See note 4 above and Mrs. Menon's letter].

16. "Artist in Action," *Facets of Radhakrishnan*, p. 50.

17. Winifred H. Dawes, "An Address to the Memory of Dr. Sarvepalli Radhakrishnan" delivered in a condolence meeting on June 4, 1975 at the Friends Meeting House.

18. In his letter to K. Satchidananda Murty, dated August 19, 1981.

19. A.J. Alston, "Letter."

20. Vernon Katz in his letter to K. Satchidananda Murty, dated September 19, 1981.

21. A.J. Alston, "Letter."

22. Quoted in T. M. P. Mahadevan, "Philosopher Radhakrishnan," *The Radhakrishnan Number*, p. 48c.

23. Vernon Katz, "Letter."

24. A.J. Alston, "Letter."

25. Ibid.

26. Ibid.

27. Katz, "Letter."

28. A.J. Alston, "Letter."

29. A.J. Alston, "Letter."

30. Ibid.

31. P.A. Schilpp, "General Introduction to 'The Library of Living Philosophers'," *The Philosophy of Sarvepalli Radhakrishnan*, p. 6.

32. Ibid., Preface, p. xi-xii.

33. Ibid., p. 12.

CHAPTER XIII

1. K. Iswara Dutt, "The Man and His Evolution," p. 96.

2. Ibid., p. 97.

3. Quoted in Hiren Mukerjee, "Reminiscences," p. 16.

4. *The Pen As My Sword*, (Bombay: Bharatiya Vidya Bhavan, 1965), p. 271.

5. *Portrait of Parliament: Reflection and Recollection 1952-77*, (New Delhi: Vikas, 1978), p. 12.

6. Hiren Mukerjee, "Reminiscences," p. 17.

7. *Distinguished Acquaintances*, (Vijayawada), p. 94.

8. "Brilliant Author," *The Radhakrishnan Number*, p. 32 h.

9. Quoted in *The Hindu*, (May 12, 1962), p. 1.

10. Quoted in Subhash Kashyap, "Dr. Radhakrishnan's Contribution to the Parliament," Paper read in the "Birth Centenary of Dr. S. Radhakrishnan, International Seminar," held from February 14-17, 1989 at New Delhi.

11. K.M. Panikkar, "In Line with Great Rishis," *The Radhakrishnan Number*, p. 41.

12. *Occasional Speeches and Writings 1952-59*, pp. 95-96.

13. Ibid., p. 96.

14. "Dr. Radhakrishnan's Secret Trip to GDR" *Sunday Amrita Bazar Patrika*, November 15, 1981.

15. Ibid.

16. Ibid.

17. Ibid.

18. *Occasional Speeches and Writings 1952-59*, p. 145.

19. Ibid., p. 149.

20. Ibid., p. 8.

21. Quoted in K. Iswara Dutt, "Nation's Patriarch," *The Radhakrishnan Number*, p. 96c.

22. Quoted in K. Iswara Dutt, "The Man and His Evolution," p. 97.

23. Ibid., p. 97. [Quoted.]

24. Ibid., p. 98. @Quoted.]

25. Quoted in K. Iswara Dutt "Nation's Patriarch," p. 96c.

26. K. Iswara Dutt, "The Man and His Evolution," p. 99.

27. *Occasional Speeches and Writings 1952-59*, p. 193.

28. Ibid., pp. 197-198.

29. Ibid., p. 31.

30. Ibid., p. 200.

31. Ibid., p. 203.

32. Ibid., p. 203.

33. J.A. Naik, *Soviet Policy Towards India: From Stalin to Brezhnev*, (Delhi: Vikas, 1970), p. 96.

34. Ibid., p. 96. [Quoted in *Pravda* June 16 and 17, 1956.]

35. *Occasional Speeches and Writings 1952-59*, pp. 200-201.

36. Ibid., pp. 40-41.

37. Ibid., p. 36.

38. Quoted in Arthur Stein, *India and the Soviet Union: The Nehru Era*, (Chicago: Chicago University Press, 1969), p. 82.

39. *Occasional Speeches and Writings 1952-59*, p. 47.

40. Ibid., pp. 49-50.

41. Ibid., p. 52.

42. Ibid., p. 204.

43. Ibid., pp. 357-358.

44. *My Search for Truth*, p. 4.

45. *Religion and Society*, p. 184.

46. R.L. Handa, *Rajendra Prasad, Twelve Years of Triumph and Despair*, (New Delhi: Sterling, 1978), p. 63.

47. Quoted in Gyanwati Darbar, *Portrait of a President*, (Delhi, 1974), p. 140.

48. Quoted in R.L. Handa pp. 63-64.

49. Gyanwati Darbar, p. 155.

50. R.L. Handa, p. 70.

51. Ibid., pp. 71-83.

52. H.N. Pandit, *The Prime Minister's President*, (New Delhi, 1974), pp. 7-8.

53. Escott Reid, *Envoy to Nehru*, (Delhi, 1981), p. 202.

54. Ibid., pp. 201-202.

55. Ibid., p. 202.

56. K. Iswara Dutt, "The Man and His Evolution," p. 100.

57. Ibid., p. 101.

58. M.O. Mathai, *Reminiscences of Nehru Age*, (New Delhi: Vikas, 1978), p. 72.

59. *Occasional Speeches and Writings 1959-62* (New Delhi: Publications Division, 1962), p. 63.

60. Ibid., p. 64.

61. Ibid., p. 226.

62. Ibid., p. 214.

63. Ibid., p. 215.

64. Ibid., p. 216.

65. Ibid., pp. 64-65.

66. Ibid., p. 72.

67. Ibid., p. 6.

68. Quoted in Dilip Kumar Roy, "A Harmonious Evolution," *The Radhakrishnan Number*, pp. 80g-80h.

69. N.M. Jaisoorya, "A Legendary World Figure," *The Radhakrishnan Number*, p. 171.

70. His Speech at Second UNESCO General Conference held in Mexico City in November, 1947. Quoted in *UNESCO and India, 1946-48*, (New Delhi: Ministry of Education, Government of India, 1948), p. 58.

71. His Speech at Tenth UNESCO General Conference held in Paris, 1958. Quoted in Mahendra Kumar, *India and UNESCO*, (New Delhi: Indian Council of World Affairs, 1974), p. 102.

72. *UN Weekly Bulletin*, (November 18, 1947), pp. 657-658.

73. *UNESCO and India*, p. 7.

74. *Records of the General Conference of the UNESCO*, Fourth Session (1949), Proceedings, p. 60.

75. Mahendra Kumar, *India and UNESCO*, pp. 59-61.

76. *UNESCO and India*, p. 6.

77. Ibid., p. 59.

78. Ibid., p. 59.

79. UNESCO General Conference, First Session (Paris: UNESCO, 1947), p. 27.

80. Quoted in Mahendra Kumar, p. 61.

81. Khushwant Singh, "Artist in Action," *Facets of Radhakrishnan*, p. 51.

82. "Sarvepalli Radhakrishnan: Some Memorable Reminiscences," *Dr. Sarvepalli Radhakrishnan, A Commemorative Volume*, pp. 40-41.

83. Quoted in R.L. Handa, p. 165.

84. The Life Insurance Company without consulting the Investment Committee had purchased shares worth rupees one crore and twenty-five lakhs of a private company owned by Hari Das Mundhra. The shares were purchased at a rate higher than the prevailing market rates and the deal was struck on a day when Bombay and Calcutta Stock Exchanges were closed. The deal was exposed in the Parliament by Feroze Gandhi. Ultimately, Hari Das Mundhra had to go to jail; T.T. Krishnamachary, the then finance minister had to resign from the cabinet; and H.M. Patel a senior ICS officer had to leave his job.

85. Sheikh Abdullah's ministry in Jammu and Kashmir was dismissed by the centre in August, 1953, and he was arrested for allegedly carrying on propaganda against India. In 1958 he was released, but as the powers that be considered that he did not mend his ways, he was rearrested a few months later (in May) the same year.

86. R.L. Handa, p. 56.

87. Ibid., p. 80.

88. Ibid., p. 80.

89. Ibid., p. 165.

90. Ibid., p. 165.

91. "Our President," *The Radhakrishnan Number*, p. 9.

92. Quoted in K. Iswara Dutt, "The Man and His Evolution," p. 102.

93. R.R. Diwakar, "The Modern Acharya," *The Radhakrishnan Number*, p. 66.

94. B. Gopala Reddi, "Dr. Sarvepalli Radhakrishnan as I Knew Him," *Dr. Sarvepalli Radhakrishnan, A Commemorative Volume*, p. 19.

95. "Dr. S. Radhakrishnan: Genial and Humane," *Dr. Sarvepalli Radhakrishnan, A Commemorative Volume*, p. 70.

96. Quoted in K. Iswara Dutt, "The Man and His Evolution," p. 101.

97. B.N. Banerjee, "Dr. Sarvepalli Radhakrishnan: The First Chairman of the Rajya Sabha," *Dr. Sarvepalli Radhakrishnan, A Commemorative Volume*, p. 11.

98. Ibid., p. 12.

99. Quoted in "Dr. S. Radhakrishnan: Chairman Par Excellence," *Dr. Sarvepalli Radhakrishnan, A Commemorative Volume*, p. 134.

100. Ibid., p. 135 [Quoted in.]

CHAPTER XIV

1. Quoted in *The Hindu*, May 13, 1962, p. 1.

2. *President Radhakrishnan's Speeches and Writings, May 1964-May 1967*, (New Delhi: Publications Division, Ministry of Information and Broadcasting, 1969), p. 93.

3. *President Radhakrishnan's Speeches and Writings, May 1962-May 1964*, p. 229.

4. Ibid., p. 230.

5. Ibid., p. 229.

6. *Occasional Speeches and Writings, Third Series, July 1959-May 1962*, p. 378.

7. M.C. Chagla, *Roses in December—An Autobiography*, (Bombay, 1973), p. 437.

8. K. Iswara Dutt, "The Man and His Evolution," pp. 111-114.

9. Court or Levee.

10. Major C.L. Datta, *With Two Presidents: The Inside Story*, (Delhi: Vikas Publications, 1970), p. 77.

11. Quoted in M.C. Chagla, p. 438.

12. H.N. Pandit, p. 14.

13. *Mission to India (A Search for Alternatives in Asia)*, (New Delhi: B.I. Publications, 1974), p. 115.

14. Quoted in C.L. Datta, pp. 133-134.

15. *President Radhakrishnan's Speeches and Writings, May 1962-May 1964*, p. 230.

16. Durga Das, *India, From Curzon to Nehru and After*, (London, 1969).

17. C.L. Datta, p. 76.

18. Quoted in H.V. Kamath, *Last Days of Jawaharlal Nehru*, (Calcutta: Jaysree Parkashan, 1977), p. 4.

19. *President Radhakrishnan's Speeches and Writings May 1962-May 1964*, p. 125.

20. C.L. Datta, p. 129.

21. M.O. Mathai, p. 182.

22. Michael Edwards, *Nehru: A Political Biography*, (Penguin, 1971), p. 308.

23. Quoted in C.L. Datta, p. 136.

24. Quoted in C.L. Datta, p. 140.

25. Durga Das, p. 365.

26. C.L. Datta, p. 119.

27. Ibid., p. 120.

28. Quoted in B. Shiva Rao, "As President," *Sarvepalli Radhakrishnan*, p. 80.

29. *President Radhakrishnan's Speeches and Writings, May 1962-May 1964*, p. 296.

30. Quoted in B. Shiva Rao, pp. 80-81.

31. *President Radhakrishnan's Speeches and Writings, May 1962-May 1964*, p. 320.

32. Ibid., p. 291.

33. Ibid., p. 292.

34. N.G. Ranga, *Distinguished Acquaintances Vol. II*, (Vijayawada, 1976), pp. 95-96.

35. Ibid., pp. 95-96 [Quoted in].

36. Morarji Desai, *The Story of My Life Vol. II*, (Macmillan, 1974), p. 199.

37. Durga Das, p. 365; C.L. Datta, p. 119.

38. "Message to MP Congress" *Patrika*, reported in *The Times of India*, August 9, 1964.

39. Quoted in S. Gopal, *Jawaharlal Nehru: A Biography*, Volume III (Delhi: Oxford University Press, 1984), p. 245.

40. Quoted in Michael Brecher, *Succession in India, A Study in Decision Making*, (London, 1966), p. 9.

41. C.L. Datta, p. 121.

42. For details see Durga Das, H.N. Pandit, Michael Brecher, and Mary C. Carras, *Indira Gandhi, In the Crucible of Leadership*, (Bombay: Jaico, 1980).

43. Ibid., p. 30 and p. 135.

44. Mary C. Carras, p. 135.

45. C.L. Datta, p. 121.

46. Ibid., p. 149.

47. R.L. Handa, p. 80.

48. *President Radhakrishnan's Speeches and Writings, May 1964-May 1967*, p. 341.

49. Ibid., p. 329.

50. Ibid., p. 337.

51. Ibid., p. 336.

52. *Jawaharlal Nehru: Homage*, (New Delhi: Publications Division, Government of India, 1964), p. 39.

53. Ibid., p. 40.

54. Ibid., p. 41.

55. Gundevia, *Outside the Archives*, p. 93.

CHAPTER XV

1. Michael Brecher, *Succession in India*, pp. 34-35.

2. Chester Bowles, *Mission to India*, p. 115.

3. Ibid.

4. Michael Brecher, pp. 34-35.

5. Krishna Bhatia, *The Ordeal of Nationhood: A Social Study of India Since Independence 1947-70*, (New York: Atheneum, 1971), pp. 71-72.

6. *President Radhakrishnan's Speeches and Writings May 1964-May 1967*, p. 138.

7. Ibid., p. 42.

8. M.O. Mathai, *Reminiscences of Nehru Age*, pp. 235-236.

9. *President Radhakrishnan's Speeches and Writings, May 1964-May 1967*, p. 51.

10. Ibid., p. 52.

11. Ibid., p. 55.

12. C.L. Datta, *With Two Presidents: The Inside Story.*

13. *President Radhakrishnan's Speeches and Writings, May 1964-May 1967*, p. 201.

14. Ibid., pp. 200-201.

15. Ibid., pp. 366-367.

16. Quoted in Tara Ali Baig, "Dr. Radhakrishnan: Philosopher-President," *Dr. Sarvepalli Radhakrishnan: A Commemorative Volume*, p. 47.

17. M.C. Chagla, *Roses in December*, p. 318.

18. Ibid., p. 321.

19. Quoted in B. Shiva Rao, "As President," *Sarvepalli Radhakrishnan*, p. 81-2.

20. Ibid., p. 83. [Quoted in]

21. Quoted in M.P. Bhargava, "Dr. S. Radhakrishnan: A Multifaceted Personality," *Dr. Sarvepalli Radhakrishnan: A Commemorative Volume*, p. 60.

22. *President Radhakrishnan's Speeches and Writings, May 1964-May 1967*, p. 298.

23. Ibid., p. 299.

24. Umashanker Joshi, "A Meditative Mind," *The Radhakrishnan Number*, p. 83.

25. *President Radhakrishnan's Speeches and Writings, May 1964-May 1967*, p. 172.

26. Ibid., p. 204.

27. *President Radhakrishnan's Speeches and Writings, May 1964-May 1967*, p. 184.

28. Ibid., p. 186.

29. Ibid., p. 186.

30. Ibid., p. 186.

31. C.L. Datta, *With Two Presidents: The Inside Story*, pp. 83-84.

32. Ibid., pp. 83-84.

33. Quoted in K.A. Abbas, *Indira Gandhi, Return of the Red Rose*, (Bombay: Popular Prakashnan, 1966), p. 157.

34. Quoted in H.N. Pandit, p. 52.

35. Quoted in M.C. Chagla, p. 322.

36. Dom Moraes, *Mrs. Gandhi*, (New Delhi: Vikas, 1980), p. 129.

37. Durga Das, pp. 408-409.

38. Basant Chatterjee, *The Congress Splits*, (Delhi), pp. 28-30.

39. *President Radhakrishnan's Speeches and Writings, May 1964-May 1967,* p. 86.

40. Ibid., p. 86.

41. Ibid., p. 85.

42. Ibid., p. 87.

43. "Dr. Radhakrishnan Bows Out," *The Statesman,* April 10, 1967.

44. *President Zakir Husain's Speeches,* (New Delhi: Publications Division, Government of India, 1973), p. 1.

45. *President Radhakrishnan's Speeches and Writings, May 1964-May 1967,* p. 93-94.

46. Ibid., p. 94.

47. S. Gopal gave this information in reply to a questionnaire sent to him by K. Satchidananda Murty.

48. *The Hindu,* April 18, 1975.

CHAPTER XVI

1. E.J. Sharpe, *Hinduism,* ed. J.R. Hinnals and E.J. Sharpe, (New Castle upon Tyne, 1973).

2. Ibid.

3. Ibid.

4. *Quack, Quack!* (London: Hogarth Press, 1935).

5. Ibid., p. 184.

6. Ibid., p. 185.

7. Ibid., p. 160.

8. Ibid., pp. 187-188.

9. Ibid., p. 192.

10. *Counter Attack from the East* (London: George Allen and Unwin Ltd., 1933).

11. Ibid., p. 73.

12. Ibid., pp. 71-73.

13. Ibid., p. 75.

14. Ibid., p. 93.

15. Ibid., p. 264.

16. "Radhakrishnan and Mysticism," *The Philosophy of Sarvepalli Radhakrishnan*, pp. 413-414.

17. Ibid., p. 86. ["Radhakrishnan's World,"]

18. *Hibbert Journal*, October, 1932.

19. *Quack, Quack!*, p. 192.

20. "Reply to Critics," *The Philosophy of Sarvepalli Radhakrishnan*, p. 803.

21. *An Idealist View of Life*, p. 152.

22. Ibid., p. 152.

23. *President Radhakrishnan's Speeches and Writings, May 1962-May 1964*, p. 197.

24. *Dhammapada*, (Oxford University Press, 1954).

25. "Fragments of a Confession," p. 10.

26. "Reply to Critics," p. 820.

27. Ibid., p. 820.

28. *President Radhakrishnan's Speeches and Writings, May 1962-May 1964*, p. 226.

29. "Fragments of a Confession," p. 10.

30. Ibid.

31. *Religion and Society*, (London: George Allen and Unwin Ltd., 1947), pp. 132-133.

32. Ibid., p. 134f.

33. Ibid., p. 192f.

34. Ibid., p. 182.

35. Ibid., p. 189f.

36. Ibid., p. 35.

37. Ibid., p. 64.

38. Ibid., p. 66.

39. *President Radhakrishnan's Speeches and Writings, May 1964-May 1967*, p. 145.

40. Ibid., p. 342.

41. Ibid., pp. 342-343.

42. Ibid., p. 145.

43. Ibid., p. 226.

44. Ibid., p. 334.

45. Ibid., p. 334.

46. Ibid., p. 334.

47. Ibid., p. 274.

48. Ibid., p. 233.

49. Ibid., p. 233.

50. Ibid., p. 274.

51. Ibid., pp. 348-349.

52. Ibid., pp. 348-349.

53. Ibid., p. 201.

54. Ibid., p. 350.

55. *Hibbert Journal*, October, 1932.

CHAPTER XVII

1. Gandhi, Introduction to his *Autobiography*, (Ahmedabad: Navajivan Publishing House, 1958).

2. Radhakrishnan, *My Search for Truth*, p. 49.

3. P.A. Schilpp, Preface, p. 12.

4. Ibid. [That's how Schilpp called it.]

5. Ibid., pp. 6-7.

6. Ibid., p. 5.

7. *My Search for Truth*, p. 1.

8. Ibid., p. 3.

9. Ibid., p. 4.

10. Ibid., pp. 42-43.

11. Ibid., p. 9.

12. *The Philosophy of Sarvepalli Radhakrishnan,* Ibid., p. 806 n.

13. S. Gopal's letter in reply to K. Satchidananda Murty's questions.

14. *President Radhakrishnan's Speeches and Writings, May 1962-May 1964,* p. 123.

15. *My Search for Truth,* p. 2.

16. This entire account depends on: "S.P.," *Sir S.R. (A Sketch), Triveni,* New Series, September 1936, pp. 6-16.

17. When he became vice-president, Sundarayya said, having followed his "multifarious activities in the interests of the country," they felt pleasure and pride that he was presiding over Rajya Sabha. When he laid down the vice-presidency, Bhupesh Gupta said, he had converted Rajya Sabha into a large family and surely as president, "he would exercise his charm to convert this huge nation into a large family."

18. Khushwant Singh, "Radhakrishnan—the man," *Sunday,* (September 18-24, 1988), p. 9.

19. *Triveni.*

20. He publicly eulogized Gandhi from the 1920s. He hailed him as the national emancipator and presented to him a book of essays and reflections on his life and work by world figures like Einstein, which he had edited; he made Gandhi the chief guest in the Banaras Silver Jubilee Convocation. In that same convocation he conferred honorary doctoral degrees on Nehru and Rajendra Prasad. He pleaded with Gandhi for Bose's presidency of the Indian National Congress. In the first meeting of the Constituent Assembly, Radhakrishnan was the first to felicitate its chairman, Prasad, hailing him as the "Suffering Servant of India." He wrote a panegyric for a Nehru *festschrift.*

21. For example his convocation address at Allahabad (1934), Agra (1941), Gurukul Kangri (1942), and his statement in *My Search for Truth* (1937) that "so long as India is dependency . . . Britain has no moral authority to question Japan's adventures in the Far East or Italy's in Africa" (p.24).

22. Cited by M.P. Bhargava in his article in *Dr. Sarvepalli Radhakrishnan: A Commemorative Volume,* p. 54.

23. His speech at Madras in March 1936 replying to felicitations.

24. Ibid.; *My Search for Truth,* p. 24; Agra Convocation Address (1941) which criticized Britain's moral lapse in its unwillingness to apply its vaunted democratic principles to India.

25. Ibid., p. 19; ["Fragments of a Confession," in Schilpp]

26. Ibid., p. 820; ["Reply to Critics" in Schilpp]

27. "Fragments of a Confession," p. 10.

28. Ibid., p. 8.

29. "Reply to Critics," p. 820.

30. S. Gopal, "Letter."

31. Andhra University Convocation Address, (1927).

32. Kamala Lectures. *Religion and Society*, Lect. III, in *Radhakrishnan Reader, An Anthology*, (Bombay, 1988), p. 185.

33. For example, the testimony of two ladies: Mrs. Tigert (G.C. Osborn, *J.J. Tigert: American Educator*, [Gainesville, 1974], p. 499), and Tara Ali Baig, *Dr. S. Radhakrishnan: A Commemorative Volume*, p. 48. Of course, they could not comprehend the significance of what he was doing.

34. *My Search for Truth*, p. 34.

35. Ibid., p. 820; "Reply to Critics".

36. Ibid., p. 14; ["Fragments of a Confession"].

37. Many ideas in this paragraph have come from Mrs. Lakshmi N. Menon's letter of November 30, 1981, to K. Satchidananda Murty.

38. S. Gopal "Letter."

39. *President Radhakrishnan's Speeches and Writings*, Second Series, p. 94.

40. *My Search for Truth*, p. 41.

41. Ibid., p. 47.

42. Her letter of November 21, 1981 to K. Satchidananda Murty.

43. *My Search for Truth*, pp. 48-49.

44. G.C. Osborn, *J.J. Tigert: American Educator*, (Gainesville, 1974), p. 497.

Index

233

18
LH